Gendered Asylum

Gendered Asylum

Race and Violence
in U.S. Law and Politics

SARA L. MCKINNON

UNIVERSITY OF ILLINOIS PRESS

Urbana, Chicago, and Springfield

Support for this research was provided by the University of Wisconsin–Madison
Office of the Vice Chancellor for Research and Graduate Education with funding
from the Wisconsin Alumni Research Foundation.

Library of Congress Cataloging-in-Publication Data
Names: McKinnon, Sara L. (Sara Lynn), 1979– author.
Title: Gendered asylum : race and violence in U.S. law and politics / Sara L
    McKinnon.
Description: Urbana, Chicago, and Springfield : University of Illinois Press,
    2016. | Series: Feminist media studies | Includes bibliographical references
    and index.
Identifiers: LCCN 2016019883 (print) | LCCN 2016008372 (ebook) |
    ISBN 9780252098888 (e-book) | ISBN 9780252040450 (hardback) |
    ISBN 9780252081910 (paperback)
Subjects: LCSH: Refugees—Legal status, laws, etc.—United States. | Asylum,
    Right of—United States. | Refugees—Government policy—United States.
    | Sex discrimination—Law and legislation—United States. | Transgender
    people—Legal status, laws, etc.—United States. | Women's rights—
    Government policy—United States. | United States—Race relations. |
    United States—Emigration and immigration—Government policy. | BISAC:
    SOCIAL SCIENCE / Women's Studies. | SOCIAL SCIENCE / Emigration
    & Immigration. | POLITICAL SCIENCE / Political Freedom & Security /
    General.
Classification: LCC KF4836 (print) | LCC KF4836 .M35 2016 (ebook) | DDC
    342.7308/3—dc23
    LC record available at https://lccn.loc.gov/2016019883

Contents

Acknowledgments

I remember many years ago when I first began thinking about gender and asylum as a topic for my research. I remember also the moment I realized that the project should be a book. These moments change the direction of a work, but they are not realized alone. Many, many people have had a significant influence on the direction of this project. This influence is evident in the project's theoretical and analytic development, the political commitments of the book, and in some cases even in the specific word choices. Thank you to my amazing editor Dawn Durante at the University of Illinois Press and the incredible anonymous reviewers who so generously thought with me about the project and its potential. There were times when you saw something bigger in the book than I could see. I thank you for pushing me to pursue those bold directions.

Thank you to those at Arizona State University who encouraged the pursuit of this investigation so many years ago. In addition to Hugh Downs School of Human Communication and the ASU Graduate Student Association for their financial support, thank you to Daniel C. Brouwer, Olga Idriss Davis, Belle Edson, C. A. Griffith, LaDawn Haglund, Jennifer Linde, Judith Martin, Thomas Nakayama, H. L. T. Quan, and Sarah J. Tracy for support, encouragement, and hours of conversation about the direction of this work.

I feel very fortunate to work in a department and university that have provided me with significant material and intellectual support during the drafting of this monograph. Support for this research was provided by the University of Wisconsin–Madison Office of the Vice Chancellor for Research and Graduate

Education with funding from the Wisconsin Alumni Research Foundation. Thank you to the faculty and graduate students in the Department of Communication Arts at the University of Wisconsin–Madison, and especially to my esteemed colleagues in the area of Rhetoric, Politics and Culture, Robert Asen, Karma Chávez, Robert Glenn Howard, Jenell Johnson, Stephen Lucas, and Susan Zaeske. Thank you so much for your continued encouragement, feedback, and intellectual stimulation. I feel so fortunate to work alongside you each day and to learn from you.

I have also had the great fortune to present significant portions of this book to fantastic audiences at the following universities: Arizona State University, College of Wooster, Northeastern University, Syracuse University, University of Copenhagen, University of New Mexico, University of Minnesota, Paris-Sorbonne University, University of Southern Denmark, and the University of Wisconsin. It is impossible to thank individually every person who heard these talks, asked questions, or offered feedback and suggestions, but a few people stand out for their particularly insightful and useful suggestions: Peter Campbell, KC Councilor, Jigna Desai, Ron Greene, Dag Heege, Annie Hill, Kelly Jakes, Jennifer Keohane, Leah Mirakhor, Amyaz Moledina, Charles E. Morris, Rachel Rosenbloom, Lou Roberts, Emily Sauter, Kyle Schneider, Catherine Squires, Lisa Villadsen, and Suzanna Walters.

In addition to these wonderful interlocutors, the following individuals have been generous with their love, friendship, and time: M. Adams, T. Banks, Shawnika Hull, Maurice Gattis, Ginny McDermott, Leah Mirakhor, Ulises Moreno, Alix Shabazz, Catalina Toma, Daniel Ussishkin, and Anders Zanichkowsky. Thank you for the diversion of wine, laughter, and juicy stories, and for always being there when I needed a hug or some words of encouragement. Your friendship means everything to me.

To my family of origin, and especially my mom, thank you so much for your unfaltering encouragement to keep studying and writing, even when it probably felt like I would probably never finish. I know there were times when I was short on the phone and not able to come home as often as you'd probably have liked. You never complained. Instead, you told me to keep going, that you were proud of me, and that I could do it. Thank you for always being so generous with your positivity, love, and support.

Finally, to Karma for endless love and faith in me, thank you. You had to read the chapters of this book too many times, and for that I am sorry, but the project would not be what it is without your criticism, insights, and endless belief in me. You make me better in all ways. Most of all thank you for getting me, even when I don't make it easy.

Introduction

In 1971 a Haitian woman named Pierre refused to leave the United States when her temporary visitor visa expired.[1] The U.S. Immigration and Naturalization Service (INS) served Pierre with a notice stating that she would be returned to Haiti if she did not leave of her own accord. Pierre promptly applied for a temporary relief status called *withholding of removal*,[2] testifying that her husband would kill her if she returned to Haiti. In this document, she reported that she was married to a high-ranking Haitian political official who, because of his position, could bar her from receiving political and legal protection in Haiti. Pierre explained to the court that her husband had not only threatened her but had also "attempted to kill her by burning down the house in which she lived."[3]

Not able to make this fear discernible as one connected to her race, religion, or political opinion, which were the recognized categories of immigration relief at the time, Pierre was without the argumentative means to be legible as a refugee to the court. The Board of Immigration Appeals (BIA) evaluating Pierre's case denied her request in 1975 and ordered her to either leave the United States willingly or be forcibly deported: "The respondent does not allege that her husband seeks to persecute her on account of her race, religion or political beliefs. The motivation behind his alleged actions appears to be strictly personal. Thus, even if the respondent had shown that the government of Haiti was unable or unwilling to restrain her husband, she could not qualify for temporary withholding of deportation."[4] Pierre was denied immigration protection because there was no category for her claim to be made legible as political persecution. Were Pierre's claim to be evaluated today, it would most likely be argued as a gender-based asylum case. But in the courtroom where Pierre gave her testimony in 1975, it was not even imaginable to think of gender or sex as identity categories for which one might be politically persecuted.[5]

Almost fifteen years after Pierre's initial request, Iranian-born Parastoo Fatin directly posed the question to U.S. judges of whether gender or sex could count as political categories in the national asylum system. Fatin had been a student in the United States since 1979. She requested asylum in 1984 because she believed she would be persecuted if returned to Iran on account of her participation in "the social group of the upper class of Iranian women who supported the Shah of Iran, a group of educated Westernized free-thinking individuals."[6] She also claimed a fear of persecution because of her "'deep[ly] rooted belief in feminism' and in 'equal rights for women, and the right to free choice of any expression and development of abilities in the fields of education, work, home and family, and all other arenas of development.'"[7] The judge hearing Fatin's case in 1986 decided that there was no evidence that she would be singled out among other women by the Iranian government, nor did the judge find that her fear of future persecution met the necessary level of "extreme hardship" to qualify her for asylum.[8]

Fatin appealed the decision. In May 1993 the Third Circuit Federal Appeals Court agreed that they could not see how Fatin could demonstrate "a well-founded fear of suffering 'persecution' based solely on her gender."[9] Not only did her religious beliefs get in the way of the court's ability to see Fatin's case as gender based, but her class, race, and nationality shaped the way she was received as a gender-based asylum applicant. Even in denying Fatin's right to relief on the basis of her gender, though, the judges acknowledged that sex or gender could be a political category in the asylum institution. Referencing the 1985 BIA decision in *Matter of Acosta*, in which the board clarified who could count as a "particular social group" in the refugee definition, Judge Samuel Alito, writing the majority opinion, explained how sex or gender could fit: "The Board specifically mentioned 'sex' as an innate characteristic that could link the members of a 'particular social group.' Thus, to the extent that the petitioner in this case suggests that she would be persecuted or has a well-founded fear that she would be persecuted in Iran simply because she is a woman, she has satisfied the first of the three elements that we have noted."[10] Fatin was denied immigration relief, but the life of her claim lived on as her arguments for relief gave refugee advocates and scholars inventional resources for conceptualizing how sex or gender might fit. Unfortunately, in the excitement about what the case might mean for other gender-based asylum seekers, advocates overlooked the way intersectionalities between gender, class, race, nationality, and religion complicated gender's intelligibility. As I'll demonstrate in chapter 2, it was Fatin's identity as upper class, Iranian, and not white that cast doubt on whether her gendered claim rose to the threshold of persecution necessary to win asylum. The intersections complicated her narrative too much to make the fear of persecution stark enough to count as persecution.

By the time INS officials explicitly addressed where gender fit in 1995, the concept was not only the preferred political term (in other words, sex was dropped from discussions), but gender had taken on definitional parameters; gender was meant for cisgender, presumably heterosexual women who requested exile based on fears that could easily be interpreted as cultural, relational, or private.[11] This meant that when Honduran Gina Ricarda Miranda appealed the negative ruling of her first asylum claim in 1995, her adjudicators would never consider whether she was eligible on the basis of fears relating to her gender. Miranda was described in court documents as "a transsexual who was born male, but has always believed she is female."[12] In her asylum application, she argued that gender-confirming healthcare options were not available in Honduras and that she would "face discrimination and governmental persecution in Honduras and cannot legally change her name and gender in Honduras."[13] Miranda was unsuccessful on both counts in her bid for asylum.

In addition to cases like Miranda's not counting as *gender-based* asylum, the fixing of gender as a referent for cisgender, presumably heterosexual women fleeing cultural, relational, and private violence, has also meant that a host of other asylum claims were situated beyond the purview of "gender." These cases, what I call *gender-related* cases, include: men and women fleeing state-sponsored family planning policies, such as abortions, sterilization and the forced use of birth control; cisgender, presumably heterosexual men whose experiences of persecution include sexual assault by military, guerrilla forces, and gang members; persons targeted for their gender nonconformity; and lesbian asylum seekers, among other claimants. What is intelligible as gendered within a gender-based asylum claim is exceptionally narrow and contingent.

This book charts the development and solidification of gender as a political category in U.S. asylum law from the 1980s, when the first gender-based violence cases begin to emerge in case law, to 2012, when the United States executive office formalized an explicit program for eradicating global gender-based violence through development, defense, and diplomacy projects, a program I take up in the conclusion of the book. Leading gender-based asylum advocate Karen Musalo explains, "Few refugee issues have been as controversial as that of gender asylum."[14] Despite international recommendations in the 1980s for nation-states to address disparities in the way refugee and asylum reliefs were distributed,[15] calls by U.S. legal scholars for gender to be added as a protected category to the refugee definition,[16] and other nation-states' formal adoption of gender as a protected category,[17] U.S. officials across three decades of presidential administrations have regulated gender's incorporation as a legal category through isolated legal decisions, allowing gender to take shape only as a contingent and segregated political category. Despite the state's unveiling of a global strategy for eradicating gender-based violence in 2012, gender is still not recognized as an established identity category for which one may experience persecution. Instead, each gender-based claimant must define that person's social group and prove that persecution is on account of that gendered social group. In addition to being a contingent category, it is also segregated from other aspects of identity and experience—such as one's religion, race, ethnicity, class, age, or sexuality—that may intersect with someone's gendered fears and also complicate the ways gender-related claims are intelligibly received by immigration officials. Taking up these developments, this book tracks gender in U.S. asylum and asks, What has enabled gender's emergence as a contingent and segregated category?

Two dynamics undergird gender's institutional life as a political concept. First, in line with scholars who critique human rights frameworks for assuming a universal male subject, the emergence of gender as a political concept in U.S. asylum is premised on a universal system of one sex (male-sex assigned subjects) and one gender (female-sex assigned cisgender women). While male-assigned subjects may have all categories of political asylum available to them, cisgender women may have only gender to ground their claim. The second dynamic is akin to what critical race theorists and feminist legal scholars have identified as western law's fundamental problem: the inability for the law to see and hear intersectionally. In U.S. asylum, gender is included, but only by being segregated from other categories like race, ethnicity, and sexuality. When claimants name the violence they experience as persecution, they can name it only as gender violence, even though this violence often stems equally from the intersections of their class, race, religion, sexuality, and age. A consequence of this segregation is that particular forms of violence are associated in the U.S. imaginary with the places and countries in which, and the bodies to which, particular gender violence happens, effectively racializing both place and body in the U.S. political-legal imaginary.[18] Lewis R. Gordon explains that people and experiences are "racialized at the point at which the values attributed to them are treated as material attributes of who or 'what' they are."[19] In the context of gender-based asylum cases, because these claims can only ever be explicitly named as gendered claims, the particular violence that they speak about are assumed as natural conditions, part and parcel of what it means to have a particular body and to come from a particular part of the world. As we will see, sometimes the racialization of violence is exactly what prompts an asylum seeker's eligibility and incorporation, for it diminishes the anxieties that are associated with the gendered subjects. In other circumstances, the racialized reading of gender violence proves too threatening; the claimants are racialized as too willful, too reproductive, or too loyal to their former sovereign. These applicants are unincorporable and thus must be removed.

Migration and refugee studies scholars have done much to examine the gendering, sexualizing, and racializing processes of immigration and displacement.[20] As Pierrette Hondagneu-Sotelo explains, the goal in this scholarship is to "look at the extent to which gender [and I would add sexuality] permeates a variety of practices, identities, and institutions."[21] Such an approach is important because, as Eithne Luibhéid argues in her foundational work, the control of non-normative gendered and sexual subjects and politics has always been the function of immigration processes: "Immigration control is not just a powerful symbol of nationhood and people but also a means to literally construct the nation and the people in particular ways . . . Yet immigration control has been equally integral to the reproduction of patriarchal heterosexuality as the nation's official sexual and gender order. . . . Nation is equated with the male subject position, and women's sexuality is reified as the property of the male nation."[22] This approach strongly resonates with feminist migration projects that articulate race as a mediating force for constructions of the immigrant and nation.[23] Parallel conversations address the discursive openings for gendered protections in asylum systems around the world[24] and the "mainstreaming" of gender discourses throughout global refugee and human rights institutions, such as the United Nations High Commissioner for Refugees (UNHCR), the Red Cross, the International Rescue Committee, and others.[25]

This focal point of understanding the gendering, sexualizing, and racializing processes of displacement and migration strongly resonates with the broader transnational feminist concern about state projects that mobilize around gender and women. For example, scholars have examined how the United States has justified political actions of occupation, militarization, and invasion in the name of emancipating and saving women,[26] advocating for "women's rights as human rights,"[27] fostering women's empowerment through education and advocacy,[28] and heralding an anti-violence against women agenda, all toward implementing neoliberal market logics as social logics.[29] My work contributes to this corpus in two ways: first, I unearth the logic underlying gender's emergence as a political category with the power to constitute transnational imaginaries and relationalities. Second, I demonstrate the racialization of the bodies and places of flight that attenuate neoliberal openings for refugee protection in the name of gender and gender violence. Guided by a rhetorical analysis of both judicial and "extra-judicial" discourses and contexts, this work examines how subjects are racialized and thus "differently coded" as worthy (or not worthy) of refuge in the United States because of what their gender, gendered claims, and countries of birth do for U.S. national and transnational state interests. To establish a foundation for this analysis, I first historicize the entrance of gender on the global stage of the international system for managing refugees and asylum seekers, outlining my understanding of gender as a legal category and identity construct before concluding with an overview of my methodology and organization for the book.

Asylum in the United States

As has been thoroughly described elsewhere, contemporary international and national refugee and asylum systems emerged directly in response to the aftermath of World War II.[30] This war was not the first in history in which people fled persecution, nor was it the first time nation-states accepted refugees.[31] Rather, this period saw the institutionalization and harmonization of international and national systems for managing displaced persons.[32] Prior to World War II, states were recognized as having rights under the Westphalian nation-state system, while individuals derived rights from states alone. This structure worked well for those who resembled the type of person desired by their state, and if they held the political opinions that were valued by state officials, but if someone did not, everyday life could be significantly more precarious.

In witnessing the violent, state-sponsored expungement of Jews, Roma, Serbs, ethnic Poles, Russians, Ukrainians, Balkans, people with disabilities, racial and ethnic minorities, homosexuals, and prisoners of war in Europe, world political leaders recognized the necessity of naming the rights of individuals in relation to states. Eleanor Roosevelt of the United States, John Peters Humphrey of Canada, René Cassin of France, and Charles Malik of Lebanon, among others, gathered to debate and draft the thirty articles that now make up the 1948 *Universal Declaration of Human Rights*. Articles 13 and 14 entitle all humans to the right to freedom of movement and residence in each state, and the right to seek asylum, or to ask for refuge in a country because they have been persecuted or fear persecution in their home country.

Two years later, toward defining who could gain asylum under this convention, the United Nations drafted the *United Nations Convention Relating to the Status of Refugees* (UN Convention), which includes the definition of a refugee that asylum seekers use today in demonstrating that they are bona fide refugees. The UN Convention states that a refugee is "any person who . . . owing to a well-founded fear of being persecuted for reasons of race, religion, nationality, membership of a particular social group or political opinion, is outside the country of his nationality and is unable or, owing to such fear, is unwilling to avail himself of the protection of that country; or who, not having a nationality and being outside the country of his former habitual residence as a result of such events, is unable or, owing to such fear, is unwilling to return to it."[33] Notably, in debates leading up to the drafting of the UN Convention, the delegate from Yugoslavia suggested that "sex" be added to Article 3, which mandated the application of the UN Convention "without discrimination as to race, religion, or country of origin." However, representatives from Austria, Colombia, Italy, Switzerland, Turkey, the United Kingdom, and the United States quickly voted this amendment down.[34] The representative from the United Kingdom elaborated that "the equality of the sexes was a matter for national legislation" and "to include the reference to sex might bring the Convention into conflict with national legislation."[35] Article 3 was purposed with ensuring that refugees, who had been exposed to persecution and discrimination in their former countries, not face the same experiences in the countries where they gained asylum.

Given the aftermath of World War II, delegates could hardly protest freedom from discrimination on the basis of religion, yet with laws in many asylum-granting countries that denied women voting rights, positioned husbands as legal guardians over wives, and allowed for different wage and working hours between men and women, delegates could scarcely say that citizen or refugee women would not experience discrimination on the basis of sex. One delegate offered the following example: "During a tobacco shortage in Austria, the ration for women had been smaller than that for men. It had been alleged in the constitutional courts that that was a violation of the equality of the sexes, but the finding of the courts had been that women needed less tobacco than men."[36] Delegates explained that refugee policy should not meddle in matters of national concern, implying that what states do with their women was, literally, up to the state to decide.

As if needing to solidify further sex/gender's place in global politics, UN High Commissioner for Refugees Gerrit Jan Van Heuven Goedhart assured the delegates that he "doubted strongly whether there would be any cases of persecution on account of sex."[37] While asylum-granting countries were not obligated on the matter of sex, the 1967 *Protocol Relating to the Status of Refugees* (Protocol) obligated them to maintain a policy of non-refoulement. This meant that states could not forcibly deport asylum seekers with a reasonable fear of persecution until their claims for asylum had been fully evaluated as far as they could go through the appeals process.

Not long after the initial crafting and implementation of these international protocols, nongovernmental service workers, policymakers, and activists began to recognize problems with their execution. The universal "human" who was supposedly protected under these guidelines was decidedly male. In refugee camps, adult men received food and water first under the assumption that they had family with whom they would share the resources (often leaving those with no adult male kin without regular access to daily rations).[38] Adult men were also often the first to leave camps for resettlement in a third country because they more frequently had the necessary identification documents (birth certificates, passports, and the like), and they were privileged for resettlement because it was assumed by refugee-granting states that they would more easily find and keep employment and would later sponsor their families through alternative immigration channels.

These discrepancies led many refugee advocates to argue that the "human" protected through refugee systems was, in effect, a man. The United Nations and its refugee agency, the UNHCR, moved to address this fissure by organizing a series of conferences and committees, including the UN Decade for Women conferences in Mexico City (1975), Copenhagen (1980), and Nairobi (1985); the UNHCR Commission on the Status of Women (1985); and the United Nations World Conference on Human Rights in Vienna (1993).[39] The 1975 Mexico City conference led, in part, to the drafting of the 1979 *Convention on the Elimination of All Forms of Discrimination against Women* (CEDAW), which defined discrimination against women as "any distinction, exclusion or restriction made on the basis of sex which has the effect or purpose of impairing or nullifying the recognition, enjoyment or exercise by women, irrespective of their marital status, on a basis of equality of men and women, of human rights and fundamental freedoms in the political, economic, social, cultural, civil or any other field."[40]

The rights of refugees and asylum seekers were not included in CEDAW, but conversations at the two subsequent conferences did include special consideration for displaced persons. For its own part, in 1985, the UNHCR formed a committee to assess the status of protection for refugee women. The committee's recommendations declare at the outset: "The policy set out in this document is premised on the recognition that becoming a refugee affects men and women differently and that effective programming must recognize those differences."[41] In total, the archive of these conferences and commissions reveals stark awareness of the need for asylum- and resettlement-granting states to address the question of gender in their asylum, immigration, and refugee resettlement programs. While some states, such as Canada and the Netherlands, took this call up through formal policies and procedures, other states remained starkly silent.

In the midst of these international conversations, the United States implemented a new national system for managing refugees and asylum seekers. Before 1980, U.S. law dictated that refugees could be admitted to the United States only when they were fleeing "Communist persecution" or when the state had "special humanitarian" interest in the violent context propelling the displacement. As Luibhéid explains, through years of narratives of persecution about fleeing Communism, an archetype of "someone heroically trying to assert his (typically male) individuality against an oppressive state" solidified as the model asylum seeker against which all claims are evaluated.[42] Seeking to wean Communist preferences from U.S. refugee law, to harmonize the national system with international law, and to manage the number of refugees and asylum seekers seeking exile from the Southeast Asian conflicts in which the United States was involved,[43] President Jimmy Carter signed the Refugee Act in 1980 as an addendum to the Immigration and Nationality Act (1965) and the Migration and Refugee Assistance Act (1962).

The Refugee Act changed three things about the United States' management of refugees. First, by ratifying the act, the U.S. government adopted the definition of a refugee as outlined by the United Nations in the Refugee Convention, with an addendum for instances where the conflict caused "special humanitarian concern" to the United States.[44] Second, the act formalized a system of refugee resettlement, allowing Congress to designate an annual cap of refugees to be admitted per year through the resettlement program, and charged federally funded volunteer agencies with managing the resettlement of refugees in the country. Through this system, hundreds of thousands of Hmong, Sudanese, Iranian, Bhutanese, Bosnian, Somali, Liberian, and Iraqi individuals, among many others, have been resettled across the country. Finally, the act formalized a system through which individuals who arrived at or within U.S. borders could seek refuge as asylum seekers. To do this, the act adopted the 1967 Protocol of Non-Refoulement, or the policy to not return to their home countries any subjects with potential claims to political refuge. It also set in place a judicial process for hearing the cases of asylum seekers through the immigration court system. Upon institution of the asylum system, immigration judges began to hear the cases of Haitians seeking refuge from political repression, Salvadorans fleeing civil war, and Guatemalans feeling guerrilla violence.

By the late 1980s and early 1990s the courts began to hear cases on the basis of past and (anticipated) future persecution, including rape and sexual assault by police officers, military, family members, and strangers; intimate violence; institutionalization for being gay or gender nonconforming; genital cutting; electroshock therapy; psychological and/or emotional torture; sterilization; forced abortion; and threats to life among other experiences—all of which challenged the gender neutrality that was supposedly present in the formulation and implementation of the 1980 system for managing refugees and asylum seekers in the United States.

Situating Gender

In the wake of early, largely unsuccessful gender-related asylum cases, the INS, in concert with both governmental and nongovernmental organizations, offered what they billed as a remedy to gender disparities present in asylum relief distributions. The INS circulated a document titled *Considerations for Asylum Officers Adjudicating Asylum Claims from Women* (Considerations) to all asylum interviewers and judges.[45] This document will be discussed fully in chapter 2, but what is important about this text is that it figures gender as a direct referent for particular kinds of women. The text also articulates what gender-based experiences specific to women include, such as: "laws and customs of some countries," "breeching social mores (e.g. marrying outside of an arranged marriage, wearing lipstick or failing to comply with other cultural or religious norms)," "requir[ing] that women live under the protection of male family members," and "discrimination because they are viewed as having brought shame and dishonor on themselves, their families, and their communities."[46] While it would have been reasonable to articulate gender as a political category that referred to all categories of gender identity and expression, this early pronouncement positioned gender as a signifier for women, figured through normative assumptions about assigned sex and heterosexuality.

Legal scholars with a critical eye toward early gender disparities in U.S. asylum also largely failed to challenge this conflation of gender with particular women in their calls for gender-based recognitions. Argumentative starting points such as the following were common throughout early legal calls for gendered protections: "A majority of the world's refugees are women. Although most refugees are fleeing wars and political violence in their home countries, a number of women seeking asylum in the United States and elsewhere are victims of more specific, gender-based persecution."[47] Similarly, many analysts grounded their pleas in the developing "women's rights as human rights" framework: "Women are human. Women seeking refuge from human rights violations are not demanding charity or special consideration because of their gender. They are, however, demanding that their gender-based claims for refuge and asylum be determined justly and fairly."[48] Mattie Stevens attempted to define gender-related persecution broadly, but as her analysis progressed, she slipped back into an equation where women were the sole targets of gender violence: "gender-specific persecution denotes persecution based on the sex of the victim, or persecution visited upon women because of their sex and/or physiological vulnerability to a specific type of harm."[49]

As the sole analyst early on to parallel challenges to gender and sexual orientation asylum cases, Peter Godfrey's work offers important possibilities for understanding the rhetoric and logic of the sex/gender system more broadly. Even Godfrey, though, circumscribes gender as a political category, assuming in his analysis of gendered cases a particular kind of gender that also assumes a particular sexuality: "The refusal to classify either 'women' or 'homosexuals' as a particular social group defeats the purpose of protection embodied in asylum law because it results in the denial of the claims of applicants who face real risks of harm upon return to their countries of origin."[50] Reviews following these early legal analyses largely fall in line with the "women only" approach, as Hondagneu-Sotelo describes it,[51] in advocating for a gender analysis to migration.[52]

Despite the continued penchant to study gender by analyzing certain women's experiences, recent scholars have moved to question the assumptions that guide their use of the term. Jane Freeman, for example, deploys gender as a "relational concept" that "is defined in terms of relationships between men and women, between maleness and femaleness, or masculinities and femininities."[53] In her comprehensive, multi-country study of state adoptions of UN gender and asylum protocol, Heaven Crawley explains that her focus on gender is not intended to "generalise or essentialise the experiences of refugee and asylum-seeking women." Rather, "because women's relationship to the state is racialised and ethicised as well as gendered, it is critically important to connect race, gender and class processes and identities and not to assume that they exist separately from one another."[54] Katherine Donato and her colleagues make a similar point when they call for a "dynamic" definition of the concept that acknowledges that "gendered ideologies and practices change as human beings (gendered as male and female, sexualized as homosexual, bisexual, or heterosexual) cooperate or struggle with each other, with their pasts, and with the structures of changing economic, political, and social worlds linked through their migrations."[55] Rejecting received formulations that link sex and gender in linear equations, Thomas Spijkerboer calls scholars of refugee and asylum policy instead to recognize that gender is as discursively constructed as those differences that are situated within the realm of biology. Influenced strongly by Judith Butler's theorizing,[56] he explains that "differences are always perceived; the notions of sex and race are *constructed* as 'real' and as prior to the social constructions gender and ethnicity. In other words: the difference between the discursive (social construction) and the pre-discursive (biology) is itself discursive."[57]

I follow in kind with Butler and Spijkerboer in conceptualizing discourse as central to the solidification of gender as a legal concept. Furthermore, I return to Gayle Rubin's articulation of the sex/gender system as a way of cueing in to the structures and institutions that produce gender in meaningful ways. As Rubin writes, the idea of a sex/gender system shares resonance with concepts such as patriarchy and modes of reproduction but offers a less normative framework in understanding the various ways that gender is made meaningful.[58] Instead of strictly articulating against the reproducing body, or law of the father, the sex/gender system enables critics to identify—with contextual and historical specificity—the logics, systems, and discourses that constitute how gender operates and is made meaningful in particular instances. Rubin elaborates that "sex/gender systems are not ahistorical emanations of the human mind; they are products of historical human activity."[59] This point leads analysts to focus on specific economic, political, and cultural interests that propel sex/gender articulations, asking what "the emergence of concepts and identities" mean as they take shape and gain lives of their own in the institutions, societies, and nations to which they belong. Joan Scott argues that this tracing of the institutional history of concepts "does not mean that one dismisses the *effects* of such concepts and identities, nor that one does not explain behavior in terms of their operations." Instead, it means "assuming that the appearance of a new identity is not inevitable or determined, not something that was always there simply waiting to be expressed, not something that will always exist in the form it was given in a particular political movement or at a particular historical moment."[60] We must approach the emergence of concepts with questions about what their appearance or circulation means in a particular space and time, assuming not that we know in advance what the concepts mean or do. We must ask instead: What does this concept mean for this moment and/or institution? How does it operate? What does it do?

I foreground how the sex/gender system intersects or interlocks with other systems of power in order for us to gain insight into gender's codification as a legal concept. While many have critiqued intersectional theories as too focused on identity, I take up intersectionality in its more structural deployment, which focuses on the ways institutions form "expectations based on inappropriate nonintersectional contexts" that then impact the ways people with a multitude of intersecting identities can be legible within institutions, state their claims, and access resources.[61] A vital aspect of this framework is its ability to illuminate how systems of domination and oppression work in tandem to produce people's emancipation and marginalization, their access and exclusion.[62] "Interlocking systems need one another," Sherene Razack insists, for "in tracing the complex ways in which they help to secure one another, we learn how women are produced into positions that exist symbiotically but hierarchically."[63]

Intersecting and interlocking conceptualizations of gender are especially necessary in situations where non-U.S. subjects must articulate their experiences to U.S. adjudicators with U.S. eyes, ears, and sensibilities. To this point, I have previously shown that immigration judges use their own experiences, knowledge, logic, and worldviews to make sense of what they hear asylum seekers describe in testimony.[64] This mode of sense-making becomes a problem because asylum seekers describe events and experiences that often "don't make sense," or make sense differently in the evaluator's view of the world. In these moments evaluators are *audiencing*; they are engaged in the active perception, reading, sense-making, and judgment processes of determining the status of particular speech and speaking subjects. This definition shifts the action implied in the noun *audience* into a verb, *to audience*. Such a shift allows the critic to examine the practices of the audience as an active subject—a subject whose practices have gone largely unexamined because of a preoccupation in critical analysis with the speaker and the text. In the context of the asylum courtroom, judges often audience by relying on essentializing discourses of race, class, nation, gender, sexuality, religion, and culture to fill in the sense-making gaps. These discourses also serve to fill in the sense-making gaps when claimants' cases do not easily fit the standard definition of a refugee as someone fleeing persecution on the basis of race, religion, nationality, political opinion, or membership in a social group, and when individuals flee contexts of violence that are rarely covered by the press. Furthermore, asylum seekers whose identities veer from those desired of immigrant subjects by the state struggle in being seen as people who warrant political protection. Thus, while asylum seekers may request refuge for experiences pertaining to their gender, other interlocking systems of power and meaning interact to produce the possibility of their access to refuge. In this context, it is not solely a question of identity but rather how subjects are interpreted, evaluated, and translated through these systems and logics that shapes how and what gender means.

A structural intersectional approach works well with a focus on the ways gendered subjects and types of violence are racialized in the national imaginary. The gendered and racialized meanings produced through these systems are not fixed or static, though they may appear on the surface as such at any given historical moment. Lisa Lowe persuasively demonstrates in *Immigrant Acts* that "legal institutions function as flexible apparatuses of racialization and gender in response to the material conditions of different historical movements."[65] Aiwha Ong argues that racialization is a central function of contemporary U.S. immigration processes. Intersections of race, class, and gender attend with neoliberal economic discourses of independence, entrepreneurship, and personal responsibility to shape how specific migrants get assessed and essentialized in the "bipolar racializing scheme" that figures one's potential and risk as a U.S. subject: "They become racialized not simply because of their perceived skin color, and ethnicized not simply because of claims of a particular ancestral culture, but because they have been assessed as belonging to a category and inscribed with a racial indeterminacy in the game of becoming self-motivated, self-propelling, and freedom-loving American citizens."[66] With this in mind, an examination of the institutional life of a concept must attend to the dynamics of power that made its emergence possible, and ask what the concept's presence and circulation reveals about the historical moment.

I understand also the institutional life of the gender concept to be constituted by transnational relationalities and disconnections. Refugee and asylum law, as kin to international human rights law, is always and already transnationally pitched and attuned.[67] The international horizon of this body of law is evident in its founding documents, such as the UN protocol and charter discussed earlier in this chapter, as well as in the way refugee boards from asylum-granting countries cite each others' decisions in forging new national precedent and policy.[68] It is also evident in the way transnational networks of advocacy, activism, information sharing, and human rights abuse documentation serve as the bedrock of evidentiary support in asylum seekers' legal claims.[69] Rebecca Dingo persuasively illuminates these connectivities, or what she describes as the ways "rhetorics travel" in feminist policy and advocacy, beyond the bounds of nation-states, connecting up with new rhetorics, getting translated, articulating anew in particular locales, and then moving again through transnational modalities of circulation.[70]

In this project, I examine the movement of gendered discourses, noting what happens when they move, but also attending to the geopolitical interests that buttress their movement and intelligibility. This latter point is done with the recognition that, as Raka Shome argues, it is "the in-between slash (between the national and international) [that] is precisely the volatile and anxious site upon, and through, which gender relations are being violently (and often un-recognizably) reconstituted in globalization."[71] A central focus of the project is thus to interrogate and explain the ways sexual and gender politics align with U.S. national and international state interests. M. Jacqui Alexander and Chandra Talpade Mohanty illustrate that a focus on state governance of/through sexual and gender politics means examining "not only the effects of governance on women or 'what happens to women' under state rule but also the way the entire apparatus of government treats women."[72] Transnational feminist research of this kind includes discussions of citizenship and immigration law,[73] state economic governance policies,[74] as well as militarism and war.[75] I contribute to this work by examining the national and international state interests that make gender and gendered subjects intelligible as persons worthy (or not) of U.S. protection.

Methodology and Chapter Overview

To analyze the implications of gender's emergence and institutional life, I conduct a rhetorical analysis of the corpus of asylum case law between the late 1980s, when the first gender-based asylum cases began to be evaluated in U.S. immigration courtrooms, until 2012. Specifically, I draw upon an analysis of more than 150 appellate-level decisions evaluated by either the BIA or one of the U.S. Circuit Courts of Appeals.[76] I pay close attention to the arguments, decisions, sources of invention, and evidence deployed in these cases.[77] As someone who approaches legal analysis not as a legal scholar or practitioner but as a rhetorical critic, I look at legal decisions and arguments as rhetoric that emerges from particular sociopolitical contexts and shapes people's material possibilities. Specifically, I am interested in how state officials, in the form of U.S. attorneys and judges, make sense of, evaluate, and ultimately make judgment on who is worthy of refuge and who is not.

I presume in my reading that the asylum seekers who file these cases are experts of their own lives who speak truthfully about their experiences and fears and who are often turning to asylum as a last option for relief. I make this move in contradistinction to popular U.S. discourse that chiefly frames refugees and asylum seekers as shifty and untrustworthy,[78] and because my ultimate focus is not a judgment of whether these claimants *should* receive asylum, but how state officials codify gender in their reading of these claimants as eligible or not eligible against the broader political landscape. With this in mind, I intend not to argue for the value of the system of U.S. asylum, to suggest how to better address people's human rights claims, or to make it easier to advocate within the system. The goal of the project is to uncover how power operates through gender's intelligibility in this massive and expansive institution with impact on thousands of people's lives. Toward understanding this operation, I draw on "extra-judicial"[79] material in the form of news media accounts, human rights reports, speeches, congressional debates, governmental reports, and historical accounts to gain insight into the political, economic, social, and cultural interests that make these constructions of gender in U.S. asylum meaningful. I do this to contextualize asylum law in the broader sociopolitical and geopolitical landscape from which it emerges. I argue that this de-naturalizes asylum decisions as a matter of fact, foregrounding instead these decisions as a matter of judgment that is redolent of and wrapped up in dominant U.S. culture and meaning making. This approach falls in line with what John Lucaites articulates as addressing "'the law' *as* a rhetoric."[80] Such an approach, he writes, "looks *between* rhetoric and 'the law' to discover the materialized practices of language-in-action which create the conditions for the collective experience of power, legitimacy, and social change."[81] This practice is also congruent with what Wendy Hesford frames as an "intercontextual" mode of analysis. She writes,

> *Intercontextual* is meant to foreground both the textual and contextual dimensions of representational practices. An intercontextual analytic also complicates analytics that focus solely on scale (such as nation-to-nation analyses) by foregrounding how meaning is produced, materialized, and experienced between and among multiple, ever-shifting contexts. Intercontextuality is a key element of a rhetorical analytic that seeks to understand how arguments and images travel across cultural and national borders, and how symbols and symbolic practices are appropriated, translated, and historicized.[82]

In summary, the chapters that follow draw on legal rhetorical studies, international political economy studies, and transnational feminist theory to examine the emergence of gendered discourses in U.S. asylum law within the context of broader global relations, and increasingly restrictive state policies. Gender-related asylum decisions reveal not only how a state recognizes gender and gendered subjects, but they also illuminate how states incorporate or exclude particular subjects for the political, economic, and cultural viability of the state.

To explicate the emergence of the gender concept and consequent racialization of gender violence chapter 1 introduces readers to asylum cases made by women from Central America who claimed intimate and sexual violence as persecution from the late 1980s to the present. While these women struggled early on for recognition, a number of the claimants have seen recent success. The chapter demonstrates how shifting political and economic dynamics between the United States and Central American countries, and transnational publicity in the form of "women's rights as human rights" activism, provide the rhetorical pressure needed for the state to recognize intimate gender violence as sufficiently political and public to warrant these women's incorporation. The asylum grants also enable the United States to mask a history of violent involvement in Central American affairs to position itself as a pastoral state that protects and defends women from sexual violence. A consequence of this incorporation is a spatial fixing of what gets framed as "femicide" and "gender-based violence" to Central and Latin America in the U.S. imaginary. Chapter 2 picks up on this analysis of early case law by examining the first cases to be recognized explicitly as "gender-based asylum cases" alongside the emerging "women's rights as human rights" framework. The rhetorics of freedom and choice so salient in feminist "human rights" discourse emerge as primary frames of recognition in the cases of those fleeing genital surgeries and social repression for feminist beliefs. The analysis demonstrates, though, that these gendered rhetorics operate to different effect as warrants in the claimants' cases. They also contribute to the racialization of the gender violence that the claimants speak about in the U.S. national imaginary.

Having articulated what is institutionally recognized under the frame of the gender concept in chapters 1 and 2, chapters 3, 4, and 5 examine logics resting under the surface of gender's conceptual intelligibility by examining what I discuss above as gender-related asylum cases. Chapter 3 looks at the gender concept's institutional life as a racializing and universalizing force in an examination of the cases made by Chinese migrants on the basis of forced abortion and sterilization. Since 1996, Chinese claimants have received the largest welcome as asylum seekers of any national group. Yet, as I demonstrate in chapter 3, this welcome comes with particular gendered exclusions, through what I talk about as coverture logics, attended by U.S. anxieties about Chinese capital accumulation and consolidation of global power. In chapter 3, I demonstrate the racialization of female migrants as reproductive threats, a gendered racialization that corresponds with a re-assertion of a national preference for male-bodied Chinese migrants.

Chapters 4 and 5, respectively, focus on the cases of cisgender and transgender sexuality-related asylum seekers as well as lesbian asylum seekers. Neither gender identity nor lesbian persecution is recognized as a gendered form of violence in U.S. case law. In these chapters, I analyze what gets walled in and out of the rhetorical categories of gender and gender violence, and articulate the logics that reinforce gender's making and unmaking across the corpus of

U.S. asylum requests. Chapters 1, 2, and 3 demonstrate particular types of gender violence to be racialized in that they are associated with particular bodies and geographies. Chapters 4 and 5, in large part, reflect a flattening effect that happens with sexuality-related asylum that returns the male-assigned sexed subject back to his position as a universal legal subject without a gender. The liberal opening for gender-based asylum as a contingent, segregated category for claiming asylum means that the universal male-assigned subject is naturalized even further as the model subject for whom refugee protections are intended.

The international system of asylum was conceptualized through the guiding universal ideal that states will hospitably care for and welcome the world's vulnerable and dispossessed when their countries of residence no longer can or will. It is widely recognized that this system has dismally failed in achieving this ideal, yet it is, nonetheless, the system we have. Much attention is drawn to the failures of asylum sending countries in producing conditions so unlivable that that people are forced to exit in order to have a chance at life. This book flips the equation and examines the interests, investments, and effects of asylum-granting-state decisions that produce conditions so precarious that people find themselves, literally, between state protections.

Transnational Publicity, Gender-Based Violence, and Central American Women's Asylum Cases

After a fourteen-year appeal, Rody Adali Alvarado Peña[1] of Guatemala won political asylum in the United States in 2009. Alvarado came to the country in 1995 after ten years of severe intimate violence, including being "kicked in the vagina, and kicked in the spine in an attempt by her husband to force a miscarriage of her second child. She survived a dislocated jaw, near amputation of her hands with a machete, and having her eye nearly pushed out."[2] Alvarado tried multiple times to leave, but her husband Osorio found her regardless of where she went. She filed reports with the Guatemalan police; officers laughed in her face. She filed for divorce, only to be told by a judge that he would not permit the divorce without Osorio's consent. As there were no women's shelters in Guatemala, invoking her rights under the UN Convention on Human Rights, Alvarado fled the country to the United States, where she claimed asylum on the basis of ten years of intimate violence and the Guatemalan government's unwillingness to intervene.

The immigration judge who first heard Alvarado's plea in 1995 granted her asylum, explaining that her case was in line with recent U.S. and international asylum protocol that addressed the specific types of violence that women experience because of their gender. The judge pointedly explained in the decision that domestic violence was a form of persecution that disproportionately impacted women and young girls, and that Alvarado had suffered enough harm in the face of a glaring unwillingness on the part of Guatemalan officials to intervene.[3]

Most important, the judge unequivocally recognized Alvarado as a political subject who fit the refugee conventions on two grounds: social group membership and political opinion. As explained in the case brief, "The social group was defined by nationality, gender, and marital status (Guatemalan women, who have been involved intimately with Guatemalan male companions, who believe that women are to live under male domination), and the political opinion was that of opposition to male domination."[4]

Upon notification of the asylum grant, the Immigration and Naturalization Service (INS), acting on behalf of the state, appealed the decision to the Board of Immigration Appeals (BIA), arguing that Alvarado was not entitled to political refuge. Specifically, the INS took issue with the constitution of Alvarado's social group and questioned the political nature of the violence.[5] Upon evaluation of the case, in 1999 the BIA reversed the judge's affirmative decision and put Alvarado into deportation proceedings, directly using language from the INS appeal to frame its decision that Alvarado was ineligible. Alvarado's lawyers immediately appealed the decision, though it would be ten years before the case would be fully evaluated again. This time, however, there was no opposition to Alvarado's eligibility; in fact, U.S. state attorneys, under the direct advisement of the U.S. attorney general wrote an amicus brief in support of Alvarado's bid for asylum. In December 2009, in yet another immigration courtroom in San Francisco, California, Alvarado would receive final word. The judge explained, "Inasmuch as there is no binding authority on the legal issues raised in this case, I conclude that I can conscientiously accept what is essentially the agreement of the parties [to grant asylum]."[6] Alvarado won asylum, for a second time.[7]

There are numerous issues in this case that might draw a critic's attention, some of which I have taken up in other venues.[8] In this chapter, though, I question what happened in the midst of this ten-year span—between the BIA's negative decision in 1999 to the 2009 affirmative decision—that enabled or, perhaps more accurately, necessitated such a drastic discursive shift in state rhetoric and recognition of Alvarado's eligibility. I interpret this shift against the broader geopolitical landscape that unfolds in the midst of Alvarado's tenuous bid for final word. Specifically, I argue that this shift is mobilized through the consolidation of transnational publicity about gender violence, violence in Central America, and women's human rights that emerge in the aftermath of Alvarado's case. This transnational publicity enabled new frames of recognition for the United States' own involvement in and proximity to the gender violence that women from Guatemala and El Salvador flee, allowing the United States to go from bloody supporter of the civil wars, which Central American women were fleeing, to pastoral protectors of women's rights. A consequence of this enabling publicity, though, is the fixing of femicide and militarized sexual violence on to the bodies and geographies of Central America. Against this transnational publicity, Central America and, by association, Mexico come to be racialized as physically and sexually violent to women—sometimes to the point of death.

Transnational Publicity

The concept of transnational publicity is jointly informed here by public sphere theorizing and transnational feminist theory. Publicity highlights the "actions and activities," as Daniel C. Brouwer and Robert Asen argue, that constitute how subjects and issues can be received in particular publics.[9] Mimi Sheller and John Urry develop this process-definition further by arguing that publicity emphasizes movement and circulation, meaning not only the ways discourse traverses different spaces but "how people (and objects) move, or desire to move, between the supposedly private and public domains."[10] Publicity draws us to think of material, events, and ideas that are announced to the world, promoted, and in their promotion made real for particular publics. This idea recognizes that an event is only an event if people have learned about it prior to the event and show up. For example, a blockbuster movie never becomes a blockbuster without the trailers, media attention, and hyping among friends that make people show up to the movie theaters on opening night and buy tickets. Much like blockbuster movies, human rights issues need publicity, or "staging," as Wendy Hesford calls it, to become real to interested publics.[11] Because the scale of human rights abuses is most often beyond the boundaries of the nation-state, these events need transnational attention—in the form of publicity—to become real to publics. While there are certain large-scale institutions that offer information about human rights problems, the production of human rights publicity is eclectic and diffuse in nature—made up of bodies of organizations, groups, and individuals with varying levels of institutional power that are interested in bringing attention to a particular issue. Toward conceptualizing the diffused mobility and circulation that publicity evokes, I combine this notion with Rebecca Dingo's term "transnational networks"[12] and Inderpal Grewal's concept "transnational connectivities," which both highlight "the myriad connections that characterize the transnational arena"[13] and produce publicity that can move, get taken up in particular contexts, and serve as attention and pressure toward particular claims. Both concepts also draw attention to the way discourse is produced through disparate and connected groups and individuals. The publicity generated in these diffused networks and connectivities shapes the options that publics have in understanding and framing particular issues and subjects. Putting these two concepts together—transnational and publicity—I deploy transnational publicity to refer to the rhetorical crafting and circulation of discourse by a broad range of advocacy groups, individuals, and organizations that intervene in particular rhetorical situations, constraining and enabling the options that publics have in responding to the issues and subjects they take up. As a concept congruent with networks and connectivities, transnational publicity allows scholars to ask, What does the publicity do within transnational publics? What story does the publicity construct? What instrumentalities does the publicity enable? What does the publicity conceal from public view? In this way, the concept shifts us from tracking movement and linking and asks us to consider how the publicity influences a public's framing, understanding, and meaning making of an issue, as well as what those hermeneutic effects enable in the political sphere.

Transnational publicity is a mediating force, paving the way for a shift in the state's recognition of its involvement in the structures of violence that women such as Alvarado flee. The publicity about gender violence that circulated in the aftermath of Alvarado's case articulated gender violence in ways that freed the United States of recognizing itself as complicit in the structures of violence that Central American women flee. It also racialized Central America in that it fixed particular types of gender violence to the bodies and lands of this geographical locale. To understand this enabling effect, I begin my analysis a few years before Alvarado's case in the late 1980s, with the asylum cases of women from Guatemala and El Salvador who also sought refuge for reasons relating to sexual and physical violence. My task in this section is to etch out the contours of U.S. involvement in the structures of violence that Central American women were fleeing, and also to demonstrate the early U.S. response to these women's requests for refuge. Part 2 will detail the staging of transnational publicity about gender violence, and violence in Central America that circulates after Alvarado's 1999 denial. My contention is that this publicity enabled the United States to recognize itself, without complicity, as a pastoral state that protects women from violence. This, in turn, constrains state officials in Alvarado's case, as they dare not refuse her right to refuge, lest they be seen as a state that is itself volatile and violent against women.

Early Central American Case Law

When President Ronald Reagan took office in January 1981, Guatemala and El Salvador had already launched into civil wars that would take both countries another decade to calm. In total, 200,000 people died in Guatemala, while another forty-five thousand (a very narrow estimation) are now considered *los desaparecidos,* or forcibly disappeared persons. Salvadorans faired no better during the decade; approximately seventy-five thousand lost their lives as the Salvadoran army tried to squelch the mounting power of leftist groups who were led by the *Frente Farabundo Martí para la Liberación Nacional,* or FMLN. Such violence caused eighteen-year-old Carmen Gomez to leave her home of El Salvador in 1979, traveling the span of Guatemala and Mexico to San Ysidro, California, where she entered the United States. Gomez had experienced personally what civil war meant in her country; from the time she was age twelve until she was fourteen, she experienced five separate instances when guerrilla soldiers forcibly entered her home and physically and sexually assaulted her. In the midst of escalating violence across the country, when her mother died in August 1979, Gomez fled the country to later claim asylum on the basis that she was a part of a large social group of "women who have been previously battered and raped by Salvadoran guerillas," and because of this she could be "subject to, and singled out for, persecution in El Salvador."[14]

Around the same time, fellow Salvadoran native Sofía Campos Guardado made a similar plea to the United States for exile.[15] In her case, Campos Guardado noted two experiences that caused her to leave El Salvador for refuge in another country. In 1984, Campos Guardado took a trip to the home of her uncle, who was the director of a local agricultural union participating in the Land Reform Movement, to take care of errands for her father. Not long after she arrived, a group of armed men and women appeared at the farm and demanded that her uncle give them the cooperative's money. The group seized Campos Guardado and her family members, and according to INS documents, "They dragged Ms. Campos, her uncle, a male cousin and three female cousins to the rim of the farm's waste pit. They tied all the victims' hands and feet and gagged the women."[16] The group murdered the men and afterward raped Campos Guardado and her female cousins; all the while, "the women who accompanied the attackers shouted political slogans."[17] Campos Guardado and her female family members were then verbally threatened and set free. They fled, and upon reaching a hospital in San Salvador, "Ms. Campos suffered a nervous breakdown and had to remain in the hospital 15 days."[18] When she exited the hospital, Campos Guardado returned to her parents' house in the city. Shortly after returning, two men her mother introduced as her cousins appeared at her parents' home. Campos Guardado recognized one of the men as her assailant and realized he was there to watch her as he "later sought her out several times and threatened to kill her and her family if she revealed his identity."[19] Recognizing that she may not be safe in El Salvador, she fled the country in the fall of 1984 and filed for asylum relief.

Traveling a similar northbound migration path two years prior, Salvadoran Olimpia Lazo Majano also arrived at the United States' southern border seeking refuge on the basis of political persecution. Lazo Majano was married to a man who had to seek exile outside of their home city because of his choice to exit *Organización Democrática Nacionalista* (ORDEN), a murderous paramilitary organization affiliated with the Salvadoran army. Lazo Majano herself chose to stay in their small town, as it had been her home since she was a child, and she didn't want to leave.[20] After her husband's exit in 1982, army Sergeant Rene Zuniga approached Lazo Majano and asked if she might work for him doing laundry. She agreed, as she had known Zuniga since she was a child. For six weeks she did his laundry on her day off without complaint. One day, Zuniga pointed out that her husband was no longer in El Salvador, and then he raped Lazo Majano. For months Zuniga tormented Lazo Majano: "He broke her identity card in pieces and forced her to eat the pieces. He dragged her by the hair about a public restaurant. He pummeled her face, causing a blood clot to form in one eye; she thought she had lost the eye."[21] The sergeant threatened to kill her and her husband if he returned: "Zuniga told Olimpia that it was his job to kill subversives . . . he would have her tongue cut off, her nails removed one by one, her eyes pulled out and then she would be killed."[22] As recalled in the court testimony, Zuniga stated, "And I can just say that you are contrary to us; subversive."[23] Zuniga backed this statement up again when he "told a friend from the police, 'in front of all the other people in the restaurant,' that she was a subversive and that was why her husband had left: because she was a subversive."[24] Threats and physical violence of this nature continued for three months; Lazo Majano then left the country.

The experiences of Guatemalan women who filed cases contemporaneously with Gomez, Campos Guardado, and Lazo Majano are replete with similar details; Sonia Juarez Lopez reported that a man nearly twenty years her senior repeatedly raped her, starting when she was approximately twelve or thirteen years old, and threatened to kill her if she told anyone.[25] An anonymous asylum seeker testified to her father's kidnapping, torture, and ultimate murder, testimony which later resulted in her own physical and sexual assault because the man who killed her father found her, threatening to kill her if she reported the murder.[26] Another woman reported severe sexual and physical violence by her father when she was a child and by her husband later on. She reported that she feared "returning to Guatemala because of the awful memories of what her father did to her, and because she is afraid her ex-husband will kill her."[27] Yet another woman suffered abuse at the hands of her common-law husband, who was a police officer in Guatemala. Before the U.S. immigration officials who evaluated their cases, these women were unilaterally denied asylum on the basis that their experiences of violence were more personal than political, that their social group didn't count in accordance with the refugee definition and precedent defining what counts as an eligible social group. Furthermore, even if the women were members of the named social group, officials often reasoned that their persecutors would not identify them by their membership in gendered social groups, thus precluding their eligibility.

The Salvadoran women faired no better. The BIA explained in its negative ruling of Carmen Gomez "that [Gomez] has failed to demonstrate that the guerrillas are inclined or will seek to harm her based on her association with a particular social group."[28] The Court of Appeals affirmed this ruling, elaborating, "Gomez failed to produce evidence that women who have previously been abused by the guerillas possess common characteristics—other than gender and youth—such that would-be persecutors could identify them as members of the purported group. Indeed, there is no indication that Gomez will be singled out for further brutalization on this basis."[29] Similarly, the judges told Campos Guardado that she was not entitled to asylum. The Court of Appeals board explained: "While the attackers may have been motivated by their own political goals such as, for example, the intimidation of other peasants involved in land reform, the record does not establish that [Ms. Campos] was persecuted on account of any political opinion she herself possessed or was believed by the attackers to possess."[30] In Lazo Majano's case the immigration judge and BIA agreed that "the evidence attests to mistreatment of an individual, not persecution,"[31] elaborating that "the fact remains that such strictly personal actions do not constitute persecution within the meaning of the Act."[32] Lazo Majano would ultimately win asylum when she revised her argument, claiming persecution on the basis that she was "imputed" with a political opinion as "subversive," when Zuniga called her a subversive. This endowment of political voice and political subjectivity, though, was never recognized as of her own accord. Rather, she was endowed with a political opinion through the voice of her male persecutor.

These cases are rife with evidentiary connections to the state itself, to state actors, and to non-state political actors as the agents of violence in these women's lives, and yet in the decisions the judges decidedly interpret these agents as either non-state actors or privately motivated state actors. In total, the women from Guatemala and El Salvador who claimed asylum in the late 1980s and early 1990s spoke intimately of the ways their gender motivated violence against them, the ways their states refused to ensure their protection, and often of the ways state and political actors were the primary agents of the persecution. Yet these cases were consistently refused recognition in the United States as political persecution warranting relief through international refugee protocol.

Despite their initial failures, what the cases did enable is a normative framework for what counts as gender-based persecution in U.S. asylum law. Specifically, the cases help solidify the definition of gender violence as physical and sexual violence against cisgender, presumably heterosexual women. This does not mean, however, that U.S. officials recognize this gender violence as *political* persecution. As my previous work evaluating these cases demonstrates, in the institution of asylum, cisgender women are recognized first as private and relational subjects: "Women who are sexually assaulted still face the discursive positioning as private subjects with personal interests when they stand before the court. Furthermore, they continue to be read as possible political subjects not of their own accord, but through their real and imagined relationalities to/ with men."[33] On another level, these cases reveal how relationships between states create the context for these cases to be heard and evaluated. This context becomes increasingly clear by examining the trajectories of these cases through time and hence through the shifting geopolitical relationship between the United States and Guatemala and the United States and El Salvador.

The CIA, Covert Operations, and Political Persecution

President Reagan took office in January 1981 at a time of high anxiety in the United States about Communism strengthening around the world. One of the president's first tasks upon election was to secure the United States' influence in a number of key political theaters, including Guatemala and El Salvador, where the "Communist threat" was evident. Reagan expediently committed support to de facto president of Guatemala José Efraín Ríos Montt after the 1982 coup d'état that secured his rule. This support included shipments of military hardware worth millions of dollars and training support for military and intelligence. Not long after amplifying its support, the United States, through state officials on the ground, began receiving secret word of increased violence in these countries. In February 1982 state officials learned, through a National Security Administration brief, that "the Guatemalan Army [had] reinforced its existing force in the central El Quiche department and [had] launched a sweep into the Ixil triangle." The brief continued: "The commanding officers of the units involved have been instructed to destroy all towns and villages which are cooperating with the Guerrilla army of the poor (EGP) and eliminate all sources of hesitance."[34] By February of the next year, officials were alerted to a further uptick in the violence. As explained in a then-classified CIA wire, "There has been a steady increase of suspect right-wing violence over the past few months. Kidnappings, particularly of students and educators, have increased in number and bodies are again appearing in ditches and gullies. Showing the telltale signs of rightist hit squad executions similar to those common under the previous regime."[35] In the same wire, though, the U.S. ambassador to Guatemala raised concerns about the attribution of culpability for the violence, explaining, "I am firmly convinced that the violence described in paragraph three is government of Guatemala ordered and directed violence and not 'right wing violence' and that these were not 'rightist hit squad executions' but again executions ordered by armed services officers close to president Rios Montt."[36]

The situation would rage on in Guatemala, with hundreds of thousands displaced, disappeared, or murdered. Meanwhile, the United States would continue its support of the army. Records show not only that thousands of Guatemalan military officers were trained at the U.S. Army School of the Americas but also that the counterintelligence strategies, including execution, imprisonment without cause, and torture were tactics developed by U.S. officials for implementation in these countries.[37]

Citizens of El Salvador also had to negotiate U.S. involvement in their bloody civil war. The United States was one of the primary promoters of the Land Reform Movement in El Salvador, in which Campos Guardado's uncle was participating as a farm-cooperative leader. Furthermore, when civil war began in the country, U.S. support followed a similar pattern as it did in Guatemala, with a channeling of U.S. resources to the Salvadoran military in the form of support and training of El Salvador's paramilitary groups, including ORDEN (which Lazo Majano's husband had participated in), but also in financial and material support for the broader military objectives. U.S. Congressman Joe Moakley of Massachusetts was fervent in his opposition to U.S. involvement in El Salvador. In a personal letter written in February 1982, he took this matter up directly with President Reagan.

> Mr. President, I have read numerous accounts and reports of the conditions and the political situation in El Salvador. Every one of these reports leads me to believe, beyond a doubt, that the present government in El Salvador lacks respect for the basic human and civil rights of its people. In fact, a recent report of the United Nations Human Rights Commission estimates that well over 9,000 political murders were committed in the first six months of 1981 alone. It seems to me that by training Salvadoran soldiers in the United States we are contributing to the oppression that already exists. We are, in essence, training Salvadoran troops to oppress their own people. . . . Our support of this government, through military means, is nothing short of unconscionable.[38]

Congressman Moakley would continue his critique of U.S. involvement in El Salvador throughout his time in office. While such pressure eventually resulted in the release of hundreds of secret CIA documents that confirm just how bloody

U.S. activity was in repressing Salvadoran and Guatemalan citizens, it did not translate into sustained relief for those displaced or fearing persecution in relation to the violence: "Approval rates for Salvadorans and Guatemalan asylum cases were under three percent in 1984. In the same year, the approval rate for Iranians was 60 percent, 40 percent for Afghans fleeing Soviet invasion, and 32 percent for Poles."[39] While those fleeing Nicaragua's Sandinista government experienced approval ratings at 84 percent in 1987 alone, Guatemalans and Salvadorans were denied asylum at rates of 99 percent and 97 percent respectively throughout the decade.[40] There was, reportedly, an informal policy of preventing Salvadorans and Guatemalans during these years of ever getting to the point where they could apply for asylum. As Susan Gzesh explains, "Salvadorans and Guatemalans arrested near the Mexico-U.S. border were herded into crowded detention centers and pressured to agree to 'voluntarily return' to their countries of origin. Thousands were deported without ever having the opportunity to receive legal advice or be informed of the possibility of applying for refugee status."[41] Many remained in Mexico, legalizing status through Mexican processes of refugee resettlement, or remaining undocumented and stateless.[42]

The U.S. Refugee Act of 1980 was supposedly designed to rid U.S. refugee law and policy of its ideological and geographical preferences, invoking in their stead humanitarian principles that could be applied to the experiences of all displaced persons. "Actual practice," as Kathleen Newland writes, "changed very little. In 1993, the overwhelming majority of U.S. resettlement places for refugees from abroad still went to people from the former Soviet bloc and Indochina" despite the large numbers of asylum applicants from countries south of the U.S.-Mexico border.[43] By 2010, though, analysts of asylum trends would see an interesting shift in the way Central Americans were receiving asylum. Guatemalans and Salvadorans continued to have approval rates hovering around 1 percent and 2 percent, yet women fleeing gender-based violence from these countries began to see their claims for asylum accepted. In order to understand this shift, I address the transnational publicity that unfurled in the aftermath of Alvarado's 1999 BIA denial.

Constructing the Frame of Gender Violence

The BIA's negative decision in Alvarado's case, discussed at the beginning of this chapter, did not signal the end of her travels and travails in the United States. The justices appointed to the BIA could see Alvarado only as a "victim of tragic and severe spouse abuse,"[44] not a victim of political persecution, but many others disagreed and began diligently addressing the matter with public attention toward the case. In February 2000, Senators Patrick Leahy, Sam Brownback, James Jeffords, John Kerry, Edward Kennedy, Russell Feingold, and Charles Schumer wrote a letter on behalf of Alvarado, asking Attorney General Janet Reno to reconsider the decision herself. They wrote, "Women's persecution often takes gender-specific forms, including 'honor killings,' domestic violence and rape. . . . As [you are] an internationally recognized leader in the field of women's human rights, your guidance and arbitration is needed to ensure that asylum laws are uniformly applied."[45] Later that year, fifty-seven members of the House of Representatives and eight members of the Senate again signed letters of support for Alvarado's bid explaining,

> Too many U.S. decision-makers fail to recognize that harms unique to women—such as forced marriage and the repressive practices of the Taliban—may constitute persecution. We are deeply concerned by the apparent gross misunderstanding of the law demonstrated by the characterization of honor killing as a "personal family dispute." We urge you to address this growing gap in the United States' protection of women fleeing severe human rights abuses. In particular, we are aware that you are currently reviewing the BIA decision in the Matter of RA [Rody Alvarado]. We implore you to reverse that decision.[46]

Further afield, international human rights groups began to put pressure on the executive office of the United States to recognize Alvarado's eligibility. In 2003 Amnesty International began calling its members to contact President George W. Bush and Attorney General John Ashcroft on the matter, arguing that the decision was in "conflict with recent UNHCR guidelines on gender persecution, and out of step with countries around the world that recognize government-tolerated gender-related violence as a basis for asylum, including Canada, the United Kingdom, Australia, and New Zealand."[47] Organizations, including Human Rights First, Family Violence Prevention Fund, HealthRight International and many others, joined the attention-generating efforts to put international pressure on the U.S. government to recognize these forms of persecution as eligible for asylum. At the same time, publicity in more diffuse form began to circulate about the violent circumstances for women in both Guatemala and El Salvador. It was this information and analysis that provided the rhetorical pressure to recognize these contexts as politically hostile to women *as* women.

First, the publicity located the violence women experience within these countries as systemic gender violence, making it impossible to deny the targeting of women as pervasive in these countries. Second, it politicized the violence, offering an analysis that made it impossible to brush the gendered forms of violence off as "personal" or "private" and thus not eligible for protection as political and state-sponsored violence. Finally, the publicity offered an analysis of the impetus of the violence that freed the United States from culpability, creating distance between the state's involvement in Guatemalan Salvadoran civil wars and the present-day structures of violence. What is so unique about this publicity, though, is the unity of voice and rhetorical invention across each of the discursive venues emergent from very different locales, for different purposes, and by different sorts of groups. This unity of voice, across transnational registers gives the frame much persuasive force in shifting state acknowledgement of the violence. Vital to the success of these cases, the transnational publicity also circulated a frame of the violence that enabled the United States to recognize itself as free from implication in the violent conditions that these women were fleeing. Instead, the violence was racialized as endemic and essential to the dominant cultural values of the countries that these women fled. Containing the violence solely within the countries and regions facilitated the United States' ability to position itself as detached outside observer, not violent participant. Such freedom from complicity then enabled the United States to begin admitting asylum seekers on the basis of gender-based violence, duly allowing the state to mobilize rhetoric about itself as a pastoral defender of women's rights around the world. An unintended consequence of this staging, though, was the way the publicity localized gender violence in place and body.

Examining how various venues, media, and messages construct violence in these countries reveals that the high rates of violence are framed as acts of gender violence, specifically, violent acts against women. The language deployed to describe the issue, including terms such as "gender-based violence," "violence against women," and "femicides" or "feminicides," solidifies the shape and scope of the violence. As a 2005 Amnesty International report explains, "Many women and girls in Guatemala live with gender-based violence: violence against women in the family, rape, and sexual harassment in the workplace are commonplace. Women and young girls are also the victims of commercial trafficking and sexual exploitation."[48] Femicide is another common framing device, which "lifts," as one report explains, "the murder of women out of the mass of violent crime taking place in Guatemala and highlights its gendered aspect."[49] Another report notes that "the term femicide is used to refer to the gender-motivated killings, carried out with extreme brutality. While violence against both men and women has increased in Guatemala in the past year, the murders of women are distinct both for their misogynistic nature, as well as the disproportionate rate at which they are increasing."[50]

Along with the framing of the violence in the region and countries as gender-based violence, there is unified publicity about the pervasiveness of the danger, emphasized through the repeated citation of numerical figures across each of these venues. A 2007 Guatemala Human Rights Commission report takes a scenic narrative approach. "This is Guatemala" the report begins, "where more than 3,000 women have been brutally murdered since 2000, and fewer than 2% of cases end in conviction. This is Guatemala, where femicide, or the murder of women, claimed the lives of at least 665 women in 2005, 603 women in 2006, and 306 women during the first seven months of 2007. The majority of the victims are young, poor women between the ages of thirteen and thirty. This is Guatemala, the most dangerous place for women in all of the Latin America."[51] Approximately the same number of women are murdered each year in El Salvador as in Guatemala, another report offers, with 160 femicides in the first three months of 2012.[52] "The rate of femicides," yet another explains, "has risen 197% in El Salvador over the past decade."[53] Rates of domestic violence in these countries are also alarming; numerous groups repeat the figure that as many as 70 percent to 90 percent of women in these two countries experience intimate abuse in their lifetime. Such statistics paint an alarming picture of the scope of the violence in the area, making it hard to imagine a scenario where a woman, no matter her identity or social status, might be safe if she were living in the area. Not only are forms of gender violence such as femicide and intimate abuse localized onto the landscape, but also the shocking descriptive statistics make a persuasive argument that to be Central American and a woman is to be always in danger. Gender violence is racialized as pervasively and precariously at the core of what it means to live as a woman in the region and these countries.

After having framed the violence in these countries as pervasive gender violence, the texts articulate an impetus, or root cause, for the gendered dimensions of the violence that frees the United States of complicity. All agree that Guatemala and El Salvador are "male-dominated states."[54] As one report conjectures, "The history of the oppression of women in Guatemala has its roots in the traditional gendered roles of Mayan culture. . . . [F]or many indigenous women of Latin America, their association as bearers of culture hindered their ability to efficaciously engage in national society."[55] Another explains, "Guatemalan society is an environment in which aggression toward women is perceived as 'natural,'"[56] a point that is elaborated in yet another source: "Guatemala has always been a deeply patriarchal society that privileges men's authority over women in general and over their wives and children in particular."[57] Amnesty International argues in one of the earliest reports that "the prevalence of violence against women in Guatemala today has its roots in historical and cultural values which have maintained women's subordination."[58] In these depictions, the violence is framed as the result of deep-seated cultural values and structures—those that purportedly existed long before civil war in these countries.

The depictions frame the violence as essential to cultural values and beliefs in Central America. It is not just a small faction or a subset of the population that commits the violence. The publicity blames culture as the root cause of the problem. This cultural explanation further facilitates the containment of gender violence to Central America because it figures the violence as essential to the values, beliefs, and rituals of the people living in these countries and in the region. And, as a cultural value, gender violence thus becomes nearly impossible to avoid. The only possibility is escape or complete cultural eradication.

Some reports blame gang violence, organized crime, and powerful drug families that wage war against common citizens. Others cast blame on the governments of these countries, urging that they have perpetuated a "culture of impunity" or a "culture of violence." This culture of impunity means, in Amnesty International's view, that "perpetrators of past violations have evaded criminal prosecution and have contributed to a spiraling level of violence in society and continuing human rights violations."[59] A number of the texts also mention the civil war in these countries, but the locus of responsibility for the culture of violence is solidly situated within the country. A fact-finding report about violence in Guatemala explains, "Behavioural patterns during the conflict were never fully addressed,"[60] while another argues that "the present government has failed to punish those who committed atrocities during the long and bloody civil war, and there remain ongoing abuses, structural inadequacies, and other indications that the government's commitment to peace and democracy is weak."[61] As one document articulates:

> Guatemala's violent past provides some context for the current wave of femicides sweeping the country, and the virtual impunity that exists for its perpetrators. . . . The conflict was marked by pervasive state-sponsored violence. . . . Women were particularly vulnerable to sexual violence, as rape was commonly utilized as a weapon of war. Numerous investigations have concluded that the vast majority of these human rights violations were conducted by members of the Guatemalan intelligence services, many of whom escaped prosecution and now participate in police activities or are members of private security forces, which have been implicated in the femicides.[62]

With these particular forms of gender violence already racialized as endemic to the cultural core of the Central America region, such descriptions facilitate a further distancing of the United States from implication in the violence. Absent in these narrations are mentions of U.S. complicity, involvement, or even knowledge of the conditions of violence. The United States, through a rhetoric of absence, is framed in this transnational publicity about gender violence as distanced, disconnected, and hence never questioned for its own complicity and culpability in the precarious conditions that require these women to flee their homes.

Instead, the United States is recognized anew as pastoral protector of women. Michel Foucault described pastoral power as state power derived from a Christian theological focus on the "salvation" of individuals and entities in the next world. Modern deployments of pastoral power interpreted "salvation" as a concern of the here and now: "It was no longer a question of leading people to their salvation in the next world but rather ensuring it in this world. And in this context, the word 'salvation' takes on different meanings: health, well-being (that is, sufficient wealth, standard of living), security, protection against accidents. A series of 'worldly' aims took the place of the religious aims of the traditional pastorate."[63] What makes this technique of state power so challenging to critique is that it organizes around questions of popular concern—well-being, humanitarian need, protection—and "is both an individualizing and a totalizing form of power."[64] Pastoral power individuates, or individualizes the locus of subjectivity, by focusing the work of institutions on addressing issues of popular concern through the personal. A question about health is addressed by supporting services for individuals targeted by domestic violence, mandating that women over a certain age do regular gynecological and mammogram check-ups, and giving financial incentive to those who eat well and go to the gym.[65] Popular concern about risk is addressed through mentorship of "at-risk" youth and adults, as well as the encouragement—even mandate—of personal insurance; homes, vehicles, health, even lives can be protected and "saved" from the dangers of various worldly risks through personal purchase.[66] By individuating all concerns of the citizenry, the state, through this pastoral technique, comes to regulate and control the populace.

As Iris Marion Young ruminates about the current security state, there is a gendered and, I would add, racial dimension to this pastoral power, one that, in accordance with a whitening/darkening schema of agency and subjectivity,[67] positions the United States in the whitened "masculine role of protector in relation to women and children" against "bad" brown men, brown culture, and brown sovereigns that are "selfish, aggressive, dominative" and "wish to master women sexually for the sake of their own gratification to have the pleasures of domination."[68] The United States imagines itself in the pastoral role of father, protector of women and children. In this schema, internal and external, the national and international "bad men" are seen by the United States as posing a danger to the vulnerable feminized citizenry. And, because the violence is framed as culturally rooted, it means that extinguishing it will necessarily

involve invasive procedures. In exchange for what it bills as protection, the security state demands "obedience and loyalty" from the populace.[69] Those inside
and outside of the nation-state who are racialized as threatening are targeted
through similar mechanisms—surveillance, militarization, criminalization,
incarceration, detention, and death.

Both elements of pastoral power, individuation and gendered logics, emerge
in the shift in recognition of Central American women's asylum claims through
transnational publicity about gender violence and femicide in Central America.
First, the asylum process, as a whole, individuates the protections offered to
those fleeing gender violence in Guatemala and El Salvador. Alvarado had to
make an individual claim for refugee relief, just as all Central American women
seeking similar protections must do to be "saved" through refugee reliefs. It is
important to note that the transnational publicity about gender violence serves
as a mediating force in these cases, reframing what had been seen as private
violence into political persecution, shifting possible U.S. involvement into distanced interaction, and the United States as pastoral observer of the violence.

There is certainly not unilateral support for Guatemalan and Salvadoran
women's asylum claims, yet there has been a marked shift in the reception of
gendered forms of violence as potentially legitimate as political violence in these
cases. In one of the earliest cases to demonstrate this shift, Mayan Angelica
Erika Castillo-Hernandez of Guatemala argued that the Guatemalan government violently targeted her on account of her gender. Like most asylum seekers,
Castillo-Hernandez included personal testimony that spoke intimately of her
fear to return to the country. Yet she also included evidence from secondary
sources such as the Amnesty International Regional Report discussed above,
which stated that "'horrific brutality' characterized the killings of women in Guatemala," that "the rape of indigenous females was common," and that "murder
victims included 'students, housewives, and professionals, domestic employees,
unskilled workers, members or former members of street youth gangs, and sex
workers,' with gender as the motivating factor in the crimes."[70] Furthermore,
Castillo-Hernandez was able to draw on U.S. State Department human rights
reports on Guatemala, which acknowledged that "'violence against women'
and 'sexual offenses' were a problem in Guatemala."[71]

Lesly Yajayra Perdomo's 2010 bid for asylum best demonstrates the individuating affirmative gestures to recognize gender as a political category in U.S.
asylum law in the wake of this staging of transnational publicity. In 1991, at age
fifteen, Perdomo fled Guatemala to join her mother, who was living in Nevada.
Perdomo entered the country as an undocumented migrant, for her mother had,
in 1985, applied for asylum on behalf of herself and her daughter on account of

her fear that they would be killed in Guatemala—a request that was denied relief. In 2003 the Department of Homeland Security identified Perdomo as unlawfully in the country and called her to appear at an immigration hearing. At that hearing in 2004 Perdomo requested asylum and other forms of immigration relief, arguing that she belonged to a social group of "women between the ages of fourteen and forty" who risked a "high incidence of murder" as Guatemalan women if they lived in the country.[72] The immigration judge and the BIA both denied this claim, explaining that the categories of "all women in Guatemala" and "women between the ages of fourteen and forty who are also Guatemalan and live in the United States" were too broad to be identifiable in line with social group membership precedent.[73] On appeal in 2010, however, the Ninth Circuit Court of Appeals decided that the question of social group may not be as clear as previously thought by the immigration judge and BIA, remanding the case back to the courts to be decided in line with their writing on the matter.

The Ninth Circuit relied on the language and evidence present in the transnational publicity about these countries' problems with gender violence to make sense of Perdomo's need for asylum. Perdomo was explicitly recognized by the courts as having a "high risk of femicide and that as a woman she has an objectively well-founded fear of future persecution in Guatemala."[74] The court was also persuaded that in Guatemala, "women were murdered at a high rate with impunity."[75] This individual recognition was possible because the frame of gender-based violence and femicide as fixed in Guatemala both successfully circulated in transnational publicity and was taken up by the courts to articulate their own meaning for gender-based violence in Guatemala:

> Perdomo testified that her fear was based on the high incidence of murder of women in Guatemala, and her own status as a Guatemalan woman. She provided the IJ [immigration judge] with several reports by the Guatemala Human Rights Commission, which is based in the United States, documenting the torture and killing of women, the brutality of the killings, the non-responsiveness of the Guatemalan government to such atrocities, the countrywide prevalence of the killings, and the lack of explanation for the killings.[76]

In contrast to the earlier decisions in Central American women's cases, gender violence in this case was unquestioningly recognized as political. The pervasiveness of gender violence in Guatemala and El Salvador as described in transnational publicity became the mediating force for U.S. immigration judges to see gendered forms of violence such as intimate abuse and sexual assault as political. Gender violence as a form of political persecution is here given an institutional life, enabling gender to be recognized as a political category in these instances. These rulings and this publicity do not enable all instances of intimate violence and sexual assault from all parts of the world to be seen as political. Instead, this gesture to recognize gender and gendered subjects is particular and localized.

The localization of such forms of violence as endemic to, or part and parcel of, a particular space and targeting of particular bodies also becomes a mediator, providing a container around the recognition of gender violence in order to guard against potential leakage to other gendered bodies, or against U.S. involvement. Framed as specific to country and region, these forms of violence are recognized as problems that only particular women living in particular locations experience—not all women everywhere. While this specific gender violence frame has also migrated to apply to the experiences of women in neighboring countries like Mexico and Honduras, the frame remains specific to country and region so as to be contained—not communicable to the United States or other geographical locales.[77] Here, what makes gender violence political is not the fact of gender violence alone but instead that there is a context in which the political violence can be placed, isolated, and contained; this locating creates an assurance to the United States that responsibility or culpability for such violence won't spread. In the early cases, the U.S. asylum policymakers were fearful that if gender, or more specifically women, were added to the definition of what constitutes a refugee, then a "floodgate" would open to all women asylum applicants—women fleeing domestic violence, rape and sexual assault, castigation for refusal to conform to social norms, and the like. This fear promulgated definitions of the "political" so tied to the state and geography that it largely left women in the lurch.

The cases of Central American women in recent years have used transnational publicity to bring the political nature of their claims for relief to the foreground. These cases demonstrate the possibilities of staging transnational publicity as a rhetorical strategy in an era of the pastoral U.S. security state, but it must be remembered that these claimants have never been truly recognized as political subjects by the institution. While the publicity has demonstrated a context of politicized violence against women, it never argued that women were themselves political agents. Instead, their positions as private subjects for whom relational and cultural violence happens remains intact. The institution is never really forced to see these claimants as political subjects of and on their own accord. Instead, violence is done to them. And, because this framing of the political attends with the localization of the violence of femicide and sexual torture, the institution never has to question whether the discursive structures of knowledge used to categorize women's subjectivities might need revamping.

It is the individual woman who, in yet another form, must be protected from the "bad" male actor. Thus, while it is tempting to laud these liberal openings for Central American women fleeing gender violence to receive asylum, we must nevertheless always pay attention also to the narrowness and contingency upon which this gendered inclusion is conditioned.

Conclusion

A state's geopolitical interests and involvements articulate in particular ways alongside asylum seekers' possibilities of gaining refuge. Transnational publicity can intervene on behalf of asylum seekers in an era of the pastoral security state, augmenting the potential that they may not only gain refuge but be recognized as political subjects. In chapter 2, I move on to examine what happens to gender-based claimants once gender is entered into the judicial record as a means of accessing refugee reliefs. I pick up with the analysis of the way gender violence fixes onto particular bodies and places, working to see how feminist rhetorics of freedom and choice differently enable those seeking immigration protections.

CHAPTER 2

Fixing Bodies, Fashioning Subjects

Constructing Gender through Rhetorics of Freedom and Choice

In her now-famous article published in 1990, Charlotte Bunch coined the popular phrase "women's rights are human rights," calling U.S. publics to recognize the various intersections between the human rights platform and women's experiences. The article addressed numerous issues, but global instantiations of violence against women were at the fore of her concern. She explained: "The most pervasive violation of females is violence against women in all its manifestations, from wife battery, incest, and rape, to dowry deaths, genital mutilation, and female sexual slavery."[1] In 1993, Bunch and seventy-five thousand other signatories brought the campaign to the United Nations Center for Human Rights. As was reported by the *New York Times*, the signatories explained to the international governance institution, "In every country of the world, violence against women occurs daily and the numbers of its victims are probably the highest of any group globally.... We demand that gender violence, a universal phenomenon which takes many forms across culture, race and class, be recognized as a violation of human rights requiring immediate action."[2] By the mid-1990s, "Women's rights as human rights" had become an anthem for a new movement. "In the three years between Bunch's inspirational call and the clear response from the 1993 United Nations World Conference on Human Rights in Vienna, Austria," writes Elizabeth Friedman "a global movement, claiming hundreds of thousands of members in over one hundred countries, has coalesced in promotion of women's human rights."[3]

Indeed, the "women's rights as human rights" slogan was reproduced time and again as the title to newspaper and magazine articles, and it served as the theme of Hillary Rodham Clinton's remarks at the UN 4th World Conference on Women in Beijing. The slogan also found its way to the U.S. Congress. While not the first citing of the term in U.S. discourse, in late September 1993 the Senate Subcommittee on International Security, International Organizations, and Human Rights conjointly with the House Committee on Foreign Affairs held a three-part hearing, titled "Human Rights Abuses against Women."[4] Representative Tom Lantos of California began the proceedings by forecasting,

> Today, the subcommittee in the first of a series of hearings, will address the full range of human rights abuses against women. As a country that has made human rights the centerpiece of its foreign policy, we can no longer permit gender-driven discrimination and violence to be relegated to the sidelines of public consciousness. These hearings are convened to ensure that abuses against women will figure prominently in all foreign assistance deliberations. Women's concerns will be an integral component of our foreign policy.[5]

The committee figured gender violence and discrimination as the key issues of address in responding to women's human rights needs. Those giving testimony explained, "No country escapes unscathed on the issue of treatment of women."[6] They then outlined the ways specific forms of gender violence are associated with particular bodies and places. "Widow burning," for example, was associated with India, "bridal kidnappings" with Georgia, and "rape as a tool of torture in Africa and Latin America," they said, "continue unabated."[7] Assistant Secretary of the Bureau of Human Rights and Humanitarian Affairs at the Department of State, John Shattuck, spent considerable time discussing "women's relegation to inferior status" in the Middle East. Women in Saudi Arabia, he proffered, were severely limited in their capacity as public and political actors, while "in Iran, women have been harassed, detained or physically attacked if they appear in public in clothing that official guardians of public morality deem insufficiently modest."[8] "Female genital mutilation" arguably received the most attention over the four days: Chairman Lantos explained, "Over 100 million women worldwide have been subjected to the brutal practice of female genital mutilation. Those that survive the operation suffer a lifetime of physical and psychological pain. Six thousand girls and women are at risk every single day."[9]

While most of the policy suggestions focused on what might be done to eradicate gender violence and discrimination around the world, at the end of the hearing Chairman Lantos questioned the panelists regarding the applicability of their comments to matters of national concern, through the U.S. system of asylum. He explained, "Two days ago the *New York Times* ran an article that focused on the increasing number of women who request political asylum in the United States in order to escape persecution that takes the form of sexual torture, including gang rapes. What is the State Department's policy on this issue? Because INS [Immigration and Naturalization Service] has not been very forthcoming in providing these women with asylum."[10] Shattuck responded first by discussing the procedural complications of claiming asylum but finally qualified his answer as an opinion based in his expertise: "It is my opinion as a human rights specialist, that someone who shows a well-founded fear of persecution and who is the victim of not only gross violations in terms of physical violence but also politically motivated violence, would be a very good candidate for asylum."[11] On this point the subcommittee ended for the day as representatives were called for a vote on a separate matter. The discussion was never taken up again. Indeed, it would take another two full years for the INS to explicitly address Lantos's concern about the adoption of the "women's rights as human rights" framework for addressing gender-based asylum claims. When gender was finally addressed, as I will elaborate below, it would be in the form of administrative suggestion to immigration officers rather than actionable national incorporation of a "women's rights as human rights" framework.

Chapter 1 began with some of the earliest asylum claims that precipitated Lantos's call to understand the reception of gender violence as political persecution in U.S. asylum. In the present chapter I examine how various forms of gender violence come to be fixed in the U.S. national imaginary to particular places and bodies, a point that is gestured to in the congressional hearing cited above about "women's human rights." Not only do representatives associate particular types of gender violence with certain nonwhite bodies, but particular forms of violence become associated with, and flatly applied to, entire geographical expanses. In this chapter, I dive further into this claim, working to consider what happens to the corporeal and spatial fixing of gender violence once gender comes to be recognized in the United States as a possible (though contingent and segregated) ground for claiming asylum. First, I analyze two asylum claims explicitly identified as gender based and then consider subsequent claimants that follow in these two asylum seekers' paths. I read these cases for what they do to the making of gender as an institutional concept and for what they do to imaginations of gender violence in U.S. legal and political discourse.

Both asylum cases articulate harmoniously with the budding "women's rights as human rights" platform as both argumentatively consolidate around rhetorics of freedom. But because of the intersections of these claimants' identities and affiliations, the rhetorics are heard differently in U.S. politico-legal discourse. Both make claims on the basis of gender-based freedom. One argument is heard as a freedom *from*. The other is heard as a freedom *to*. Because of the intersections of geopolitics, gender, and class, this freedom *to* is audienced all too easily through Western logics as another prevalent feminist rhetoric—choice. I use this chapter to demonstrate the ways that feminist rhetorics apply differently to the various subjects they are deployed to make intelligible. Secondarily though, I aim to articulate the political stakes of associating particular forms of gender violence with particular bodies and geographies in the context of what I describe in chapter 1 as the pastoral U.S. security state. Because of the growing prominence of the "women's rights as human rights" frame in the West about the non-West, when these claimants present arguments about specific types of gender violence they fear, their claims can all too easily be used to promote the liberal Western impulse to castigate and eradicate people and nation-states recognized as contrary to the principles of freedom from incorporation.

Feminist Freedoms

In 1995 the INS finally offered an explicit statement in response to the mounting political pressure to include gender-sensitive provisions for evaluating asylum claims. Their contribution, a nineteen-page document, *Considerations for Asylum Officers Adjudicating Asylum Claims from Women*, provided suggestions to immigration officials evaluating women's claims.[12] The document neither codified gender as an unquestionable social group nor mandated adherence to the guidelines in evaluating gender-based claims. Yet it made explicit the state's understanding of gender and gender-based violence as political-legal concepts.

First, the "women's rights as human rights" framework initiated in the early 1990s was the primary guide in framing the articulation of these concepts. The INS began by acknowledging, "Human rights violations against women are not a new phenomenon. Yet, only recently have they risen to the fore of the international agenda."[13] They then outlined international protocols that "contain gender-related provisions and recognize and promote the principle that women's rights are human rights, and that women's rights are universal," including CEDAW, the 1993 United Nations Declaration of the Elimination of Violence against Women, the 1985 UNHCR Conclusion, and Canada's 1993 "Guidelines on Women Refugee Claimants Fearing Gender-Related Persecution."

Gender is deployed as a stand-in signifier for woman in the *Considerations* document. The INS questions neither what it means to have a gender nor what makes a woman a woman but instead defines the two concepts as one in the same. More specifically, the INS prefigures presumed-to-be-heterosexual cisgender women as the subjects for whom gendered considerations are necessary. As explicated in the document's purpose statement: "Although women applicants frequently present asylum claims for reasons similar to male applicants, they may also have had experiences that are particular to their gender. A woman may present a claim that may be analyzed and approved under one or more grounds. For example, rape (including mass rape in, for example, Bosnia), sexual abuse and domestic violence, infanticide and genital mutilation are forms of mistreatment primarily directed at girls and women and they may serve as evidence of past persecution on account of one or more of the five grounds."[14] In this justification, the *Considerations* recognize that cisgender women and men may have similar reasons for claiming asylum. A distinction is made with the gender-based claims, which are made by women and must be "particular to *their* gender." One questions, in this formulation, whether cisgender men or transgender asylum seekers can also make claims "particular to their gender," or what a claim that is "particular to one's gender" even is.

Finally, the document continues by filling in the argumentative gaps in outlining the discursive parameters of gender-based violence, explaining that "rape, sexual abuse and domestic violence, infanticide and genital mutilation"[15] are all forms of persecution that are particular to cisgender women and girls as gender violence. The INS explains, "The laws and customs of some countries contain gender-discriminatory provisions. Breaching social mores (e.g., marrying outside of an arranged marriage, wearing lipstick or failing to comply with other cultural or religious norms) may result in harm, abuse or harsh treatment that is distinguishable from the treatment given the general population, frequently without recourse to state protection."[16] Though specific targeted bodies and geographies are extracted from this document, when asylum officers and judges begin to hear the cases of women fleeing what they, the women, articulate as gender-based persecution, the imaginations of bodies and geographies so prevalent in the "women's rights as human rights" discourse emerge again to solidify subjects worthy of refuge. The rhetoric of freedom so palpable in certain Western feminist discussions becomes central to the invention and reception of arguments in these cases. Yet this rhetoric operates and applies differently to asylum claimants, and with different racializing implications.

Freedom From

At age nineteen, Fauziya Kassindja of Togo entered the United States with the passport of another person. Kassindja told the officers that she came to the

United States to apply for political asylum upon being held by immigration officials for questioning about the passport. She feared returning to Togo because she refused genital cutting and forced marriage to a man more than twenty years her senior. Circumcision, arranged marriage, and polygamy were prevalent in the Tchamba-Kunsuntu community Kassindja grew up in, yet she and her immediate family did not follow these conventions. In 1993 Kassindja's father died suddenly from an asthma attack. Shortly thereafter Kassindja's paternal aunt, Haja-Mammud, took control of the family house and ordered Kassindja's mother to return to her own family in Benin. Haja-Mammud removed Kassindja from school and told her that she soon would marry Ibrahim Isaka, a forty-five-year-old community leader; she also told Kassindja that she would soon be circumcised for the marriage. The circumcision was scheduled for a few days after the wedding ceremony, but with the help of her mother and older sister, Kassindja fled from Togo to the United States, by way of Ghana and Germany, to claim asylum.[17] In her application and asylum hearing Kassindja argued that she was a member of a group of "young women of the Tchamba-Kunsuntu tribe who have not had FGM [female genital mutilation], as practiced by the tribe, and who oppose the practice."[18] In 1996, after being detained and first denied asylum, the Board of Immigration Appeals awarded Fauziya Kassindja asylum. In this landmark decision the BIA recognized female circumcision as political violence on account of Kassindja's gender. *Re Kasinga* is arguably the most notable gender-based U.S. asylum decision to date, for it was the first time U.S. federal courts recognized a particular form of violence as *political* gender violence. Given the unilateral refusal to recognize gendered social groups and forms of violence as valid in the U.S. asylum system up to this point, I question here just what made Kassindja eligible for incorporation. To understand this incorporation we first have to investigate how circumcision was imaginable as gender violence in the U.S. imagination[19] and how Kassindja's subject position was discursively constituted. To answer these questions we must look first to the political and public messages that circulated in the midst of her appeal, rendering Kassindja and circumcision intelligible to U.S. publics.

In December 1995 the *New York Times* published a story, "Female Genital Mutilation by Immigrants Is Becoming Cause for Concern in the U.S.," that introduced U.S. publics to Kassindja's cause for fleeing Togo and her subsequent confinement in a U.S. prison that was doubling as an immigration detention center.[20] The *Washington Post* followed a month later with a direct appeal to the U.S. government to grant Kassindja asylum or at least release her from prison while she awaited her appeal. Journalist Judy Mann explained, "This is a plucky young woman who has shown a lot of courage. She's the kind of person we should want to protect, not further persecute."[21] Kassindja's story became so popular that the *New York Times* took the case up again on April 15, 1996, in a front-page story spotlighting the injustice of Kassindja's detainment.[22] Within ten days of the story, federal authorities released Kassindja from prison to await her appeal. U.S. popular press magazines, including *Time, Newsweek, Newsday,* the *Village Voice, Marie Claire,* and *Ms.,* as well as local newspapers from around the country, quickly followed in the steps of the *New York Times* and *Washington Post* in figuring female circumcision in the U.S. imaginary.[23] In these venues, female circumcision is depicted through the following discourse: The *New York Times* journalist to first report on Kassindja's struggle for asylum focused on the way circumcision curtails women's freedom of sexual pleasure, describing it as a "procedure, which is done, usually without anesthesia, in the name of destroying sexual sensation. It is sometimes fatal. In societies where it is practiced, men have traditionally demanded that their wives come to them as virgins and never succumb to sexual temptation afterward. In strong family settings, women—often grandmothers—have been the enforcers of the practice, exerting tremendous pressures on succeeding generations of mothers and daughters."[24] The *Tampa Tribune* wrote: "Just a few years ago, female circumcision—that benign name for ritual mutilation—was considered a cultural tradition."[25] While the editor for the *Providence [Rhode Island] Journal* explained: "The practice is sheer torture, involving the cutting off of the clitoris and sometimes other genital tissue to truncate women's sexual pleasure. No anesthesia is used, and often, serious health problems and even death result."[26] Former *New York Times* executive editor and then-columnist A. M. Rosenthal became most preoccupied with describing, in one of his numerous editorials on the subject, how genital surgeries impinge on women's freedom:

> Genital mutilation has been inflicted on 80 to 100 million girls and young women. In countries where it is practiced, mostly African, about two million youngsters a year can expect the knife—or the razor or a glass shard—to cut their clitoris or remove it altogether, to have part or all of the labia minora cut off, and part of the labia majora, and the sides of the vulva sewn together with catgut or thorns. *Often, the operation is prettified as "circumcision."* . . . In a man it would range from amputation of most of the penis to "removal of all the penis, its roots of soft tissue and part of the scrotal skin." Short-term results include tetanus, septicemia, hemorrhages, cuts in the urethra, bladder, vaginal walls and anal sphincter. Long-term: chronic uterine infection, massive scars that can hinder walking for life, fistula formation, hugely increased agony and danger during childbirth, and early deaths. But mutilation brings the desired result: painful intercourse and loss of sexual pleasure for women. That is supposed to

keep women virginal until marriage. Presumably it relieves men from any fear of not being able to satisfy women.[27]

Taken together, this framing positions female circumcision as barbaric and painful—something women should have freedom *from* experiencing. The accounts also position genital surgeries as abhorrent because they limit women's right to sexual freedom. Circumcision is described as done to "suppress women's sexuality and make them submissive," as the Philadelphia Inquirer explains,[28] or to "assure that girls will stay virgins until they are married and will remain faithful afterwards by removing the source of sexual pleasure," as was argued in the *Charleston Gazette*.[29] In first introducing U.S. publics to Kassindja in the *New York Times*, Crossette ends her story with the narrative of Ms. Ramsey, an opponent of female circumcision who was circumcised herself at age six:

> Physically, she comprehends now why she had difficulty giving birth to a son 21 years ago. Psychologically, she is tormented by the thought of sensual experiences she has missed, and she searches for a doctor who may be able to rebuild her. "I want to feel how American women feel," she said. She tells a story of inviting a young American couple to stay with her some years ago. When the woman screamed one night, Ms. Ramsey ran to their room to help, only to be told kindly that her friends were just making love and that the woman had had an orgasm. "I didn't understand," she said. "I thought there must be something wrong with American girls. But now I know that there is something wrong with me."[30]

Ms. Ramsey's body, as imagined by U.S. readers, is rhetorically marked with the scars and the pain of some other place. The United States, in contrast, is figured as free—free of such practices, free of physical and psychological pain, and a place free for women to experience and express sexual pleasure. Interestingly enough, in Kassindja's own testimony before the court, she framed the decision to leave Togo through rhetorics of choice, explaining that in her community circumcision was how one became a "woman," and that many women were "proud" of it, but that she and her family didn't believe in the practice and so rather than be "forcibly circumcised" she chose to leave the country. In contrast, interpreted through U.S. logics, concern about female circumcision as a violation of a woman's freedom as a sexual subject became the dominant framing device in the BIAs affirmative decision in *re Kasinga*: "FGM 'has been used to control women's sexuality'" the board writes. They continue:

> It is also characterized as a form of sexual oppression that is "based on the manipulation of women's sexuality in order to assure male dominance and exploitation." . . . We agree with the parties that, as described and documented in this

record, FGM is practiced, at least in some significant part, to overcome sexual characteristics of young women of the tribe who have not been, and do not wish to be, subjected to FGM.[31]

We learn through their decision that circumcision is performed in order to sexually dominate women; thus, it is a violation of a woman's freedom.

The public discourse that frames circumcision as persecution through rhetorics of freedom also solidifies in the U.S. imagination the bodies to which such persecution happens—ultimately essentializing in very racializing ways what U.S. publics "know" about Africa and African women writ large. The racialization solidifies through frames of genital surgeries as "cultural tradition" that truncates "women's sexual pleasure," and that takes place in "African countries." The effect of such racialization is to transform the subjects with agency who speak candidly about their fears and need for refuge into subjectless bodies in need of rescue instead.

Cut bodies are imagined as sexed and sexualized bodies, not white, not of the West, and ultimately vulnerable—precariously vulnerable to the dangers of cultural tradition. These non-Western black and brown women are imagined as having reason to claim political refuge when their bodies are in danger, and when they "expect the knife." While black and brown women are often figured in U.S. discourse as too willful, too dangerous, too vocal in their subjectivities,[32] the rhetoric of freedom cuts claimants' bodies off from their voices in these cases. Circumcision is gender violence not necessarily because of a woman's opposition to it on account of her gendered subjectivity, but because it cuts her off from the ability to experience bodily pleasure as a sexual subject. These messages, while rhetoricizing circumcision as gender-based persecution, also rhetorically constitute the positions of women who may fear persecution as vulnerable bodily subjects without dangerous political voices that are often associated with women of color in the United States, black women most of all.

The cases of asylum seekers following in Kassindja's footsteps only reiterate this positioning as vulnerable, endangered (voiceless) bodies. Not only have adult women gained asylum for their personal fear of future cutting, but claimants have also been able to gain asylum derivatively for fear on behalf of their young daughters who might also be circumcised if deported to their home countries. This limn of youth further reinforces the vulnerable and voiceless subject position that claimants are interpreted into when they speak in U.S. immigration courts, increasing the persuasiveness of rhetorics of freedom when deployed in these cases. For example, Hafza Hassan was first denied asylum because she was circumcised as a young child in Somalia. The court wrote: "Hassan does not have well-founded fear of persecution as she cannot be subjected to FGM a second time. In essence, the government argues that FGM cannot be done to her again so she should not be afraid."[33] Yet because Hassan's case also involved her daughter, a U.S. citizen who had not been circumcised, the Eighth Circuit judges reasoned that she was entitled to derivative asylum because her daughter would not be free from a risk of circumcision in Hassan's home country. This was also the case for Ethiopian Almaz Abebe and her family.[34] Abebe's claim involved her entire family, including her husband and their two U.S.-citizen children. The first asylum judge denied their case, finding it questionable whether their daughter would be subject to circumcision or cutting. The Ninth Circuit court sided with the parents, finding probability that neither parent could prevent their child from being circumcised if deported to Ethiopia. In the cases where the daughters were not U.S. citizens the courts have also been favorable. The Sixth Circuit's reasoning in Yayeshwork Abay's claim demonstrates how the courts have evaluated these claimants as eligible for asylum on behalf of their daughters: "Given the evidence in the record that female genital mutilation is 'nearly universal' in Ethiopia; that Abay herself underwent the procedure at a young age . . . we conclude that a rational factfinder would be compelled to find that Abay's fear of taking her daughter into the lion's den of female genital mutilation in Ethiopia and being forced to witness the pain and suffering of her daughter is well-founded. Accordingly, we find that Abay is also a 'refugee' within the meaning of the Act."[35]

Acceptance of these cases (and subsequent decisions) rhetorically figures women in the United States as free from practices that may restrict their expression of gender—free from the constrictions of a regressive state or culture, free to wear lipstick and buy silicone breasts, and free to participate in the market as entrepreneurs and consumers;[36] of course, this freedom comes at a price. These subjects—both those who fear cutting and those who purchase it—are corporeal subjects, as they are always figured first as subjects through what is done or what they are doing to their bodies. This is a form of political positionality that doesn't necessarily attend well with subjects who voice opinions and beliefs as grounds for their political recognition. In order to be incorporable as rescue-able, black women fearing circumcision must be cut off from their voices and subjectivities in the U.S. imaginary. This framing doesn't even recognize these women's bodies as having agency expressive of their political voice. Those who are successful in claiming asylum on the basis of genital surgeries are recognized as all body—body that is innocent, in danger, and certainly in need of rescue. Bodies, as political matter without voice, are interpretation-based resources of rhetoric making, forever vulnerable to the whims of those

with power to interpret and make meaning of the bodily matter in accordance
with their interests. As corporeal subjects disconnected from their voices who
are imagined as innocuous and acquiescent—possibly the ultimate governable
subjects—the figuring of these black women as incorporable subjects serves
as a counterexample for the state in the racialization of other black and brown
subjects as "willful" and "criminal" when their bodies and voices are deemed
too challenging to the state and its structures of governmentality.

Freedom To

Parastoo Fatin of Iran, whose case I used to open this book, is the second claimant to argue her case explicitly through gendered warrants. As explained in the
introduction, Fatin described her fear of persecution as relating both to her
political opinion and to her social group membership, which were in concert
with Iranian women's rights groups that also held feminist political opinions.
"As a feminist," Fatin explained to the court in evidencing the validity of her
political opinion and social group membership, "I mean that I believe in equal
rights for women. I believe a woman as a human being can do and should be
able to do what they want to do. . . . [In] Iran at the time being a woman is a
second class citizen, doesn't have any right to herself."[37] Like Kassindja, Fatin
argued for recognition as a subject through feminist rhetorics of freedom. She
argued that she should have the freedom to wear, or not wear, a headscarf in
accordance with her political and religious beliefs, and that she should be free
of the threat of violence for not conforming to social norms. Fatin was first in
making this claim, but she was not alone. Shortly thereafter, Soroya Sharif, Azar
Safaie, Saideh Hassib-Tehrani (discussed in court documents as Fisher), and
others would file similar claims.[38]

Central to each of the Iranian women's cases was a refusal to fashion their
bodies in particular ways, for they argued that, as feminists—and political subjects more broadly—they should have the freedom to fashion their bodies in accordance with their own political opinions about gender, religion, and politics
and to be free from the risk of bodily violence for doing so. Fatin testified that
she feared returning to Iran "[because] I refused to wear a veil which was a sign
or badge that I favored Khomeini."[39] Her resistance to wearing a veil enacted
her political and religious preferences, signaling and providing public proof of
her contrary opinions. Living in Khomeini-Iran, she argued, would most likely
require her to be a "visibly practicing Muslim woman" or else face public punishment or imprisonment. This mandated visibility, as explained in testimony,
was not in accordance with either her beliefs or identity. She emphasized this

point by explaining that she was "raised in a way that you don't have to practice if you don't want to";[40] thus, wearing a veil would be in opposition to her identity and political opinions as well as her beliefs in women's rights. Azar Safaie positioned her political voice in opposition to Khomeini and her beliefs about women. She first expressed aversion to the Khomeini government, explaining, "were [I] to be returned to Iran [I] could be imprisoned and possibly killed for ... opposition to the Khomeini regime and to its treatment of women."[41] She then explained that she belonged to a group of "Iranian women who advocate women's rights or who oppose Iranian customs relating to dress and behavior" and who want to be free not to conform.[42] Saideh Hassib-Tehrani was not as explicit in citing feminism or "Westernized" beliefs about women and gender.[43] Her opposition, instead, was toward the Iranian government's position on women and gender. Hassib-Tehrani applied for asylum for both herself and her son who were first sponsored for immigration entrance through Hassib-Tehrani's U.S.-citizen fiancé in 1984.[44] After arriving, plans for the marriage went awry. Consequently, Hassib-Tehrani applied for asylum, stating that "she did not believe in 'the way [the Khomeini government] treat[s] people,' the covering of the face, and the way of life 'dictated by the government.'"[45] Elaborating on this point, she explained that she was particularly in opposition to "Iran's rules concerning the interaction between men and women and clothing restrictions, which require all women to wear 'ultraconservative dress.'"[46] This, they argued, disallowed women the freedom to be public subjects in the way they would choose. Hassib-Tehrani detailed several incidents that gave her reason to fear limits on her freedom to comport as she chose in Iran. While in Iran, she was detained and threatened by state officials after she went to a party at the house of a man who walked around in a bathing suit in her presence. Second, as reported in court documents, "Fisher [Hassib-Tehrani] testified that four government officials stopped her on the street and ordered her into their car at gunpoint. She said she was stopped because she 'had a few pieces of hair hanging out [of her chador or veil] by mistake.' The officials told her that she was not dressed properly, returned her to her home, and admonished her not to appear on the street like that again."[47] Finally, Hassib-Tehrani testified that just before she exited Iran, state officials came to her father's house, where she lived, and searched the home for "political dissidents."[48]

These claimants' arguments resonate strongly with the U.S. public discourse circulating at the time about life in postrevolution Iran in the 1980s and 1990s. While U.S. media made mention of mullahs and clerics with influence in the country, women were overrepresented as figures for U.S. publics' learning about social changes in Iran in the aftermath of the "Islamic Revolution." Through these figures U.S. publics came to recognize Iran as a place of extreme social repression and punishment for going against the grain—especially for women. "The one program the mullahs seem able to agree on," the *New York Times* reported, "is that women's hair must be covered. Conversations are filled with tales of people carted off to jail—and sometimes death—for such crimes as coed swimming."[49] Others detailed death penalties for straying too far from social conventions. Two women were "stoned to death" for prostitution; others were "sent to firing squads" for sexual offenses. As one report explained, "Last week, the revolutionary leader urged the Government to eradicate all remnants of the deposed Shah's regime, and since then officials have been vying with each other to demonstrate revolutionary fervor. All Government departments have instructed women to wear Islamic dress to work."[50]

On the surface, the Iranian women's bids for asylum and the media discourse play into Orientalist U.S. notions of liberating Muslim women through the logics of what Gayatri Chakravorty Spivak has called "white men saving brown women from brown men"[51] and Western discourses of veiled women. The United States has arguably not witnessed the same excited flurry of concern over women's wearing of veils and headscarves as has been evident in the Western European context,[52] but as the previous description reveals, the lack of explicit politicization does not mean that veiling discourse has been absent or neutral. To the contrary, Muslim women's covering practices have had special function in contemporary U.S. discourse as a means to legitimize all sorts of symbolic and material actions toward various countries, especially when Muslim women are the rhetorical figureheads leading the charge against the veil. Lila Abu-Lughod and others explicate that images and imaginations of veiled women in U.S. public discourse often serve as the warrants to justify war and occupation toward "liberating women."[53] Such rhetorical maneuvers animate, as Chandra Talpade Mohanty famously argued, because Western discourse assumes a universality of oppression whereby an "analytic leap" is made "from the practice of veiling to an assertion of its general significance in controlling women."[54] Scholars in accord with Mohanty variously demonstrate the way the veil has been articulated in Western discourse to symbolize "submission," "passiveness," "tradition," "being unenlightened," "servitude," and "domination" in the places where women veil. While Saba Mahmood, Minoo Moallem, Nilifur Göle, Afsaneh Najmabadi, and others vociferously argue that the veil signifies agency and is a dynamic, modern, and political symbol in Muslim social-cultural contexts,[55] the logical leaps and actions that track with the veil in Western discourse assume a singularity to the subjectivity of Muslim women.

In evaluating the asylum claims, the courts did not discount the political nature of these women's identities and opinions as gendered subjects. Rather, the courts turned to the rhetorical impermanence—the choice to adorn—to render negative rulings. The appellate judges who evaluated Fatin's final asylum bid took up the political symbol itself as evidence in denying her claim. The court agreed that her membership in a group of "upper class of Iranian women who supported the Shah of Iran, a group of educated Westernized free-thinking individuals," satisfied the precedential requirements in defining how a successful gendered social group might be constituted.[56] Where she failed was in the certitude of future persecution if she returned to Iran. The court seemed suspicious of her refusal to comply with Iranian law. The majority explained in its decision:

> When asked whether she would prefer to comply with that law or suffer the consequences of noncompliance, she stated only that she "would try to avoid" wearing a chador as much as she could. Similarly, her brief to the BIA stated only that she would seek to avoid Islamic practices "as much as she could." She never testified that she would refuse to comply with the law regarding the chador or any of the other gender-specific laws or social norms. Nor did she testify that wearing the chador or complying with any of the other restrictions was so deeply abhorrent to her that it would be tantamount to persecution. Instead, the most that emerges from her testimony is that she would find these requirements objectionable and would not observe them if she could avoid doing so. This testimony does not bring her within the particular social group that she has defined—Iranian women who refuse to conform with those requirements even if the consequences may be severe.[57]

Despite Fatin's explanation of her political commitments as adversarial to the policies of the government at the time, the court consumed itself with trying to surmise—to guess, in fact—if Fatin would wear a veil if she was returned to Iran. The court found it unlikely that, facing possible penalty from state officials, Fatin would decide to move through public spaces without the necessary wardrobe. Her explanation that she "would try to avoid" the veil as much as she could did not give her much leeway in convincing the courts of the persistence of her political commitments. The judges evaluating Fatin's case were suspicious of the "bodily adornment as political enactment" argument; clothing, they reasoned, could be put on and taken off at the whim of the adorned subject. The argument that these women should have the freedom to practice their political and religious beliefs is translated into another salient feminist discourse in this reasoning—choice, which weakens the power of the warrant. Claims on the basis of freedom *from* violence work because there is an external actor or force—the persecutor—who can be recognized by the courts as the primary actor. For women asylum claimants, this dynamic is especially helpful because it allows the subject who is "gendered" to the court (the woman) to remain easily intelligible as vulnerable, innocent, and thus not threatening as an actor speaking to/against states. Claims on the basis of freedom *to* need no external force; the locus of agency is the subject who speaks and acts. In gender-based asylum cases this means that the primary actor is the gendered subject, the woman who claims refuge. She not only directly calls her country of birth violent, but she directly acts against that state and insists that another state recognize her agency as political and worth protecting. Building on Julietta Hua's work in understanding the racializing discourses that produce the intelligibility of "feminism" and "Islam" in these asylum cases,[58] in a context where gendered subjects must be vulnerable, this argument of freedom *to* racializes claimants as willful and unassimilable.

The claimants are also racialized as potential immigrant subjects in this interpretation of the rhetoric of freedom as a rhetoric of choice. In large part because of clothing's impermanence, there is a wily and sly signification of the veil or chador when adorned by these speaking subjects. That the claimants are vocal, educated, upper-class women who name themselves as "Westernized" makes them further suspicious as crafty, cunning, and shrewd. Indeed, when the primary signifier of one's political agency is a material signifier that one must put on or refuse to wear, it is equally likely, some assume, that one's political commitments and loyalty may be just as malleable, cunning, and crafty. While it would be about five years before the "War on Terror" amplified after the September 11, 2001, bombings, racialization of these women as cunning figures through clothing eerily likens them to terrorist figures who use international asylum protections to gain access to the states they will bomb, or to women "suicide bombers" who use their clothing to conceal their weapons.[59]

Toward denying her claim, the adjudicators of Hassib-Tehrani's bid offered an alternative interpretation of her threatening experiences with the police: "There also is no evidence suggesting that if she returned to Iran, Fisher would not conform with the regulations. Indeed, she testified that the 'veil incident' occurred because she had *mistakenly* left several strands of hair outside her veil, not because she intended to make a political or religious statement."[60] Similarly, the court told Safaie that she could not demonstrate that, were she to return to Iran, she would actually act on her beliefs about gender. The justices explained: "To prevail on an asylum claim on account of her political opinion based on her public expression of general opposition to the Islamic government, Safaie cannot merely contend that the government's policies are repressive or that she disagrees with the policies; she must demonstrate that she fears particularized persecution directed at her personally on the basis of her political opinion . . .

Safaie failed to present evidence of a particularized fear or of a situation which shows a risk of danger different than that faced by other citizens in Iran."[61] This decision came despite evidence that Safaie had previously refused to conform to dress codes. As she explained, she "was discharged from her job as secretary to an Iranian official in 1981 because she demonstrated her opposition to the government's rules relating to women by refusing to wear traditional clothing. She had refused to give up western dress, makeup, and perfume."[62] Furthermore, as described in the final decision, "after her termination, she enrolled in the University of Tehran, where members of the Revolutionary Guard confronted her over her western clothes and smoking; a member of Hezbollah told her she would be caught alone and punished."[63]

Such interpretations of Iranian women are reinforced in U.S. media, figured as at risk of social sanction, yet they are also heralded as vocal in their refusal to conform to social norms. The *New York Times* followed up their reporting on the executions with a story two days later that documented how two thousand Iranian women had gathered outside of the president's office to protest "the Islamic dress code" that he imposed.[64] Other willful women were recorded as saying, "'The clergy wants to put the country back 1,400 years by applying Islamic law. . . . But Iranian women are stubborn. We will not sit with folded arms. We will demonstrate if necessary.'"[65] It is important to note that this willfulness is framed to U.S. publics as a question of freedom. The *St. Petersburg Times* reported, "Women are fighting for freedom in surprising ways. By showing a bit of hair under their scarves, they are battling strict dress codes that require women to cover their heads and bodies."[66] *USA Today* reiterated this message, explaining that, after the revolution "Suddenly, women who had enjoyed Western-style freedoms found themselves having to get permission from male relatives to study, travel and work."[67] At an early postrevolution protest U.S. news described the women protestors as "most wearing black to mourn their 'loss of freedom' and disdaining any head covering [as they] lined the sidewalks."[68] The message that U.S. publics glean from this discourse is that "many women want more freedom, or at least more freedom of movement" in Iran, yet also that "the most heated battle for women's rights is still fought through their wardrobes."[69]

Much like in the asylum decisions, though, because feminist struggles for freedom are framed primarily as questions of adornment, Iranian women's calls for freedom easily slip into being heard as questions of choice. This slippage is reinforced when the fashion choices of these Iranian women are given arguably more attention than the political subjects themselves. Journalist Jonathan Randal was transfixed with details of women's wear, his accounts reading more like a story for the style section than the front page of the news. He described one interviewee as "a beautiful young upper-class woman, dressed in matching pink blouse, pants and shoes," while another, a "well-established woman lawyer," was figured as someone who "goes to court in short sleeves, considered dangerously erotic by the clerical purists, and without covering her head." His report continued: "'No one can force me to put a scarf on my head or change my thinking,' she said, 'but other women can wear the chador. That doesn't bother me as long as they are not dominated by their fathers, husbands and brothers.'"[70]

"Would you believe there is a country in which wearing bangs is a counter-revolutionary act?" a journalist from the *St. Petersburg Times* asked at the beginning of the 1990s in detailing Iranian women's social struggles. Guest writer Elaine Sciolino for the *New York Times* was effusive in her image-conscious descriptions of life in Tehran in her article "The Chanel under the Chador":

> On a street blocked to traffic in the wealthiest section of Teheran, a white-gloved honor guard salutes a parade of women swathed in black as they hurry into an opulently furnished guest house that once belonged to the Shah. The women remove their black floor-length chadors—garments that cover all but their faces and more than anything else symbolize the 1979 revolution that transformed Iran and returned its women to a shrouded life. Beneath their chadors, the women are clearly ready for a party, with lacquered hair, careful makeup and stylish clothes. One wears a black taffeta party dress with a plunging neckline and a big black bow at the shoulder; another, a form-fitting black suit trimmed in fake zebra.[71]

Juxtapositions of contrasting dress billow throughout the archive. An article titled "In Iran, Women's Fashion Ferment," began with startling flair: "The woman refused to sit down," the journalist wrote. "Dressed in a black chador and sunglasses to emphasize her militant modesty, the woman stood among 400 other women and lectured Parliament Speaker Ali Akbar Hashemi Rafsanjani at the Second International Women's Congress last week." The account was directly followed by descriptions of the thousands of Tehran women who "replaced the ubiquitous black scarves and full-length chadors with brilliantly colored scarves that show at least a tuft of the stylish perms underneath. Elegant evening gowns and designer dresses with plunging necklines fill the windows of North Tehran's boutiques."[72] Indeed, public discourse of this time is rife with rich details of women "half-buried by a cumbersome dress code of chadors, overcoats and stifling head scarves," directly contrasted with descriptions of "coats in colors other than black can be seen now along with frosted lipstick and bright-colored shoes."[73] Or women "preen[ing] in miniskirts and décolletage" during private dinner parties while the streets of Tehran are "clogged with veiled women on their way to work."[74] These juxtapositions invite the U.S. reader to believe the analysis of a state that constrains choice in what in a very different context the character Carrie Bradshaw in the series *Sex and the City* once called a "woman's right to shoes"—the choice to decide how to express one's feminist self publically and privately through attire.

Across these legal and public texts, readers are compelled to believe that for "the Westernized women of Iran, who wear off-the-shoulder outfits and tight miniskirts at evening gatherings in their homes . . . it is a daily battle between divided selves—the public personality and the real one."[75] That women in these same articles call the veil their "uniform" or "dress code" only reinforces the notion of conformance to social appearance norms as a choice. As one explained, "For a growing group of women artists, professionals and business owners, the scarf itself has become a small formality—but not its implications. 'I look upon it as a professional dress code,' commented an architect who studied and worked in New York. 'If I worked on Wall Street, I would hate to be strapped in one of those tight suits and ridiculous shoes.'"[76] A university student expressed it bluntly: "'I accept [the head-covering] just like a uniform.'"[77]

Of course, the classed nature of the descriptions of Iranian women seeking "freedom" both in the asylum cases and in media accounts further solidifies the claims of freedom that the asylum seekers express as a choice cultivated by the conspicuous consumption of the leisure class in postrevolution Iran. Chanel, Thierry Mugler, Issey Miyake, Armani, and Prada are name-dropped across the media accounts, as are fashion-forward hairstyles of the time like "the Cleopatra, a blunt cut with long bangs, and the Cartier, a geometrical cut longer on one side."[78] One woman interviewed by Sciolino was described as "dispens[ing] with her chador, and her head scarf and coat as well, and stands revealed" on a women's only night in her house. The journalist seems almost surprised when she writes, "With her perfectly tailored lime-green-and-white Chanel-style suit, pale hose and pumps and a single strand of pearls, she looks, well, modern."[79] In the context of making an asylum case about political persecution because of castigation on account of feminist freedoms, the ability to wear (or buy) Chanel hardly seems repressive.

The judges in each of the asylum cases place emphasis on the body and its adornment as the discursive site of truth, and on the feminist ability to choose, as the rhetorical means to cast shadows of doubt on their eligibility. In each instance, the courts imply that they have some evidence of corporeal failure to justify the judgment that the claimants lack evidence of future persecution. Fatin is recognized by the courts as wavering in her resistance when she states that she would "try to avoid" conformity to corporeal codes, while Hassib-Tehrani is dismissed of a fear of persecution because her past behavior in Iran had at least tried to conform to codes of piety. Safaie demonstrated past resistance and admonishment for that refusal, but the justices reasoned that these past experiences were not severe enough to prove that she would likely experience persecution in the future. Despite what these women express about their fear of future persecution, it is their bodies that do the speaking for the judges of these courts. Quite simply, the courts are not convinced that when faced with the choice between enactment of their beliefs or possible reprisal, the claimants would choose fashion-conscious clothing and thereby risk sanction. Instead, bodily enactment is envisioned as malleable, shifty, and crafty—itself a choice. Gendered corporeal enactments, in this context, are not performative but are rather figured as performances by the courts—capable of being changed in their theatricality, demonstrative of a surface of signification but not of substance connected to that surface. This is in contradistinction to the positioning as voiceless bodies of African women claiming female circumcision, which enables their incorporation. While Iranian women are figured through their corporeality, intersections of their gender, race, class, and nationality make it such that their voices always accompany their bodies. These claimants are subjects who are willful, willing, and able to use their voices and bodies to challenge the state and its governance practices.

Rhetorical Fixing

The application of rhetorics of freedom has meant differential access to asylum protections, but it has also contributed to the flattening and fixing of gender violence onto particular bodies and geographies. For example, in Kassindja's case the court insists on codifying the gender violence as "female genital mutilation" or FGM as the legally recognized terminology. Though Kassindja explained in written and verbal testimony that her fear was of being circumcised, the Board consistently deployed mutilation or the term FGM in discussing her case. Mirroring public discourse, the BIA described cutting as "a tribal practice" that is "of an extreme nature causing permanent damage," "a practice in which portions of the female genitalia are cut away," one that "shocks the conscience" and is thus persecution.[80]

In later cases this insistence on naming the fear of persecution as "mutilation" became a fixation of the courts. Khadija Mohammed found the Ninth Circuit judges so in support of her case that they insisted in their decision, "We note that many courts and the BIA refer to the practice at issue here as FGM. We see no need for using initials rather than the full three-word phrase. We are short neither of paper nor of ink. The use of initials, if it has any effect, serves only to dull the senses and minimize the barbaric nature of the practice."[81] Such a move parallels public discourse of the time that monolithically deploys the term mutilation, eschewing terms like circumcision and cutting as "prettified" and "benign." The deployment of "genital mutilation" solidifies circumcision as persecution that endangers a physical body and persecution that is located anachronistically in another space and time. The term "circumcision" connotes religious ritual; genital mutilation connotes destruction. Even though the United States is a predominantly Christian nation, circumcision is a familiar, modern practice. Genital mutilation, however, is presented as destructive: invasive and sexual on the one hand, and distant and problematically traditional on the other. The Western insistence that women and young girls in these countries are "mutilated by tradition" through "cultural torture" or "an ancient ritual" figures this form of persecution as born of culture, but culture that manifests elsewhere. Public discourse about circumcision frames it univocally as an "African genital rite." The repetitive focus on Africa flattens circumcision onto the expanse of the continent and fixes this sort of gender violence as something that African women, uniquely, should be free from.

As a way of distancing the United States from the corporeal and geographic markings of female circumcision, a few months after Kassindja[82] was granted asylum, the president and Congress incorporated Sections 644 and 645 into the Illegal Immigration Reform and Immigration Responsibility Act of 1996 (IIRIRA), criminalizing the practice of female genital circumcision in the country. Section 644 obligated the immigration service to inform those offered new visas to the country of "the severe harm to physical and psychological health caused by female genital mutilation" and of the "potential legal consequences" for performing or allowing the performance of female circumcision on someone younger than age eighteen. Section 645 criminalized the act of performing or permitting genital surgeries on minors in the country. In one of the lone public arguments for this provision, Representative Patricia Schroeder of Colorado urged House members to join her in "mak[ing] it illegal to mutilate women in the name of tradition."[83] "The practice of FGM" she explained in introducing an earlier (bill) version of the provision, "stems from an intricate mix of traditional African perceptions of gender roles, sex, health, local customs, superstition, and religion. . . . While we welcome immigrants from countries that practice FGM, we do not welcome their practice of such mutilation here."[84] Sections 644 and 645 were included in IIRIRA without further debate.

In addition to ensuring that the here and now of the United States is void of genital surgeries, these legislative measures also participate in the national U.S. discourse that racializes particular subjects as criminal. Criminalization discourse targets particular bodies—black and brown bodies—rather than particular practices as the site of meaning making. For example, body-focused racialization turned Tamir Rice of Cleveland, Ohio, from a kid playing with a toy gun in the park into a "criminal" whose bodily presence was dangerous. It turned twenty-two-year-old Rekia Boyd who was walking home in Chicago after a party with friends into someone who was threatening. And, in my current home of Madison, Wisconsin, it turned nineteen-year-old Tony Robinson, who was unarmed, high on hallucinogenic mushrooms and struggling with mental illness, into an aggressive, assaulting figure. In the context of asylum cases and immigration more broadly, black African immigrants are assumed to be already suspicious either because they have already engaged in criminal behavior, maybe even on U.S. soil, or because they are framed as unlearned in U.S. laws and customs such that they are likely to do something incorrect, something "criminal." Black African immigrants, the thinking goes, need be warned: A number of years ago I was doing qualitative research with Sudanese refugees resettled in Phoenix, Arizona, and every September, when a new group of refugees would be placed in the city through the volunteer agencies, one of the first sessions the new immigrants would have to attend was with law-enforcement officials.[85] The officers weren't there to welcome the refugees to their new country or to hear about the violent conditions that had brought them to the United States. The message was clear—do not mess up. The police listed off actions and activities that the police assumed were allowed in refugees' home countries that are prohibited in the United States: You cannot assault people or steal things that don't belong to you. You must not batter your wife or rape a woman. You should not perform rituals like mutilating women's and girls' genitals, which might have been accepted back home. The police officers' admonitions continued on. In that moment the logics of rescue and vulnerability that facilitated the refugees' incorporation in the United States were replaced with criminalizing logics of being black in America. Against this context, criminalizing particular types of genital surgeries becomes a way to incorporate African immigrant subjects into an already existing U.S. racial/ legal discourse that equates blackness to criminality. While African women claiming asylum on the basis of genital surgeries are incorporable as rescueable voice-less bodies, from the moment they step foot on U.S. soil the latent corporeal logics of blackness in America constitute them as racialized subjects whose mere bodily presence renders them dangerous, threatening, criminal.

Much like genital cutting is fixed onto African women's bodies and flattened over the continent of Africa, and criminalization is fixed and flattened onto black and brown bodies in the United States, the public discourse about Iranian women also has a flattening effect. Media reports from the 1980s and 1990s that cover Iranian women's struggles are quick to turn to other countries in the region and beyond in order to show that these countries, in total, suppress women: "In all Muslim countries, including the former Soviet republics of Central Asia, women have come under increased social pressure to veil. Iranian, Saudi and Sudanese women face criminal penalties if they fail to cover themselves."[86] The *New York Times* references an expert on women's rights, Wassyla Tamzali, in assessing the state of women's rights in these countries: "Islamic countries have modernized many laws—in the economy, education, commerce, politics, you name it. . . . But there is practically no movement in the status of women. When it comes to women's rights, religion and theology are invoked."[87] Saudi Arabia, Kuwait, Pakistan, Afghanistan, Morocco, and Algeria also take center stage in U.S. media discussions of women's rights in Iran. Many make mention of Saudi Arabia forbidding women to drive. The reader also learns that "in some countries, like Algeria or Afghanistan, women who assert themselves may be in physical danger."[88] Another source explains, "Women are not allowed to vote in Kuwait. After the gulf war, during which many Kuwaiti women rallied for their country's liberation from Iraq, Kuwait's monarchy promised they would soon have the right to vote. But in elections afterward, women were still denied the vote. In many Middle Eastern countries, a woman must have her husband's approval to get a passport."[89]

Much of the U.S. discourse about Iran goes one step further toward a comparison model of the political theater. While Iran is clearly represented in U.S. media as a constraining place for some Iranian women, in contrast to other countries the situation seems more inconvenience than actual repression: "The medieval measures imposed by the Taliban faction in Afghanistan are having an unintended consequence: giving Iran a chance to look better by comparison."[90] Another report backs this point by detailing the experiences of migration for one twenty-year-old Afghan woman to Iran:

> Here in Mashhad, 80 miles from the Afghan border, she enjoys the relative liberties of young womanhood, Iranian-style. Many Americans find it hard to see beyond the head coverings prescribed for Iranian women to realize that women here enjoy significantly more freedom than their counterparts in many pro-Western Islamic countries, such as Saudi Arabia. In Iran, women make up nearly one-third of the workforce and nearly half the university population. Primary-school education is mandatory for both girls and boys.[91]

Indeed, across the various media outlets, U.S. publics learn of the relative freedoms Iranian women hold in comparison to their neighbors: "Women drive here [in Iran], do not have to cover their faces and have many more career opportunities. Women run successful businesses, are prominent members of parliament, serve as judges on family courts, and often write into their dowries conditions under which they can get a divorce, something unheard of in many Muslim countries."[92] These comparisons are supported with data that further paint a picture for U.S. audiences of Iran as not so bad. For example, literacy rates amongst women ages fifteen to twenty-four and a country's per capita incomes are used to demonstrate just how good Iranian women have it compared with those in other countries. While Iranian women had in 1992 a literacy rate of 81 percent and the country a per capita income of $13,561, in Egypt the rate was 54 percent with $746 annually; Morocco, 41 percent with $1,079; and Pakistan, 25 percent with $452. To U.S. eyes and ears, the contrast between the countries makes Iran seem not so bad. While codes for social conformity exist for women in each of these national contexts, the media discourse does the dual function of flattening social conformity onto the expanse of the Middle East yet also hierarchizes the conformity—making some forms of conformity seem more like hindrance than persecution. Iran exists in the social imaginary as a place that castigates women for not conforming, yet the class narratives of the asylum seekers in these cases intervene to complicate the imagination of social repression—turning what was framed as a question of freedom into an appearance of a concern about choice.

Conclusion

Gender-based asylum and gender violence are discursively constituted in the institution of U.S. asylum, and imaginations of particular forms of gender violence are racialized onto particular bodies and geographies. Gender and gender-based persecution have been constituted narrowly in U.S. asylum as referents for cisgender, presumably heterosexual women who experience relational, sexual, and cultural violence. In chapter 3 I examine how another form of gender violence—forced sterilization and abortion—enter U.S. law and politics as a mode of refugee relief. In chapters 1 and 2, claimants have been shown to carry the bulk of the argumentative work in order for them to be received as eligible asylum seekers; but in the cases of Chinese fleeing opposition to forced sterilization and abortion, the U.S. Congress intervenes. While these cases are not recognized as gender-based asylum cases in the strict sense, I read them as gender-related claims to understand the political borders etched around gender's incorporation. Gender violence is yet again racialized as endemic to body and place; the racialization of China enables the U.S. state to intervene and cover—through federal legislation—Chinese people who are imagined as in peril to their state, all the while skirting the burden of the gendered migrants it fears most.

CHAPTER 3

Standing in Her Shoes

U.S. Asylum Policy for Chinese
Opposing Population Control

In the wake of the 1989 Tiananmen Square protests, as the U.S. public and international human rights community were made starkly aware of China's restrictive state policies, the *Golden Venture* freighter ran aground on Rockaway Beach in Queens, New York. The vessel, operated by an immigration smuggler, carried 286 Chinese nationals who paid nearly $30,000 each for a trip on the ship. The passengers started their voyage in Thailand in 1992, docked in Mombasa, Kenya, for six months, and boarded the *Golden Venture* on March 28, 1993. As Wesley Hsu reported in summarizing the passengers' testimony, conditions on both legs of the journey were dismal:

> Each of the passengers boarding the *Golden Venture* received a small sleeping space in the cargo hold and a blanket. "They were confined to this space for the entire trip, an area roughly the size of a coffin. . . . It was six inches on either side to the next body." One toilet served the entire ship, so the men began relieving themselves on the upper deck. There was no running water. . . . Although the smugglers provided one paltry meal a day, by the end, many were eating anything they could. One passenger was quoted as saying that "some days [we] don't have food." She added, "[W]e only had rice and some spoiled dry peanuts."[1]

The ship ran aground in the early morning hours on June 6, 1993. Passengers, having not seen land for three months, jumped into the water, shimmied down ladders, and swam to land. The *New York Times* reporter covering the near-dawn scene described what he saw upon arrival to the shoreline:

> Some wore suits, maybe the best clothes they owned, as they leaped frantically into the dark, whitecapped water only 200 yards from America's shore. Perhaps it was a sign of high hopes in a new land. But there was likely no time to think as they surged to the deck when their ship ran aground, plunking one after another into the sea as they clutched all they owned in plastic bags. When rescuers arrived, they found the surf off Rockaway Peninsula dotted with Chinese refugees in a desperate flailing dash to the beach. The air echoed with screams for help.[2]

Seven passengers were found dead on arrival, and as Queens resident Edward Morrissey explained after a third body from the *Golden Venture* washed ashore days later, "Last year we had hypodermic needles and garbage washing up; now we have dead people."[3]

The U.S. public expressed shock as they witnessed the scene on their televisions. For some, the passengers represented the fear of an immigration system that could not handle "floods" of migrant subjects desiring access to the country. For others, the *Golden Venture* symbolized a humanitarian crisis, a clear signal of restrictive state policies that constituted a life so unlivable that flight was the only viable answer. The passengers of the *Golden Venture* also expressed shock as they were directly transferred from the sandy U.S. soil to prisons and immigration detention centers for processing. Four years later many of the detainees were still imprisoned, waiting for their immigration claims to be processed and evaluated.[4] Immigration attorneys from around the United States came to the aid of *Golden Venture* detainees, helping them to file for asylum. While the requests ranged in scope—some claiming political persecution on the basis of participation in pro-democracy demonstrations, others citing persecution because of their Christian beliefs—many of the passengers asked for asylum on the basis of their opposition to China's population-control policies, disallowing its citizens from having children outside of state-sanctioned marriages, and using birth control, forced abortions, and, sometimes, sterilization to ensure that some heterosexual married couples only had one child.

These early asylum cases were, in total, unsuccessful. In fact, in 1989 the Board of Immigration Appeals had formally decided in *Matter of Chang* that opposition to family-planning polices could not make one eligible for asylum.[5] In following this precedent, most *Golden Venture* claimants were denied asylum; consequently, vociferous and outraged attention began to mount in the United States around the question of the morality and ethics of state family-planning policies in countries around the world.[6] The sentiment is captured in a letter to the editor in the *New York Times* co-written by past president of the Asian American Bar Association Jan C. Ting and Temple University Professor of Law Kathleen Blanchard: "We agree that Haitians are discriminated against by the U.S. Government compared with Cubans. But we think U.S. treatment of Chinese boat people is even more egregious. This is consistent with the Administration's selective hostility toward Chinese asylum seekers manifest in the imprisonment for more than a year now of those from the Golden Venture. Asylum seekers of no other nationality are subjected to such harsh treatment."[7] The voices articulating this opinion came from individuals and groups with significant political sway in U.S. politics, including U.S. Christian Right organizations and leaders of anti-abortion organizations such as Operation Rescue, Human Life International, Life Coalition International, as well as anticommunist organizations. At one point, founder of Operation Rescue, Randall Terry, "staged a protest at Newt Gingrich's office to stop the deportation of those aboard the Golden Venture. Those arrested included Pat Mahoney, of the Christian Defense Council, and Joseph Slovenec, director of the U.S. Taxpayers Party."[8]

After several years, the work of these organizers proved effective. In 1996, Congress included Section 601 in the Illegal Immigration Reform and Immigrant Responsibility Act, a provision included as an addendum to the refugee definition that is used to determine the status of asylum seekers who claim the need for political and humanitarian relief in the United States. The provision mandates that immigration officials recognize people who leave their country because of opposition to their state's population-control policies as eligible for asylum under the political opinion category. While China is not named specifically in the provision, the congressional hearings that precipitated Section 601's inclusion in IIRIRA center China directly. Section 601, the congressional hearings that inform Section 601, and the precedent-setting asylum cases that follow Section 601 are the texts I analyze to understand the rhetoric of refuge as it relates to imaginations of who is harmed by state family-planning programs and how such programs constitute persecution. This chapter, in other words, does not analyze or comment on the actual *practices* of the Chinese state (around reproduction), but the *rhetorical ways* these practices get taken up in asylum cases and in U.S. public and political discourses.[9]

There is a purposeful disconnect between the rhetoric of Section 601 and the protection offered to Chinese women through Section 601, wherein noncitizen women, namely Chinese women, serve as the rhetorical "babes in the woods," the innocent victims who prove the point of China as a "bad sovereign" toward its citizens in U.S. political discourse. The construction of Chinese women as victims in need of protection, in material terms, then serves as a tool to enable the mobility of particular kinds of *men*, reinstituting an informal policy of coverture through this specific immigration policy and naturalizing the universality of the male-assigned subject as the a priori subject for U.S. immigration.[10] This mobility is a contemporary turn on a historical preference for male-assigned subjects in immigration contexts, who, while threatening in their own right, do not pose the same threat as female-assigned migrants to the nation—the reproductive threat to the primacy of the white nuclear family and nation. All of this occurs while the United States appears as if it fiercely defends the rights of women and admonishes the Republic of China for its volatility toward its citizens. This global admonishment explicitly articulates as directed toward human rights injustices within the Chinese state, yet I argue that the United States' anxieties about China's global politico-economic growth serve as a more compelling explanation for Section 601's incorporation. Here, a double coverture happens: not only do male-assigned subjects become, once again in this context, the privileged subjects for U.S. belonging, but U.S. fears about the state's waning global influence get masked as human rights rhetoric and concern. In accord with the analyses in chapters 1 and 2 that demonstrate how gender is incorporated as a contingent and segregated political category and how gender violence is racialized, this chapter investigates the sexual and racial logics that undergird gender's contingent, segregated status. The incorporation of gendered protections in U.S. asylum law, I argue, serves as yet another device to naturalize male-assigned bodies as universal subjects for U.S. asylum. In these cases, protections that organize around women's reproductive bodies are deployed as rhetoric to facilitate the mobility of male-assigned subjects. Meanwhile, the bodies of the women imagined as vulnerable in these cases are racialized as less desirable for incorporation because of the threat of reproductivity associated with their female-assigned bodies. This racial logic of reading gender violence serves U.S. transnational interests regarding its own position as the pastoral moral authority in matters of human rights over other states and also enables the non-incorporation of asylum seekers who are less-desirable immigrant subjects.

Chinese Women as Victims

In the summer of 1995, members of the House of Representatives Subcommittee on International Operations and Human Rights met to address the issue of "Coercive Population Control in China." Members of the committee included several representatives from New York, whose prisons two years later still held most of the detainees of the *Golden Venture*. Christopher Smith of New Jersey, chair of the committee, opened the hearing by stating, "Civilizations can be judged by how they treat women, children, old people and strangers," and continuing: "The Government of China now routinely compels women to abort their 'unauthorized' unborn children. The usual method is intense 'persuasion' using all of the economic, social and psychological tools a totalitarian State has at its disposal. When these methods fail, the woman is taken physically to the abortion mill. Forced abortions are often performed very late in pregnancy, even in the ninth month."[11] Evident here, and throughout the hearing, is that the committee located Chinese women as the primary subjects persecuted by the family-planning programs in general and the Chinese state in particular. Consequently, state officials figure Chinese women as the primary subjects in need of U.S. aid because their rights, as humans, are being violated. The subjectivity is further specified as experts who testified in the hearings indicated that women and young girls who were poor and who lived in rural areas were the primary targets for persecution:

> In a society where the preference for sons is strong and longstanding, the "one child only" campaign has quite predictably resulted in the surreptitious killing of baby girls. Anecdotal reports about the practice, depicted to have occurred in many different regions of rural China, have circulated in the international press for more than a decade. For obvious reasons, an accurate figure for the total number of infanticides in China is hard to come by. By the late 1980s, however, 111 baby boys were counted for every 100 baby girls in China as a whole—a disparity far greater than would be expected in a naturally constituted human population. Selective abortion may have accounted for much of that disparity, but given rural China's limited access in the late 1980s to technology for identifying the sex of a fetus, it is hard to imagine that selective abortion could have accounted for all of the disparity.[12]

The Chinese state, by contrast, is figured by U.S. representatives as forceful and determined in their "eugenics" practices against women. State family-planning policies are likened to "Nazi Germany" tactics: "In a move that is eerily reminiscent of Nazi Germany, the Communist Chinese Government is implementing forced abortion against handicapped children and forced sterilization against parents who simply do not measure up in the eyes of the State."[13] This framing, as well as other mentions of "Nazi Germany," "Eugenics," and "What was learned from the Nuremburg Trials" throughout the 136-page document, rhetorically positions China as the "bad sovereign" against its citizens, as their internal control of the citizenry is framed as invasive, acute, and excessive. The narrative of a draconian Chinese state victimizing its citizen women serves as the primary motivating evidence that Congress uses in warranting the necessity for some gesture of intervention. While state representatives could not call for actual intervention in Chinese policies, the subcommittee members urged for a gesture of admonishment using national legislation. Because of its importance in international human rights law, the likely move for this transnational admonishment was refugee and asylum policy. As Jacqueline Bhabha, Sherene Razack, Mireille Rosello, and others note, refugee and asylum admissions serve to call out another sovereign state as "bad," but they simultaneously serve as messages, what Mimi Thi Nguyen calls gifts,[14] for the state doing the calling.[15] In this context, calling out China as "bad" to its women serves to repudiate China's sovereignty, and it positions the United States as the pastoral moral authority regarding the rights of women—arguably over all of humanity.

Section 601 of IIRIRA, then, stands as the actual gesture that Congress offered to aid Chinese citizens. As stated in the provision: "[A] person who has been forced to abort a pregnancy or to undergo involuntary sterilization, or who has been persecuted for failure or refusal to undergo such a procedure or for other resistance to a coercive population control program, shall be deemed to have been persecuted on account of political opinion, and a person who has a well founded fear that he or she will be forced to undergo such a procedure or subject to persecution for such failure, refusal, or resistance shall be deemed to have a well founded fear of persecution on account of political opinion."[16] What is interesting about the drafting of this provision is its abstraction in the face of the specificity of the target subjects in the congressional hearings as Chinese women victims. Instead, the provisions are drafted in generality, naming neither country nor specific gender in the actual wording of the provision. What I address next, then, is the actual development of asylum precedent that ensues following Section 601.

Standing in Her Shoes—Male Mobility for Female Subjectivity

After the introduction of Section 601, the cases that were most successful involved Chinese women who could prove that they were sterilized against their will.[17] An applicant who goes by her initials, X-P-T, was at first denied asylum for her claim on the basis of forced sterilization. Fortunately for her, IIRIRA passed soon after the immigration judge's denial on October 5, 1995. She appealed after IIRIRA was passed and the BIA granted her asylum in December 1996. Soon after X-P-T's case, immigration judges and the BIA started hearing the cases of married men who were affected, via the sterilization or abortions performed on their wives, in the state's population-control policies. While there are a few cases of men citing forced sterilization themselves as a form of persecution,[18] the primary method that Chinese men used to claim asylum in this case law was through the actual or threatened forced sterilization of and abortion performed on their female partners.

C-Y-Z, a Chinese father of three, had been married for seven years when he arrived in the United States in 1993. Despite being forced to use an intrauterine device as birth control, his wife had given birth to two daughters and one son; then, after the birth of their son, she was sterilized. Shortly after his wife's sterilization, C-Y-Z left the country to apply for asylum. The first immigration judge to hear his case decided that C-Y-Z did not qualify for asylum because it was not he who had been forced to endure the invasive procedures. The immigration judge wrote: "In effect, the applicant seeks to ride on his wife's coattails or claim asylum because of alleged adverse factors to his wife, including forced sterilization. He, himself, has never been persecuted and he cannot show either past persecution or a reasonable fear of future persecution."[19] Much like the gender violence discussed in chapters 1 and 2, the immigration judge in this case located persecution in the invasive procedures forced upon one body, one subject. In the judge's reasoning, emotional and psychological pain could not count as persecution; it was the body that needed to experience or fear the violence for it to count as persecution. Additionally, the judge seemed suspicious of the applicant, questioning C-Y-Z's character for claiming persecution "on his wife's coattails." The immigration judge's framing might first be interpreted as a calling out of C-Y-Z's masculinity in that he would try to get refuge for something that happened to his wife's body all the while she herself remained in China. It sounds eerily similar to the discourses of suspicion that framed Chinese immigrants' reception in the United States during the exclusion era of immigration. Toward this point, Kitty Calavita illustrates the vexing problem that customs officers had in determining which Chinese migrants were laborers (and thus deportable under the exclusion laws) and which were of more elite classes.[20] Customs officers relied on corporeal cues such as calloused hands and dress to determine class status; Chinese migrants assimilated to customs officers' techniques of corporeal reading and began to fashion themselves to meet the classed expectations of officers. This also happened with the necessity that Chinese migrants hold identification documents. As Estelle Lau explains, "The more stringent exclusion became, the more Chinese found increasingly subtle means to evade immigration regulation."[21] Exclusionary laws and the fastidious documentation of customs officers prompted the purchase of family records, the changing of names, adding "fictitious" brothers to family trees, and memorizing family histories so that migrants, who would otherwise be deported, could gain entrance. The formation of "fictive kin" and "paper sons and daughters" continued until 1965, with the passage of new standards for immigration that privileged profession over family ties. Yet, as Lau and others approximate, 80 percent of Chinese migrants before 1965 involved paper family formations. "Real histories," Lau says, "became subsumed or mixed within the new family story. Generations of fictive kinship ties had to be purchased to maintain lived relationships that existed in real life but did not conform to immigration requirements."[22] Taking such license with family legacies certainly provided the means for many to access the country, but the tactics were also used in political discourse to warrant the framing of Chinese and Chinese Americans as inherently dishonest, shifty, and depraved.

In reviewing C-Y-Z's case, the BIA mulled over the question of the "threshold" of persecution in deciding whether the claimant was eligible. Specifically, the board deliberated whether the actual or threatened forced sterilization/abortion of a female partner rose to the level of persecution for male applicants. In a twist of logic, the board disagreed with the immigration judge, stating that a male partner could indeed "stand in her shoes" in making asylum claims. The BIA stated that "the husband of a sterilized wife can essentially stand in her shoes and make a bona fide and non-frivolous application for asylum based on problems impacting more intimately on her than on him,"[23] and that "the applicant in this case has established eligibility for asylum by virtue of his wife's forced sterilization . . . he suffered past persecution."[24]

This 1997 ruling provided the legal maneuvering for thousands of heterosexual and legally married men to claim asylum on account of the harm that their female spouses experienced. Ke Zhen Zhao first came to the United States in 1992 and promptly applied for asylum after immigration officials at the Honolulu Airport realized that he was traveling with another person's passport.[25] In his first asylum application he wrote that he left China "to escape the threats and persecution of the Chinese Communist government and to avoid imprisonment and sterilization as a consequence of my political views and supposedly anti-government activities regarding the government's Birth Control policy."[26] Zhao's wife had been sterilized in 1989 after the birth of their second child; Zhao himself believed that he would be arrested if he returned to China for voicing opposition to the policies and for not paying the fines demanded by the state for not following the policy. The immigration judge denied Zhao's petition, however, stating that he and his wife had had two children, so despite roadblocks put up by the government, it seemed that they got what they wanted. By chance, it took Zhao's case four years to get through the appeals process. By that time the BIA had ruled on C-Y-Z, which meant that Zhao was able to gain asylum under the precedent that allowed him to "stand in her shoes."

Guang Hua Huang applied for asylum in 1993 because his wife not only was forced to use an intrauterine device for a time, but family planning officials forced her to have an abortion and, after their second child, sterilized her by tubal ligation.[27] While the first immigration judge did not find Huang credible due to translation issues, Huang ultimately received protection. The same is true for Wang He, whose wife was forced to have a tubal ligation after their second child, and countless other husbands of Chinese women whose bodies bore the burden of evidencing the asylum claim.[28]

In each of these cases the men are seen, unquestioningly, as "standing in the shoes" of their wives, not actually having experienced the persecution themselves.[29] It is important to note that unless their spouses are physically present as co-applicants, wives have not gained the right to asylum. As Heidi Murphy explains, of the ten thousand people who have gained asylum via Section 601 since 1996, three-fourths of them have been men.[30] And while people who have been granted asylum can apply for sponsorship of spouses and minor children (younger than eighteen), the process of actually getting the spouse or child to the United States can take years and significant financial resources.

While erasing the implications about deceit and subterfuge, the BIA's decision continued the reduction of the persecution of coercive population control to the body—the reproductive female body—ignoring the emotional and psychological trauma that plays out in persecution, which may more appropriately describe what male-assigned partners may experience. Second, having reduced persecution to the body, this decision permitted male-assigned subjects to take the place of female-assigned subjects whose bodies bear the responsibility for the asylum claim. In this way, the "standing in her shoes" precedent reasserts an informal policy of coverture into U.S. law and politics. Coverture is typically figured as an English policy that was assimilated into U.S. law during the formation of the colonies. In the English legal system, coverture meant that marriage between a man and woman would turn the woman into a *femme couvert*, meaning that her legal presence was now "covered" by her husband.[31] In the nineteenth and twentieth centuries, coverture (in United States) meant that if a U.S. citizen woman married a non-U.S. citizen, she would lose her citizenship.[32] It also meant that women could not vote and that married women could not legally own property. Margo Canaday notes that U.S. coverture laws were significantly weakened with the adoption of the Nineteenth Amendment and also "in the 1970s, as a part of a broader feminist revolution in law that further weakened the principle that a husband owned a wife's labor."[33] Despite this explicit weakening, coverture laws remain on the books in many U.S. states, and coverture endures as a logic for receiving women as political subjects across a variety of legal contexts.[34]

Much like other legal realms, the "standing in her shoes" precedent in asylum law positions married women as extensions of their husbands' political subjectivity. A more insidious implication of this precedent, though, returns coverture to its older, more traditional interpretation. As Linda Kerber writes, coverture laws meant that husbands covered their wives' political subjectivity, but it also meant "at marriage the husband controlled the physical body of the wife. . . . By treating married women as 'covered' by their husbands' civic identity, by placing sharp constraints on the extent to which married women controlled their bodies and their property, the old law of domestic relations ensured that—with few exceptions, like the obligation to refrain from treason—married women's obligations to their husbands and families overrode their obligations to the state."[35] In the Chinese asylum cases, women's bodies are the property of their husbands. Women's experiences of gendered violence and violation become rhetorical matter useful to their husbands in materializing their own fears and claims for protection. Perhaps what this shows is just how consolidated and sedimented the logics of coverture are in U.S. law and politics. Female-assigned cisgender women, we find across many of the cases addressed in this book, rarely enter U.S. law and politics as subjects of their own accord. They may gain access on account of their relationalities with men (husbands, fathers, others) or on account of the places they flee. But, as gendered subjects, these women's subjectivities—as well as their bodies and voices—are already spoken for. They are covered.

In this covering, Chinese women's subjectivities are displaced from bodily experience, rendering women immobile so that their husbands can appropriate their bodily experience as their own. The primary way persecution is defined in asylum law is as *bodily* persecution. These cases remove the condition of bodily persecution as a criterion for asylum; perhaps more accurately stated, these cases remove the subject from the bodily persecution itself, transferring the experience, the fact of bodily persecution, to the subjectivity of another, to the one who is always and already universally recognized as a political subject in U.S. law and politics because of his assigned sex. All the while, the women who have been sterilized, or forced to abort a fetus, remain fixed and immobile.

Geopolitical Anxieties

Several years after permitting male partners to "stand in her shoes" the courts were confronted with the question of whether heterosexual couples, who were not legally married, could also employ the coverture-logic "standing in her shoes" precedent to receive the same protections as state-recognized married asylum seekers. Kui Rong Ma attempted to marry his partner, Lei Chiu, and register the marriage after he and Chiu found out she was pregnant.[36] Unfortunately, neither Ma nor Chiu were yet of age to legally marry in China. Soon thereafter, family planning officials found out Chiu was pregnant and forced her to have an abortion. Ma fled to Guam to seek protection while Chiu reportedly stayed in China, physically and mentally distraught.

The judge in Ma's asylum hearing denied his request, explaining that Ma did not have a credible claim. In Ma's appellate case before the BIA, the board both affirmed the immigration judge's negative ruling and clarified their decision, stating: "Only a spouse in a marriage 'legally' registered with the Chinese government can establish past persecution and qualify as a refugee on the basis of his wife's forced abortion or sterilization."[37] Similar determinations have been made in other cases: Shi Liang Lin was told that he did not qualify for asylum on account of his girlfriend's forced abortion. The immigration judge stated that it would not be "appropriate to expand . . . *Matter of C-Y-Z* to include unmarried couples," as "opening the immigration floodgates to non-spouses could jeopardize the ability of those individuals more directly harmed by coercive family-planning policies to secure immigration relief."[38] The judge in Xian Zou's case declared that there was "absolutely no way" Section 601 could apply because he and his girlfriend were not married.[39] While the Ninth and Seventh Circuits have allowed "unofficial" male spouses, or nonmarried male partners, to gain asylum "in her shoes," the majority of circuits follow the BIA's ruling on the matter, arguing that nonmarried male partners do not qualify under the intentions of the "in her shoes" provisions offered through the C-Y-Z precedent.

This newest interpretation of the "standing in her shoes" precedent demonstrates important information about U.S. transnational anxieties regarding the country's moral vitality and global placement. First, this interpretation further asserts the logic of coverture by explicitly articulating Section 601 as an entitlement primarily available to men in state-recognized marriages with Chinese women, positioning heterosexuality and state-sanctioned marriage as the morally responsible, proper orientation of desire and belonging for U.S. citizens. Luibhéid writes that IIRIRA (in which Section 601 was incorporated) was not the only piece of U.S. legislation from the mid-1990s that used state policy to push marriage. The Defense of Marriage Act and the Personal Responsibility and Work Opportunity Reconciliation Act also figured heterosexual state-sanctioned marriage as the "right disposition of sexuality."[40] The "right-ness" of heterosexual marriage was intended to advance marriage, and it was used to promote childbearing within the heterosexual marriage as a key toward re-moralizing the nation. As Luibhéid explains, according to legislators who implemented these policies, "bearing a child within marriage provides a mechanism whereby members of the marriage supposedly overcome their individual needs and desires to consider the larger good. Marriage, in this line of thinking, also provides the child with the best environment for growing up, and the greatest possibilities for becoming a moral and productive member of society."[41] In codifying asylum on the basis of opposition to forced family-planning practices as an entitlement primarily available to state-recognized married couples, and even more so accessible by the men of those couples, the state similarly asserts its faith in the power of marriage to be a moral filter for those desiring to *become* the nation. The precedent following Section 601 goes one step further in re-moralizing the future of the nation by removing the immediate threat of nonwhite reproductivity from those incorporated into the nation through asylum by privileging Chinese male-assigned married men. This is a move eerily similar to its nineteenth- and twentieth-century exclusion-era legislative predecessors.

Asian women were the first specific group to be prohibited entrance to the United States through the Page Laws during the flurry that is now known as the exclusion era of U.S. immigration. The rhetoric surrounding the Page Laws' passage drew on intersections between race, gender, and sexuality to racialize Asian women (predominantly Chinese women) as sexually immoral, easily led in to prostitution, and as compelling factors in the moral denigration of white citizen men, and thus the country.[42] The effect of this racialization was staggering. The Page Laws "almost completely stopped the entry of women; fewer than 220 entered during that period [between 1875–1882], and their numbers dwindled thereafter throughout the period of exclusion due to fears of subjecting wives and young girls to the difficulties of detention and interrogation."[43] While there were already a disproportionate number of Chinese men in the United States because of early migration flows for labor, this exclusion only exacerbated the gendered ratio. Because of the vastly gendered demographic gap in early U.S. Chinese migrant communities, Chinese men were imagined in U.S. dominant discourse as members of "bachelor" societies that "hindered the creation of Chinese American families."[44] In addition to preventing Chinese reproductivity on U.S. soil (and therefore the birth of Chinese American citizens), the prevalence of single, male-assigned Chinese migrants perpetuated effeminizing and Orientalizing stereotypes of Chinese men as accustomed to "playing house" and "playing wife" and doing "women's work."[45] In the late 1800s, for example, Chinese men were depicted in impressionistic journalistic images and cartoons as effeminate in dress, hairstyle, and nonverbal cues. While some might call political cartoons innocuous to social imaginaries, Clare

Sears argues that "In depicting men in feminine apparel, such cartoons not only framed Chinese immigrants as deceptive interlopers, sneaking into the country in disguise, but also as effeminate, deviant men, unable to perform normative masculinity and hence unworthy of inclusion in the nation."[46]

Section 601 and the legal precedent that ensued in its adoption similarly return Chinese migrants to "bachelor societies"; Chinese male asylum seekers are figured as the preferred subjects for access because of their state-recognized matrimonial affiliations and nonreproductive bodies—both characteristics that lead to their recognition as morally responsible migrant subjects. Yet this incorporation comes with a racializing of their gendered subjectivities through what David Eng has termed racial castration as a precondition.[47] Relying on Orientalist discourses, Chinese male migrants are both sexualized through effeminizing logics of Asian masculinity and rendered asexual—not the virile, sexually active masculine migrant subjects that the U.S. state should fear as it does other nonwhite male-assigned migrant men;[48] rather, Chinese men are figured as loyal patriarchs—loyal to their wives and children who prompted their flight to the United States, loyal to the ideal of family values, and because they have now been granted the "gift" of asylum in the United States, they are also figured as loyal subjects to the U.S. state. In this instance, as was the case for African women fleeing genital surgeries (chapter 2), the racialization process enables the incorporation of these male-assigned asylum claimants.

Within the transnational sphere of geopolitical publicity, the incorporation of Chinese men may be read as a double castration of Chinese state power and sovereignty. Just as the patriarchal husband should "cover" his wife, so too should the sovereign state "cover" and protect its citizens. As shown above, U.S. representatives frame the Chinese state as the "bad sovereign" whose control of its citizenry is overly severe and invasive. Such framing provides the warrant for stepping in to offer protection—a "cover"—for those Chinese fleeing family-planning policies and procedures. This covering can be interpreted as a rebuke of China's human rights record, yet it is not human rights alone that likely propelled U.S. concern.

Just as the developing international human rights discourse matters, so, too, does the context of the global economy and U.S.-Sino relations of the 1990s. While the United States was recognized as the global economic hegemon during the immediate post–World War II years through what John Ruggie has termed an era of "embedded liberalism" that was guided by U.S. interests integrated into a multilateral approach of global recovery and rebuilding, by the 1990s the global politico-economic landscape had shifted considerably.[49] Indeed, even by the 1960s and 1970s the United States was suffering what Beverly Silver and

Giovanni Arrighi described as "simultaneously a crisis of profitability and a crisis of legitimacy."[50] One signal of the weakening hegemony was Western Europe's and Japan's competiveness with the United States in key markets during the 1970s.[51] Even more illustrative was the oil crisis, the devaluation of the dollar, and the abandonment of the dollar-gold standard during this decade, which ended significant elements of the Bretton Woods agreement and the embedded-liberalism economic framework. The shift from Keynesianism to neoliberalism in the late 1970s and early 1980s, then, may be thought of as a desperate effort by the United States to maintain global dominance. Silver and Arrighi elaborate:

> It was in this context that in the closing years of the Carter administration, and then with greater determination under Reagan, there occurred a drastic change in U.S. policies. . . . [T]he U.S. government began resorting to economic policies— a drastic contraction in money supply, higher interest rates, lower taxes for the wealthy, and virtually unrestricted freedom of action for capitalist enterprise— that liquidated not just the legacy of the domestic New Deal but also and especially the legacy of the Fair Deal for poor countries launched by Truman in 1949. Through these policies the U.S. government started to compete aggressively for capital worldwide to finance a growing trade and current account deficit in the U.S. balance of payment, thereby provoking a sharp increase in real interest rates worldwide and a major reversal in the direction of global capital flows.[52]

The neoliberal privatization and retrenchment of social welfare services, cuts in taxes for those in high- and middle-income brackets, liberalization of credit, reworking of industrial regulations and law, and harmonization of branches of the financial sector during the 1980s created space and financial means for the private sector to develop a more global approach to capital accumulation.[53] But by the early 1990s worries were rising that U.S. capitalists might not be the only power actors riding the global wave. Tides were pointing in the direction of a political-economic hegemon that didn't always follow the whims of the United States.[54]

Throughout the 1980s, China also incorporated "market-oriented" elements into its national economy that facilitated transnational capital accumulation. For example, the state began to permit foreign direct investment in particular instances and developed "special economic zones" in locales prime for access and ease in international shipping. One year after the *Golden Venture* ran aground, the People's Republic of China began opening up state-run companies for private ownership, "Thousands of people lined up at banks in Beijing on Sunday for a chance to buy stock in four state-run companies, the first such public offering by the city. Police and security guards were mobilized to prevent a recurrence of the rioting that broke out two years ago in the southern boomtown of Shenzhen over a similar stock offering. . . . The money raised will be used to buy equipment, develop products and build plants."[55] This sale was a significant indicator of China's entrance in the global economy as it demonstrated a shift from state ownership to private-sector control. Individuals who held stock could now accumulate capital in their own names. Risk also shifted to the private sector. Each stock bought was a transfer of responsibility for economic loss from the state to the individual.

Another indicator of China's rising presence on the global economic stage was President Clinton's 1994 decision to continue China's Most-Favored-Nation status despite global attention and concern regarding the country's human rights record.[56] Many groups were shocked by Clinton's decision to delink trade from human rights policy. President Clinton justified the decision by arguing:

> Extending M.F.N. will avoid isolating China and instead will permit us to engage the Chinese with not only economic contacts but with cultural, educational and other contacts, and with a continuing aggressive effort in human rights—an approach that I believe will make it more likely that China will play a responsible role, both at home and abroad. I am moving, therefore, to delink human rights from the annual extension of Most Favored Nation trading status for China. . . . I don't want to be misunderstood about this. China continues to commit very serious human rights abuses. Even as we engage the Chinese on military, political and economic issues, we intend to stay engaged with those in China who suffer from human rights abuses. The United States must remain a champion of their liberties. I believe the question, therefore, is not whether we continue to support human rights in China but how we can best support human rights in China and advance our other very significant issues and interests. I believe we can do it by engaging the Chinese. . . . The actions I have taken today to advance our security, to advance our prosperity, to advance our ideals, I believe are the important and appropriate ones. I believe, in other words, this is in the strategic economic and political interests of both the United States and China, and I am confident that over the long run this decision will prove to be the correct one.[57]

Clinton's cautious maneuvering in this speech showcases the anxiety that Chinese participation in the global economy produced for the United States. Calling for engagement rather than isolation, Clinton's words demonstrate the careful navigation the United States was working in order to maintain control and influence—even if only marginal—over China's global political-economic integration. The unstated warrant in Clinton's remarks was that if left to integrate its economy independently, China might play by its own rules, using its own power against the United States. Even worse, China might rise as the hegemon with the greatest global political-economic influence among states and private transnational capital actors. While this was certainly not the first time in U.S. history that human rights concerns were deployed to manage and mitigate economic anxieties in transnational political discourse, it did signal a shift in U.S. political strategy toward pastoral power. In pastoral fashion, the United States relied on an imagination of itself as highest moral authority in human rights concerns to exert influence in the political and economic domain of other sovereigns. Clinton's announcement signaled a national shift in political-economic strategy toward the pastoral and what would continue to be a constant source of consternation throughout the rest of his presidency—how to get China to play by Washington Consensus rules.[58]

"Now, it's China's economy, stupid," *Washington Post* writer Paul Bluestein predicted two years later; "China is emerging as Washington's No. 1 trade headache. For Clinton, one of the biggest challenges of the second term will be trying to integrate China's fast-growing, heavily controlled economy into the global free trade system. . . . As a result, China—like Japan before it—threatens to become a destabilizing force in global commerce; trade experts fear that the world's free-trade regime will come under increasingly severe pressure if one of its biggest participants continues to play by such totally different rules."[59] The solution for compelling China to play by rules was to permit the state's request to enter the World Trade Organization (WTO). *New York Times* journalist David Sanger summarized the decision as such: "The Chinese Government next week will face the first test of its resolve to speed the opening of the country's economy since the death of its paramount leader, Deng Xiaoping. The moment will come not in Beijing, but on the shores of Lake Geneva, in the giant mansion that serves as the headquarters of the World Trade Organization . . . for both China and the United States the talks transcend questions of commerce. They are really about the pace at which China will reform its economy and open its society."[60] Privileging pastoral integration over isolation, Clinton spearheaded China's entrance into the WTO. The theory behind this decision was that if China were guided by hand into global integration, like a parent grasping the fingers of a child, the United States might maintain a semblance of control over how they integrate. Others were not as optimistic that this maintenance of influence was possible. Nor were they spirited about the idea of China having a seat at the global economic table:

Many in Washington view China's desire to enter the trade organization as a last opportunity to use economic incentives to change China's behavior, not only in trade, where its mounting surpluses with the United States have caused alarm, but also as leverage over China's treatment of Hong Kong, Tibet and Taiwan and a host of other political issues. On the left and the right, from the Democratic minority leader, Richard Gephardt of Missouri, to the Republican chairman of the Senate Foreign Relations Committee, Jesse Helms of North Carolina, critics of the Administration's China policy argue that Mr. Clinton should recognize that separating the issues of trade and human rights, the major shift he made in 1994, has failed. By the State Department's own accounting, China's treatment of dissidents is as harsh as it ever was before Mr. Clinton took office."[61]

Indeed, human rights groups, U.S. labor unions, lobbyists for U.S. industry, and even "conservative religious groups" all balked at the idea of China joining the WTO;[62] their concerns were expressed in vain. WTO members voted to approve China's entrance at the 2001 Doha conference.[63] For its entrance, China agreed to a series of conditions, including decreasing import tariffs, canceling rent-seeking programs like subsidies for farmers or public firms, and tightening control over pirated goods made in the country that violated international intellectual property right law by disregarding patents and copyrights.[64] The move was intended to make China align its actions with the West's version of global economic integration. Goldman Sachs Asia Vice President Kenneth Courtis believed a different effect to be looming: "China is a big player, and it is going to demand a seat at the front of the table."[65]

Permitting China to join to the WTO certainly may be read as an effort by the United States to rein in China toward playing by the "global rules" designated by the West;[66] the targeting of the state through U.S. asylum policy functions to parallel these efforts in maintaining influence over the global political-economic infrastructure. The United States would foreseeably never threaten military intervention against China in order to maintain global influence and control, but it can wage a discursive battle in order to maintain sovereignty as the supreme global moral authority. Section 601 and the subsequent precedent, then, traffic in this discursive struggle.[67] They do this by first rebuking the state for treating its citizens harshly and then offering refuge to those vulnerable subjects fleeing the excessive and invasive sovereignty that initially provoked the rebuke. At a geopolitical level, this gesture of incorporation, through rhetoric about the pervasiveness of gender violence, racializes the country that these claimants flee. It then discursively castrates the state from its sovereign power on behalf of the imagined innocent women victims who are subjected to these state programs. The United States can no longer ensure its authority and supremacy in global economic matters (or even political matters, if we want to parse these elements out), but as this chapter and book reveal, the state is struggling to maintain control as global moral authority regarding questions of human rights. This moral authority is particularly apparent when we look at issues relating to gender and women's rights, but as this study demonstrates, such geopolitical concern does not always bear the fruit of tangible relief for those imagined as precarious gendered subjects. Rather, maintaining its position as moral authority in human rights concern enables the United States to use discourse about forms of gender violence and human rights concerns to continue advocating for, and insisting on, the U.S. position at the center of the global political-economic table. Pastoral rhetorics are the mechanisms used to wage discursive battles over political economic control in the global arena, all in an effort to maintain international moral supremacy. Such political staking allows the United States to continue to rhetorically enact and evidence its preeminence, but the *need* to do so potentially has unintended consequences in bringing the state's geopolitical anxieties to the surface, showcasing the fear of waning dominance, diminishing power.[68]

Conclusion

One strand of asylum law—opposition to state population-control policies for Chinese nationals—has deployed rhetoric constructing Chinese women as victimized by their invasive state in order to create access to mobility and migration for married Chinese men. Not only does this deployment of women's experiences of gender violence on behalf of male mobility reassert the male-assigned subject as the universal subject of U.S. immigration through logics of coverture, but it also re-emphasizes the ideal that immigrants to the United States conform to U.S. conventions for sexuality, morality, and, consequently, citizenship. The implementation of this coverture policy duly enabled the United States to respond to its own geopolitical anxieties by figuring China as a bad sovereign that does not protect its citizenry. Having challenged Chinese sovereignty in national political discourse about human rights, the state then uses asylum policy to extend coverage and protection to the Chinese nationals it imagines as vulnerable. While not a material admonishment, this move deploys concerns about gendered subjects and gender violence as rhetoric in the geopolitical sphere to challenge the rationality and validity of Chinese sovereignty. As we will see in the conclusion of this book, this enactment signals a new frontier in the United States' role in global geopolitics. Gender violences—having been racialized onto particular bodies and geographies around the world—now become the rhetoric mobilized in the state's struggle to remain global sovereign.

The target is to maintain global authority; with global political and economic dominance in question the state consolidates around moral matter, centering on rights of vulnerable global subjects, like women in places around the world, in order to maintain its prominence as a global state authority. Chapter 4 examines the segregation of gender as an institutional category for claiming refugee protection and, through an analysis of gay and transgender sexuality-based asylum cases, elucidates the tacit logics undergirding gender's institutional life as a category of relief.

CHAPTER 4

The Rhetoric and Logic of One Sex, One Gender

Nancy Arabillas Moreles was born in 1968 in the town of San Luis Potosi, Mexico. At age fourteen she began to identify as Nancy and use feminine pronouns. At age fifteen, because of her father's abuse in response to her transgender identity, she left her parents' home and began supporting herself by working at a bar, later moving to Matamoros, Mexico, where she was able to secure better employment.[1] Over the course of the next three years Arabillas Moreles would experience numerous incidents of physical and sexual assault at the hands of police and strangers because of her transgender identity. Arabillas Moreles came to the United States in 1986 as an undocumented migrant and in 2002 was convicted of a misdemeanor, thus instigating her movement through the immigration system. Though Arabillas Moreles herself identified as transgender, she applied for asylum, withholding of removal, and Convention Against Torture relief on the basis of her membership in "a group of gay men with female sexual identities" from Mexico who are particularly vulnerable to persecution in their home countries. The immigration judge in Arabillas Moreles's case stated that "he would have found her eligible for asylum under *Hernandez-Montiel v. INS*" as a "gay man with a female sexual identity" who is particularly vulnerable to persecution in Mexico if it hadn't been for the misdemeanor, which he interpreted as a crime of moral turpitude.[2] The judge denied her claims to immigration relief, though the Ninth Circuit Court of Appeals later reversed the decision in 2007—granting her asylum.

Despite identifying in court proceedings as transgender and being identified in the court record as a woman, Arabillas Moreles was granted asylum as "a gay man with a female sexual identity" and consequently as a sexual-orientation asylum claimant. In this chapter I examine the logic of sex, gender, and sexuality that undergirds the recognition of Arabillas Moreles as a "gay man with a female sexuality identity" that necessitated first discursively returning her to her assigned sex as a precondition for incorporation as a refugee. As the previous chapters demonstrate, gender is only ever given contingent and segregated status as a legal concept in U.S. asylum law, and the way it is legible can renaturalize male-assigned persons as the universal subjects for whom refugee reliefs are intended. This chapter analyzes the rhetoric and logic that serve as the foundation for gender's categorical parameters as a contingent and segregated concept. I excavate these elements by considering how the category articulates alongside another social-group category that emerged in U.S. asylum discourse at roughly the same time—sexuality. We will see that, despite calls for intersectional understandings of identity and subjectivity, especially those made by legal scholars,[3] when gender and sexuality are categorically recognized in U.S. asylum law, they have almost no intersections. Gender stridently signifies as a referent for cisgender, presumably heterosexual women who flee violence easily recognizable as both corporeal and cultural; sexuality is equally constrained.

This discursive fixing happens through immigration judges' reliance on particular narrative genre conventions in evaluating asylum claims, ultimately providing the opportunity for significant numbers of asylum seekers to be incorporated in the country as claimants fleeing sexuality-related persecution. Yet just as these conventions enable the incorporation of some, they also foreclose the possibility of refuge for many others with seemingly less-conventional sexuality-related asylum claims—a point made clear in chapter 5. Before investigating what is beyond the frame of intelligibility for sexuality-related cases, I seek to identify what *is* sayable and hearable as a valid sexuality-related asylum claim and then to interrogate the rhetoric and logic of gender that undergird that articulation.[4] Through these genre conventions sexuality is figured as something that is evident in the outward expression of one's comportment and appearance. Second, in the content of one's claim, it is expected that sexualized violence will be the primary mode of persecution. Finally, it is assumed that claimants will know about their nonheterosexuality early on in their lives. These genre conventions, taken together, demonstrate the court's method of reading sexuality in the court. Largely figured through particular cisgender and transgender sexuality asylum narratives of persecution, these conventions traffic in conflating and collapsing gender and sexuality in what first appears to be whim. Yet upon further reading there is a clear logic to constructions of gender and sexuality in U.S. asylum law.

Readers familiar with widely recognized gender theories might first assume this system to be reliant on a binary matrix where two sexes become two gendered subjects whose objects of sexual desire are differently gendered subjects. I demonstrate a different logic in play, one that situates those assigned as male at birth with sex and those assigned female at birth with gender. This one sex, one gender system gives cisgender women gender as a special contingent and segregated category of relief, while those assigned with male sex are figured as the neutral subjects for whom the entire system of asylum is intended. The narratives received as legible sexuality-related cases by the courts only reinforce the notion of sexuality as disparate from gender. Before discussing the particulars of one asylum case where these conventions convene in the reading practices of the judges in line with a "one sex, one gender" logic, I reveal the incumbent rhetoric of these narrative conventions and the logics that enforce them. This analysis emphasizes the importance of reading for the narrative genre conventions that are used to audience and evaluate asylum seekers. I conclude by considering how the racialization of violence in the U.S. national imaginary of other countries plays out in cases where gender violence is legible as sexuality-related violence.

Genre Conventions

Rhetorical scholars have long been interested in identifying genres of rhetoric, for, as rhetorician Edwin Black explained, there are a limited number of speech situations in which rhetors may find themselves and hence a limited number of ways to respond appropriately to rhetorical situations.[5] Lloyd Bitzer elaborated on this point: "From day to day, year to year, comparable situations occur, prompting comparable responses; hence rhetorical forms are born and a special vocabulary, grammar, and style are established. . . . The situation recurs and, because we experience situations and the rhetorical responses to them, a form of discourse is not only established but comes to have a power of its own—the tradition itself tends to function as a constraint upon any new response in the form."[6] This chapter attends to how the narratives and testimonies of cisgender and transgender male-assigned asylum seekers create a "traditional" sexuality-related asylum claim that then has power over, or comes to constrain, those applicants who don't or can't conform to the rhetorical genre in their own bids for refuge.

Defined by Karlyn Kohrs Campbell and Kathleen Hall Jamieson as a "complex of elements—a constellation of substantive, stylistic and situational characteristics,"[7] conventions for a genre are present in the style, content, and context expectations of the speech situation, which then become the rhetorical modes of hearing and seeing used to evaluate who and what fits the genre. These conventions equally delineate what is beyond the frame of intelligibility. Genre conventions have been identified in speaking situations as traditional as presidential address[8] and apologia,[9] and as seemingly peripheral as romance novels.[10] Rhetoric scholars have also extensively demonstrated that rhetoric itself is heralded by gendered genre conventions. As Campbell explains, good public discourse is constituted by genre conventions of "cogent argument, expertise, and skill in rebuttal . . . qualities associated with masculinity, whereas defects in rhetorical presentation—sentimentality, weak logic, and timidity—are traits that have stereotypically been linked to femininity."[11] This framing of public speech in masculine terms has meant that women have not only struggled in gaining access to the public through their speech, but also that women have had to turn to alternative persuasive means to do so. One alternative, scholars argue, has been that successful women rhetors have created their own style—what some have called a feminine style—in successfully addressing the public.[12] Yet this style also has its own logic, for as Shanara Rose Reid-Brinkley demonstrates, the "feminine style," as theorized, is a style of white, straight, middle-class women, "a citation of a privileged performance of a culturally normative femininity."[13] Genre conventions, as we learn from this literature, obscure intersectionality.

Such conventions also exist in the narratives that immigration officers expect they will hear (and read in the application) when an asylum seeker gives testimony. As Amy Shuman and Carol Bohmer explain, the process of claiming asylum is often one of "translating" personal experience into recognized rhetorical conventions: "To meet the criteria for political asylum status in the United States, applicants need to reframe what they often understand as a personal trauma into an act of political aggression. Many asylum applicants who have had traumatic experiences construct their stories only in bare-bones narratives and rarely represent their traumas in political terms. . . . [T]he 'translation' process involves pushing the claimants to provide the often gruesome details of their persecution."[14] In previous work, I have demonstrated genre conventions in immigration judges' assessment of credibility in gender-based asylum cases.[15] Here, we will see that genre conventions extend beyond the mere issue of credibility to condition all that judges expect to see and hear when they evaluate asylum claims. Genre conventions frame the entirety of an asylum seeker's argument construction as well as the rhetoric through which immigration judges read asylum seekers.

Genre Conventions of Reading Sexuality

STYLE

One of the first ways we access rhetors is through their style—how they speak, move through space, and affectively engage the speaking situation. While some might argue that rhetorical style inheres in the language usage of a rhetor, many scholars call us to attend to the relation between body, subjectivity, and language in understanding the significance of style. The body of the subject who appears before an audience to speak and use language is discursively significant; informed by dominant messages about gender, race, class, sexuality, age, ability and nation, the audience who attends to the speaking subject has a sense of what they expect to see, hear, and feel from the subject before them.

For sexuality-related asylum seekers, expectations about what sexuality looks, sounds, and feels like constrain claimants' possibilities of gaining access to U.S. asylum. Gay people have long negotiated the strictly formed relationship between sexuality and societal beliefs that gayness was evident on the surface of their bodies, in their voices, and how they comported themselves. In the late nineteenth century, for example, it was largely believed that gayness could be read on the surface of someone's physiological body. As many have noted of this period, medical and scientific communities subjected a range of marginalized groups, including people of color, gay people, women, criminals, and disabled persons, to a comparative study of their bodies against the model of "normal" bodies.[16] It was during this time that these communities developed the first model of bodily difference for gay people, known as "inversion," proposing "homosexuals exhibit characteristics of the opposite sex because they are 'trapped' in the wrong bodies."[17] The homosexual invert, in other words, was believed to be recognizable because they would identify with the gender opposite to their sex within the heterosexual matrix. Gender performances, according to this theory, signaled difference in sexual desire. Of course, as Jennifer Terry explains, this construction of inversion was set directly against a normative and idealized image of heterosexuality and consequently "tended to posit a generic, monolithic or stereotypical type ('the homosexual')."[18] As she and others archive, "inversion" has been identified by characteristics of gay people that could be perceived in their genitalia, physical stature, beauty or ugliness, emotional nervousness, and in the way gay people talk, move, dress, and comport themselves.[19] While long challenged by critical scholars of gender and sexuality, these theories continue to circulate in the popular imagination,[20] political and legal discourse,[21] as well as in some medical and scientific scholarly circles.[22]

This expectation of sexuality's publicness—that it will be evident in one's manner and comportment in inverted fashion—serves as a primary narrative genre convention as sexuality-related claimants are assessed and evaluated in U.S. immigration courtrooms.[23] As Fadi Hanna asks in the opening of his comment about visibility politics in gay asylum cases, "Does a homosexual asylum seeker need to prove he is 'gay enough' to win protection from a U.S. court?

Increasingly, and troublingly, the answer is yes."[24] Indeed, the majority of the cis- and transgender gay asylum cases I analyzed included explicit description of bodily, vocal, and affective stylistics that might lead an asylum claimant to be recognized as "gay."

Jose Antonio Grijalva was described in the court record as "effeminate" from an early age. A Guatemalan guerrilla group reportedly threatened him because of his style. As evidenced in the court record, "The guerrillas noticed Grijalva's long hair and effeminate manner, and threatened to rape him, saying 'you look like a woman, you're good for us, we're going to use you as a woman.'"[25] Dennis Vitug of the Philippines also articulated corporeal styling as central to his fear: "From the age of three, Vitug knew he was 'different.' He was effeminate and played with Barbie dolls and other toys meant for girls, which his family resented. Throughout his childhood, Vitug was teased and bullied by his classmates for 'being a sissy.'"[26] Adem Ozmen reported being abused and harassed in his home country of Turkey as an adolescent because of his feminine comportment, explaining that authorities refused to do anything to assist him because "they hoped such treatment would make him 'more a man.'"[27] To be sure, Rafael Castro Martinez of Mexico, Lay She Liong of Indonesia,[28] as well as the claimants described as "gay men with female sexual identities" (on whom I'll elaborate shortly), take explicit care to articulate their sexuality as apparent in the way their bodies move, in their voices, and in the way they fashion themselves.[29] In these cases, outward cues unmarked as gender serve as inventional resources for claimants that enable them to persuasively demonstrate that they are recognizable as persecuted on account of their sexuality, and thus that there is a clear nexus between their identities and the sexuality-related persecution they fear.[30] Here we see an invisible intersection at work between gender and sexuality that appropriates the gendered messages as messages about sexuality to render these male-assigned subjects eligible for inclusion.

Immigration judges also often confirm that they read claimants' style as noticeably different in their decisions. Brazilian Marcelo Halmenschlager, for example, explained to the courts that he was persecuted because he was "a homosexual with effeminate traits." In evaluating the case, the immigration judge made note of this point, affirming that Halmenschlager, indeed, is "very feminine."[31] In these cases, historical discourses of "inversion" serve as the rhetoric that immigration judges use to read sexuality as legible in a claimant's style through invisibly intersecting gendered discourses. On bodies assigned as male, words like "effeminate" and descriptions such as "long hair" signal to judges in these cases that the claimants' bodies are visible as gay. In "inverted" fashion, these signifiers of comportment, sound, and affect traffic through silently present gendered discourses. Here it is not whom one desires or consorts with that marks a claimant as demonstrably gay, but gendered signifiers—long hair, painted fingernails, being called effeminate—that persuade the courts that the claimants are publicly gay. One's "felt sense" of gender or the way one "does" gender matters not; nor does the largely held social belief that one's trans-ness or gender nonconformity is a mismatch between one's assigned sex and felt gender.[32] As concepts of the state, when attached to bodies always, already assigned with the male sex, both are legible in U.S. asylum as expressions of sexuality.

PERSECUTION

Witnessing gay and trans friends and acquaintances killed, experiencing institutionalization for being gay and gender nonconforming, and suffering harassing slurs are other common forms of violence cited in sexuality-related asylum cases, though almost all of the claimants speak about past *and* feared future sexual violence as the basis of their plea. While family members are sometimes the perpetrators, it is frequently political or state officials (in other words, police officers and military officials) who are named as the perpetrators in applicants' discussions of their experiences of sexual violence. In fact, it was challenging to find a sexuality asylum case that did not involve some past experience of sexual violence or the credible threat of it in the future. The narrative contention is that pervasive. For example, Grijalva, whose case I mentioned above, reported being "gang raped" by Guatemalan soldiers. As explained in the court record, "the soldiers forced Grijalva to go to their camp, telling him that he would enjoy what they were going to do to him. He begged them not to kill him. Grijalva was locked in a room for three days and nights and was gang raped, usually by four soldiers at a time. While raping him, the soldiers yelled obscenities about Grijalva being a homosexual. He thinks he was raped about two or three times a day by about thirty soldiers. He was in great pain, humiliated, and felt like a prostitute for these men."[33] Revolutionary Armed Forces of Columbia (FARC) members physically assaulted a Colombian citizen who goes by the initials J. P. S. approximately ten times before the claimant escaped and fled to the United States.[34] Daniel Shahinaj was "beat[en] and sodomized" by Albanian police officers who "threatened to harm Shahinaj and his family, and made repeated derogatory references to Shahinaj's homosexuality."[35] In each of these instances, and many others, the claimants cite experiences that are easily recognized as severe enough to meet the standards of persecution. Moreover, the persons inciting the violence are often actors with clear political or state associations (police officers, military officials), making their cases more neatly fit the definitions of political persecution that are necessary for winning asylum.

AWARENESS

In addition to evaluating whether applicants are recognizable as persons who might be persecuted on account of their social-group membership, narrative conventions of sexuality also frame sexuality and nonconformity as a constant in one's life, such that they are fundamental to a claimant's selfhood. To do this, immigration judges assess applicants' awareness of their sexuality and nonconformity as the means of deciding who fits within the frame and who doesn't. While awareness and "coming out" are commonly pinned together in U.S. American culture, in the conventional gay asylum case "coming out" doesn't always follow awareness.[36] Some claimants publically identify as "gay" later on in their lives, some are ascribed as gay by others, some strategically "come out," and some not at all. What is important to the genre is that gay asylum seekers are *aware* of their sexuality and nonconformity early in their lives.

Early awareness narratives help applicants establish the standard of immutability to which immigration judges listen as they are evaluating cases. As articulated in the introduction, the immutability standard is derived from the court's ruling in *Matter of Acosta*, which articulates immutability as shared group characteristics that "members of the group either cannot change, or should not be required to change because it is fundamental to their individual identities or consciences."[37] Typically the courts have interpreted immutability to mean something "biological" or "innate" about the asylum claimant, especially in sexuality-related cases.[38]

In following the definitional parameters of immutability as "biological," or "innate," then, the earlier the persecution narrative starts, the more sexuality and nonconformity sound like they may be fundamental to a person's sense of self. For example, Leonel Euro Ayala of Venezuela told the judge that he knew he was gay from an early age but didn't tell his family. When his family found out (a family friend had seen Ayala at a "gay party" in Caracas), his family "verbally harassed him about his sexual orientation and rejected him."[39] Nasser Mustafa Karouni from Lebanon also never told his family he was gay, though he testified "he has 'always been gay,'" and that as a youth he and his gay cousin would secretly meet other gay men.[40] Halmenschlager, introduced previously, also realized he was gay at an early age. The court record reveals that "by his first year in school, [Halmenschlager] realized he was different from other boys. Schoolmates called him names, laughed at him, and beat him. Other children, especially boys, would not play with him. He changed schools in the third grade but he was still harassed and beat by other children. He was afraid to tell the teachers because he believed the more people who knew of his problems, the more he would be subjected to mistreatment. Most of his friends in high school were girls. He had a troubled relationship with his stepfather who said Halmenschlager was not the type of son he expected."[41] This genre convention of early awareness is undeniably present across the range of these asylum claims.[42]

The citation of early awareness of same-sex desire demonstrates to the judge that one's sexuality and/or gender nonconformity are inherent and fundamental to one's sense of self and identity. This citation not only harks back to biological theories of gayness that figure sexual desire and identification as "something in our genes," a characteristic passed down through families, and thus innate, unchangeable, and fundamental to the person. The citation also figures sexual desire and practice as uni-directional and singularly oriented in its aversion to heterosexuality. In addition to knowing that they are gay early in their lives, none of these claimants note having had relationships with someone of a different sex. That none of the asylum claimants mention intimate different-sex relations further demonstrates that their sexuality is so fundamental that it cannot be changed.

The genre of sexuality derived from these cases positions sexuality and nonconformity as a constant in one's life. According to the genre, cis- and transgender sexuality asylum seekers are not only aware of their sexuality early on, but their desire never goes away, changes, or even just happens upon an exception. This genre assumes a fixed, singular, and perhaps even biological definition of sexuality that aligns with the legal definitions of immutability that also have biological roots. Knowing about your sexuality from an early age helps to establish that your sexual desire is part and parcel to who you are, such that requiring you to change it—even for your safety—would change *you*. Coming out later in life, having and continuing relationships with differently sexed persons, as well as having children muddies the neatness of the constructions of immutability that immigration judges rely on in making sense of sexual-orientation claims. This genre convention thus denies the very different ways that people come to an awareness of, experience, and express their sexuality, assuming instead a singular model—a male model—of sexual awareness and expression.

Taken together, in invisibly subsuming gender into sexuality for subjects assigned with male sex in the eyes of the law, these conventions, as rhetoric used in evaluating asylum claimants, work in tandem to forge the logic of reading sexuality in U.S. asylum courtrooms as a one-sex, one-gender logic. The assumption in U.S. asylum law is that gender and sexuality are discrete conceptual categories. In these asylum cases (where transgender or gender nonconforming identity or expression is evident) there is a mismatch between one's sexed body and one's gender "feeling," as Gayle Salomon describes it, which reifies dominant constructions of transgender and gender nonconformity.[43] Yet what the courts do with this mismatch is arguably something altogether different than what is evident in U.S. discussions of trans and gender nonconformity—they codify these gender expressions as expressions of sex and sexuality. This not only mirrors dominant societal beliefs that trans subjects are psychologically out of alignment with the physicality of the body, but it also refuses recognition of gender in these cases—naturalizing a one-sex, one-gender logic to the conceptual life of gender and sexuality in U.S. asylum law. This figures gender-based asylum as a special, segregated category reserved for cisgender women, while those assigned with male sex are naturalized as universal and neutral subjects for whom the entire system is intended.

"Feeling" Gender

Mexican national Giovanna Hernandez Montiel's case fit easily into the narrative conventions that frame the way sexuality is read in the U.S. asylum courts. Hernandez Montiel began to identify as Giovanna and dress in women's clothes at age twelve.[44] This public pronouncement of selfhood prompted a string of incidents that would ultimately compel Hernandez Montiel to leave Mexico in 1993. Not only was Hernandez Montiel kicked out of school, reportedly on account of being "gay," and threatened by classmates' parents who told Hernandez Montiel not to "pervert" their sons, but Hernandez Montiel was arrested and sexually assaulted by police officers because "it was illegal for homosexuals to walk down the street and for men to dress like women."[45] Later in life, family members institutionalized Hernandez Montiel. While in the psychiatric ward "the program staff cut his hair and nails, and forced him to stop taking female hormones" to "'cure' his sexual orientation by altering his female appearance."[46]

Hernandez Montiel attempted to enter the United States multiple times and was finally successful on October 14, 1994. Shortly after crossing, Hernandez Montiel applied for asylum on the grounds of sexual orientation persecution, and approximately one year later the immigration judge first heard the case. The judge found Hernandez Montiel to be credible and sincere as an asylum applicant but ultimately denied the asylum request, reasoning that the way Hernandez Montiel's social group definition was framed did not showcase immutability, or how Hernandez Montiel's identity was so fundamental that it could not or should not be changed. The judge wrote, "If he wears typical female

clothing sometimes, and typical male clothing other times, he cannot characterize his assumed female persona as immutable or fundamental to his identity.
The record reflects that [sic] respondent's decision to dress as a women [sic] is
volitional, not immutable, and the fact that he sometimes dresses like a typical
man reflects that [sic] respondent himself may not view his dress as being so
fundamental to his identity that he should not have to change it."[47] Hernandez
Montiel appealed the decision to the Board of Immigration Appeals, which sided
with the immigration judge, stating that the "tenor of the respondent's claim
is that he was mistreated because of the way he dressed (as a male prostitute)
and not because he is a homosexual."[48] Fortunately, Hernandez Montiel's final
appeal before the Ninth Circuit Court of Appeals resulted in the court reversing
the previous two negative decisions as the court revised the social group membership to which they recognized Hernandez Montiel belonging.[49] Hernandez
Montiel was convincingly read through the narrative conventions as a legible
sexuality-related asylum seeker. The claimant was granted asylum. The weight
of this individual achievement cannot be understated. What this case does for
the conceptual fixing of sex/sexuality and gender onto particular bodies is what
I examine here.

Rather than relying fully on the precedent set when Attorney General Janet Reno, in 1994, established in *Re Toboso Alfonso* that gays and lesbians were
protected social groups, in accordance with the amicus brief co-written by the
American Civil Liberties Union of Southern California, the Lambda Legal Defense and Education Fund Inc., the National Center for Lesbian Rights, and the
International Gay and Lesbian Human Rights Commission, which argued that
Hernandez Montiel should be awarded asylum as an "effeminate gay man,"[50]
the court did something entirely different. The Ninth Circuit judges agreed with
the previous two courts that the social group of "homosexual males who dress
as females" was not sufficient to demonstrate immutability in accordance with
court precedent. Instead, they recognized Hernandez Montiel as a member of a
group of "gay men with female sexual identities" who are particularly vulnerable to persecution and thus in need of refuge.[51]

The court could have turned to the trans concepts that were in circulation at
the time to articulate Hernandez Montiel's social group as immutable. While
there is considerable disagreement about how these concepts should be properly defined and deployed as their meanings are mutable and in flux, Susan
Stryker notes that they were in circulation in the United States at least as early
as the 1960s and definitely by the 1990s.[52] This is particularly true in U.S. legal
discourse. For example, the 1984 *Ulane v. Eastern Airlines* case set binding precedent for questions of employment discrimination against trans people. While

Ulane, a trans flight attendant, was not awarded relief for being fired on account of her trans identity, the case shows the recognition and deployment of trans concepts in the legal arena. The Seventh Circuit justices evaluating Ulane's claim even go as far as to define (albeit problematically) what they mean by "transsexual" in assessing the discrimination claim: "It is clear from the evidence that if Eastern did discriminate against Ulane, it was not because she is female, but because Ulane is transsexual—a biological male who takes female hormones, cross-dresses, and has surgically altered parts of her body to make it appear to be female."[53]

The Ninth Circuit, in a nod to this concept in their evaluation of Hernandez Montiel's claim, explains in a footnote that Hernandez Montiel "may be considered a transsexual" or in their understanding "a person who is genetically and physically a member of one sex but has a deep-seated psychological conviction that he or she belongs, or ought to belong, to the opposite sex, a conviction which may in some cases result in the individual's decision to undergo surgery in order to physically modify his or her sex organs to resemble those of the opposite sex."[54] It is not evident from reading the case if the appellation is Hernandez Montiel's own avowal or the court's ascription; whatever the case, the judges quickly move on from the question, stating, "We need not consider in this case whether transsexuals constitute a particular social group."[55]

The judges also avoid the term gender identity used in other arenas of U.S. case law.[56] As early as 1974 gender identity appeared in U.S. legal cases as a concept to describe the experiences of people whose assigned sex at birth did not match in binary fashion their expressed gendered self.[57] By 1980 the U.S. federal court of appeals began recognizing this concept in cases where someone's gender nonconformity was the basis for discrimination,[58] and by 1997 the Ninth Circuit Court of Appeals—the same court that evaluated Hernandez Montiel's claim in 2000—was hearing the complaints of people diagnosed with "gender identity disorder" who were refused hormonal therapy in prison.[59]

While both of these discursive options were possible sources of rhetorical invention in articulating Hernandez Montiel's identity as immutable, the court took the most expedient argumentative route and fit the framing into the already acknowledged sexual orientation precedent, but with a twist. They did this by taking up the language of Professor Thomas M. Davies, who wrote an affidavit in support of Hernandez Montiel. Davies's language and analysis provided them with the quickest argumentative means to etch out their recognition of gender nonconformity as a valid and immutable reason for claiming asylum. In this affidavit, Davies explained that in Latin America, "a man who is perceived to assume the stereotypical 'female,' i.e. passive, role in these sexual relations is 'ostracized from the very beginning and is subject to persecution, gay bashing as we would call it, and certainly police abuse.'"[60] Furthermore, he wrote that these persons "[are] heavily persecuted by the police and other groups within the society. They are a separate social entity within Latin American society and in this case within the nation of Mexico."[61] Notably, in my archival research I could find no evidence of Davies's expertise concerning constructions and expressions of gender and sexuality; he is a scholar of Latin American studies who has written or edited books with the following titles: *Indian Integration in Peru: A Half Century of Experience, 1900–1948*, *The Politics of Antipolitics: The Military in Latin America*, and *Guerrilla Warfare*, none of which concerns configurations of gender and sexuality in Latin America. Additionally, scholars of Latin@ sexualities including Tomás Almaguer, Michael Hames-Garcia, Lionel Cantú, Héctor Carrillo, Carlos Decena, and Salvador Vidal-Ortiz stridently refute the thesis about Latin@ sexuality proffered by Davies in their own analyses.[62]

And yet the Ninth Circuit appropriated his language regarding gender and sexuality as its own, arguing,

> Professor Davies is helpful to our analysis.... Professor Davies did not testify that homosexual males are persecuted simply because they may dress as females or because they engage in homosexual acts. Rather, gay men with female sexual identities are singled out for persecution because they are perceived to assume the stereotypical "female," i.e., passive, role in gay relationships. Gay men with female sexual identities outwardly manifest their identities through characteristics traditionally associated with women, such as feminine dress, long hair and fingernails. Gay men with female sexual identities in Mexico are a "small, readily identifiable group."[63]

Davies's affidavit helps the court define Hernandez Montiel's identity as immutable within the confines of sexual orientation, skirting the question of whether individuals who are recognized by the courts as male sexed/bodied can also have a gender. Specifically, Davies explains that "their female sexual identities unite this group of gay men, and their sexual identities are so fundamental to their human identities that they should not be required to change them."[64] Here, the court is persuaded that immutability may be connected to what congeals through the repetitive doing of discourse on and through one's body, yet invisibly so as to articulate this expression as one of sex/sexuality not gender, explaining, "We therefore conclude as a matter of law that the 'particular social group' in this case is comprised of gay men with female sexual identities in Mexico."[65]

The term "sexual identity" may be new to some readers, but it too has a history, albeit one not neatly composed. As a legal concept sexual identity seems to have two institutional referents—the field of psychology and that of biomedical studies. The derivative of the term in psychology is the concept of sexual identity development, which is most commonly applied to theorize patterns in the development of gay, lesbian, and bisexual identities. In this context, sexual identity would be thought of as an identity on the basis of sexual orientation, and nonheterosexual identities would be even more accurate.[66] Biomedical research, however, deploys "sexual identity" to refer to one's avowed sex, or as Milton Diamond explains, "the personal core awareness of being male or female."[67] This identity is categorically distinguishable from gender identity and sexual orientation, Diamond argues: "Gender identity, as a recognition of a social phenomenon distinct from sexual identity, develops before or concomitant with the acceptance or awareness of preferred gender patterns. This awareness of preferred patterns develops prior to an acceptance of a stable sexual identity, and one's sexual orientation develops later."[68] In this way, we might also understand sexual identity as a person's avowed sex identity, which may or may not match the sex they were assigned at birth.

As if that was not confusing enough, both sexual orientation and avowed sex appear as referents for sexual identity in other bodies of U.S. case law. In family, adoption, and custody law, sexual identity refers to an identity on the basis of sexual orientation. In employment law, by contrast, sexual identity refers to the sex that a person identifies with, while sex itself is figured as one's assigned sex at birth. The *Ulane v. Eastern Airlines* decision keenly demonstrates the rhetorical barriers placed around these two categories, as the Seventh Circuit judges explain:

> Other courts have held that the term "sex" as used in the statute is not synonymous with "sexual preference." The district court recognized this, and agreed that homosexuals and transvestites do not enjoy Title VII protection, but distinguished transsexuals as persons who, unlike homosexuals and transvestites, have sexual identity problems; the judge agreed that the term "sex" does not comprehend "sexual preference," but held that it does comprehend "sexual identity." The district judge based this holding on his finding that "sex is not a cut-and-dried matter of chromosomes," but is in part a psychological question—a question of self-perception; and in part a social matter—a question of how society perceives the individual. The district judge further supported his broad view of Title VII's coverage by recognizing Title VII as a remedial statute to be liberally construed. He concluded that it is reasonable to hold that the statutory word "sex" literally

and scientifically applies to transsexuals even if it does not apply to homosexuals or transvestites. We must disagree.[69]

As if that severing of sex and sexual identity was not clear, the justices later speak directly to Ulane's bid:

> The phrase in Title VII prohibiting discrimination based on sex, in its plain meaning, implies that it is unlawful to discriminate against women because they are women and against men because they are men. The words of Title VII do not outlaw discrimination against a person who has a sexual identity disorder, i.e., a person born with a male body who believes himself to be female, or a person born with a female body who believes herself to be male; a prohibition against discrimination based on an individual's sex is not synonymous with a prohibition against discrimination based on an individual's sexual identity disorder or discontent with the sex into which they were born.[70]

Marriage certification cases, a jurisdiction of state but not federal law, also take up this usage of sexual identity as avowed sex that is distinguishable from sex; but this case law includes yet another discursive twist. In some states—Kansas, Florida, and Texas, for instance—people are ceaselessly recognized as their assigned sex, which means that sex and sexual identity are forever fixed as disparate categories.[71] In other states, though, a person's sex and sexual identity can become congruent again through gender confirming surgery, which then enables them to change the sex listed on legal documents such as their birth certificate and ultimately to marry someone of the same or different sex in a marriage that is endorsed by that state.[72]

In asylum cases, though, the social group framing of sexual identity works by conflating sex and sexual identity under the broader framework of sexuality, which then enables trans and gender nonconforming asylum claimants to make successful bids for refuge. Arabillas Moreles (at the opening of this chapter) identified as a transgender woman and was given asylum as "a gay man with a female sexuality identity." Salvadoran citizen Luis Reyes Reyes gained withholding and Convention Against Torture because there was a reasonable chance of persecution if returned to El Salvador, evidenced by a long history of prior personal violence in the country. Drawing on the success of Hernandez Montiel's "sexual identity" claim, Reyes Reyes requested asylum as "a homosexual male with a female sexual identity." As continued in the court record, "[h]e dresses and looks like a woman, wearing makeup and a woman's hairstyle. Although Reyes has not undergone sex reassignment surgery, he has had a characteristically female appearance, mannerisms, and gestures for the past sixteen years. He has a 'deep female identity' and has gone by female names such as Josephine, Linda and Cukita."[73] Reyes Reyes was not granted asylum relief (a result of untimely filing) but would gain the right to stay in the United States through the conjoined Convention Against Torture and Withholding of Removal applications. In affirming these two forms of relief, the court recognized that Reyes Reyes's visibility as "a homosexual male with a female sexual identity" would more than likely instigate violence against the claimant in El Salvador.

The court evaluating Francisco Ornelas Chavez's bid was also persuaded by this language. Ornelas Chavez left Mexico in 1998, according to court records, to "escape a lifetime of abuse suffered on account of his female sexual identity" and to claim asylum in the United States.[74] Ornelas Chavez endured sexual and physical assault as a child from friends and family for wearing traditionally feminine clothing and for playing with "girls'" toys. Threats from teachers, employment supervisors, and police officers for "being a fag," "sleeping with men," and for "dressing like a woman" continued throughout Ornelas Chavez's adolescence and adulthood;[75] co-workers tried to smother Ornelas Chavez with a pillow, exclaiming "they were 'finally going to get rid of another homo.'"[76] Ornelas Chavez saw many gay and trans friends murdered at the hands of police while living in Mexico. The tipping point for the claimant came in 1998, when "his father, who had discovered his whereabouts, came to Mexicali and beat him severely, breaking his nose with a bottle."[77] Shortly after this incident, Ornelas Chavez entered the United States without documents, residing in the country until 2003, when U.S. Immigration and Customs Enforcement (ICE) officials began removal proceedings against Ornelas Chavez for unlawfully entering the country; at that time, Ornelas Chavez filed for asylum and withholding of removal for fear of persecution and torture if returned to Mexico, ultimately gaining immigration relief as "a gay man with a female sexual identity."

Read against this record of sexual identity as a legal concept, it is unclear exactly what the courts are referring to when they recognize Hernandez Montiel, Arabillas Moreles, Reyes Reyes, and Ornelas Chavez as "gay men with female sexual identities." Both sexual orientation and sex seem to be referents of this concept. What is not present, however, is gender, despite the fact that the genre conventions that make these individuals so intelligible as "gay men with female sexual identities" are so reliant on the invisible intersections of gender as the silent argument signaling the necessity of their incorporation. Hernandez Montiel, Arabillas Moreles, Reyes Reyes, and Ornelas Chavez express their gender through signifiers traditionally associated with womanhood and femininity, and they even identify as women—and yet in discussing their cases, court officials consistently first reorder these claimants back onto the male side of the sex/ gender system. In early decisions Hernandez Montiel was told that comporting as a woman does not a woman make;[78] Hernandez Montiel's preferred gender expression was instead legible as a "persona," not an identity; a "volitional" decision to dress in a certain way exists as surface matter, not as matter that can itself engender gender. Hernandez Montiel is constantly figured as a man and, even more important, a man with a "female sexual identity," which, when read in relation to the psychological, biomedical, and legal discourse on this term, further sediments Hernandez Montiel as a male-assigned subject.

The turn to sex and sexuality as the primary descriptive mechanism circumvents gender completely through what feminist scholar Monique Wittig addresses as the constant conflation of sex and sexual orientation: "The category of sex is the political category that founds society as heterosexual. As such it does not concern being but relationships (for women and men are the result of relationships), although the two aspects are always confused when they are discussed."[79] Legal scholar Francisco Valdes explains that this conflation is embedded in the Western legal tradition wherein sex (external genitalia at birth) is conflated with the social construct of gender, gender as an expression of sexual relations is confused with sexual orientation as desire, and sexual orientation as defined by the sameness or difference of the genital parts of the sexual partners one desires is once again conflated with sex.[80] And yet I posit a different logic at work—one that is derivative of a much older conceptualization of sex, gender, and sexuality—a one-sex, one-gender system. Instead of a two-gender system that is organized discursively through the heterosexual matrix as contemporary theorists of gender have argued, the logic of thinking sex, gender, and sexuality in the modern U.S. asylum courtroom congeals in the likeness of what Thomas Laqueur articulates as the pre-Enlightenment one-sex system:

> [I]n these pre-Enlightenment texts, and even some later ones, *sex*, or the body, must be understood as the epiphenomenon, while *gender*, what we would take to be a cultural category, was primary or "real." . . . In the world of one sex, it was precisely when talk seemed to be most directly about the biology of two sexes that it was most embedded in the politics of gender, in culture. To be a man or a woman was to hold a social rank, a place in society, to assume a cultural role, not to be organically one or the other of the two incommensurable sexes. Sex before the seventeenth century, in other words, was still a sociological and not an ontological category.[81]

In the present-day legal context, sex rarely appears ontologically, and even when it does—as in *Matter of Acosta* (discussed in the introduction)—it is never explicitly *applied* ontologically as grounds upon which one's life, one's being, may be at risk. As Barbara Young Welke shows, while gender does enter the Western system of legal discourse as an ontological status, it does so attached to a particular subset of bodily subjects[82] and, as Wittig argues regarding women's entrance into language, this entrance often happens through force:

"I" [*Je*] as a generic feminine subject can *only* enter by force into a language which is foreign to it, for all that is human (masculine) is foreign to it, the human not being feminine grammatically speaking but he [*il*] or they [*ils*]. "I" [*Je*] conceals the sexual differences of the verbal persons while specifying them in verbal interchange. "I" [*Je*] obliterates the fact that *elle* or *elles* are submerged in *il* or *ils*.[83]

In this formulation, not only is the subject who enters when "I" is written or spoken decidedly male assigned, but also for gender to be intelligible as associated with a subject position in language it must be through force. Though Wittig never specifies what force she had in mind, the way gender can enter as a concept in the language of U.S. asylum law—most often through violence done to cisgender women's bodies—makes very real what it may mean when Wittig says that the feminine enters into language as a subject through force. Moreover, when subjects with bodies interpreted through the law as fixedly assigned male—regardless of how they see themselves, what names they use, what pronouns they prefer, what bodily configurations they desire, or how they enact their felt sense of gender— describe experiences that are typically associated with femininity, the only logical extension from the one-sex, one-gender system is that they must be talking about sexuality, and that they are ultimately male-assigned subjects.

In this framework, the male subject is not a gendered subject but rather a neutral and universal subject recognized as such because of assigned sex. When male-assigned subjects make claims to asylum, they need not find a language to speak from, or enter it through force, for they already belong in the language as the naturalized and appropriate subjects for belonging in the U.S. nation-state. When male-assigned applicants claim asylum for reasons involving what could be described as their gender identity, their claims are intelligible—though they must be read through sexuality, because in this political context the male body does not have a gender. These cases, read together, demonstrate the persistent return of those assigned at birth as male back to sex; meanwhile, gender remains a segregated referent for cisgender women.

This framework solidifies the courts' earlier equation that gender equals cisgender woman, and persistently maintains male-sex as both neutral and universal. In this neutrality, male-assigned subjects continue to be figured first as the appropriate subjects for belonging in the U.S. nation-state, while female assigned persons are given gender as a special, exceptional category when their claims exceed the frame. As scholars of gender and refugee studies note, the asylum system was constituted around the model refugee as a male-assigned subject who was persecuted by his state for his public opinions or actions against that state.[84] This preference continues not only in what the courts imagine political persecution to look like but also whom the courts imagine as a political subject with particular claims. When male-assigned applicants claim asylum for reasons involving what could be described as their gender identity and expression, their claims must be read through sexuality so as not to challenge the undergirding, naturalized logic of male as the immutable sex for which asylum (and arguably the nation) was originally intended.

Chapters 1 through 3 demonstrated how particular types of gender violence are fixed on to particular bodies and places. The logic for including claimants on the basis of sexuality operates differently. What is interesting about the conceptual life of sexuality-related persecution is the flatness of its corporeal and geographic applicability. While it is true that there are racialized versions of sexuality associated with particular bodies and geographies in the Western imagination,[85] when cases of male assigned claimants are argued as sexuality-related persecution, these differences are largely effaced, rendered irrelevant. The genre conventions insist that claimants will be visibly nonconforming and aware of their non-normativity from an early age, which solidifies the nexus between persecution and social group, as well as the standard of immutability. Additionally, because the claimants are intelligible in the one-sex, one-gender logic first and foremost as male assigned subjects, the persecution that is expected in accordance with these genre conventions—sexual violence—is easily recognized as political.

As scholars of sexual violence demonstrate, much more than being about desire, sexual assault is an act of power and domination.[86] In heterosexist thinking, male-male rape is seen even more stridently as motivated by power rather than desire.[87] This means that male-assigned sexuality claimants, regardless of their gender, who experience sexual forms of persecution more easily fit into the frameworks of political persecution that are necessary for winning asylum claims. This is the case no matter where a claimant comes from. Now, there are certainly geopolitical, racial, and corporeal nuances in some of these cases. For example, all of the cases of "gay men with female sexual identities" come from Mexico and Central America, which, as Lionel Cantú has argued, evokes an idea that "Mexico [and arguably Central America] is represented as an oppressive country where homosexual relations exist but where only the passive partner is stigmatized."[88] Yet diverse types of violence are not grafted onto particular bodies and geographies as stridently as happens with women's gender-related asylum cases. All sexuality-related persecution is sexual violence. The continent or country a person flees, the identity of the persecutor, and the details of flight become mere backdrop for the ultimate offense, which is male-male rape. The U.S. imaginary conjures the victim of male-male rape as having lost masculinity, as able to be physically overpowered, and as possibly gay. Sandesh Sivakumaran argues that these beliefs support the "power dynamic theory behind rape," which posits "a hierarchy of power in society, with men placed at the top and women at the bottom. The threat of the existing power dynamic being usurped and those at the top losing their positions of power explains why those at the top of the hierarchy rape those lower down. Such threats do not stem from active challenges but simply from being the 'other.'"[89]

In Western heterosexist thought, power is linked to masculinity and heterosexuality. When immigration judges hear about sex as persecution between those assigned as male—no matter the individual's country of citizenship, sexual preference, or gender expression—the act or threat is recognizable as an act intended to eradicate power or to "achieve the total and utter humiliation of the individuals concerned, stripping them of any semblance of dignity."[90] Against this heteromasculinist logic a judge would never dare to ask of the male-assigned claimant, as an immigration judge did to a gender-based asylum case, "Now, how do I not know this was a consensual arrangement?" or to imply that the sexual violence was motivated by the perpetrator's personal desire for the victim, sentiments that have been conveyed in the asylum cases of cisgender women claiming sexual assault as grounds for their claim.[91] Male-male rape—as a universal—is always, already imagined as political. It does not need corporeal particularity or geographic specificity to be intelligible as political persecution. It is already, a priori, imagined as such.

Conclusion

We have seen how gender is cordoned off from sex and sexuality as concepts in U.S. asylum law. Chapter 5 takes up the implications of this one-sex, one-gender system to understand what happens when gay men who might be described as gender-conforming and cisgender women claim the need for protection on behalf of their sexual orientation. I question the invisible intersectionalities that are produced in the segregation of gender from sexuality, helping to demonstrate even more clearly what gender can mean as a political concept in U.S. law and politics.

CHAPTER 5

The Reading Practices
of Immigration Judges

Intersectional Invisibility and the Segregation
of Gender and Sexuality

I n a *New York Times* story titled "Gays Seeking Asylum in U.S. Encounter a New Hurdle" published on January 29, 2011, journalist Dan Bilefsky alerted U.S. publics to the politics of reading sexuality and gender in U.S. asylum hearings. The story detailed the experiences of Brazilian-born Romulo Castro, who was in the process of claiming asylum for persecution relating to his sexuality. In Brazil, Castro explained to Bilefsky, "I was persecuted for being fruity, a boy-girl, a fatso, a faggot"; in applying for asylum in the United States, Castro was encouraged that "flaunting it was now his best weapon against deportation." Bilefsky used Castro's experiences to demonstrate that "homosexuals seeking asylum may risk being dismissed as not being gay enough."[1] The story features comments by Human Rights First lawyer Lori Adams, who reiterates this point: "Judges and immigration officials are adding a new hurdle in gay asylum cases that an applicant's homosexuality must be socially visible. . . . The rationale is that if you don't look obviously gay, you can go home and hide your sexuality and don't need to be worried about being persecuted."[2] Legal Director of Immigration Equality Victoria Neilson was also cited, referencing the case of an Albanian lesbian who was first denied asylum for "not conforming to the officer's stereotype of a lesbian."[3] Moving from this "new hurdle," the reporter ended the story by implying that some claimants try to "fake" gayness in order to win asylum cases. A few immigration lawyers, Bilefsky noted, had even been convicted of setting up an asylum consulting business where they "coached straight people on how to file gay asylum claims." The "new hurdle," readers learned, concerned what immigration judges expected to hear and see when a gay asylum applicant entered their chambers.

The immigration law experts cited in the story were understandably upset by the coverage. Not only had the journalist perpetuated the myth of "fraudulent" refugees, but he had also implied that immigration officials and judges—the same people to whom these two lawyers had to advocate for clients—might be reliant on gay stereotypes in evaluating LGBT cases. A week after the story ran, Victoria Neilson and Lori Adams published their response as a letter to the editor:

> While we appreciate your coverage of lesbian, gay, bisexual and transgender asylum seekers, the article is not consistent with our experience in several ways. . . . In our experience, however, it is exceedingly rare for asylum seekers—whose families and home countries often stigmatize gay and transgender people—to present themselves falsely as lesbian, gay, bisexual or transgender to immigration officials. We have not seen an emerging trend of straight individuals claiming to be gay for immigration purposes. Indeed, asylum seekers undergo rigorous evaluation by immigration officials to ensure that their claims are authentic. Nor have we seen a "new hurdle" for L.G.B.T. asylum seekers having to prove that they are "socially visible." While there have been a few cases where adjudicators have demonstrated a bias in L.G.B.T. cases, we have found that most United States officials do their jobs, and verify claims made in asylum applications while respecting an individual's identity as an L.G.B.T. person. Until L.G.B.T. rights are respected around the world, asylum remains a lifeline for those fleeing persecution.[4]

Taken together these two comments illustrate that there is indeed awareness that immigration judges are guided by a sense of what a sexuality-related persecution narrative might look and sound like. These authors differ only in questions of the scale and the stickiness of the narrative genre conventions. The disagreement, in other words, is in how widespread and pervasive the reliance on these narratives is in immigration judges' decisions. These articles also demonstrate the problem of making generalizing statements about something like inclusion of sexuality-related asylum seekers without looking at the nuances and details, or how subjects who differ dramatically from one another because of the intersections of their identities, geopolitical associations, and the particularities of their lives come to be evaluated against the rhetoric of the narrative conventions. Charting these nuances is the focus of this chapter.

Chapter 4 outlined the rhetoric and logic of immigration judges' reading practices of sexuality-related asylum cases. This chapter takes up the narrative conventions again to understand what happens to claimants whose experiences are not as easily legible in the rhetoric of the conventions codified through the male-assigned cis and trans sexuality cases. I see the reading practices of judges as a particular aspect of the process of audiencing that I describe in the introduction of this book. As we will see in this chapter, immigration judges base their reading of particular claims on the conventional sexuality-related persecution narrative that I outlined in chapter 4. Reading as a practice then involves looking for alignment between the signs and cues present in the conventional narrative and those evident in the specific claim. When there is not alignment, asylum seekers struggle in being audienced as eligible or bona fide political subjects who've been persecuted because of their sexuality. Due to the constraints of the archive, I will focus first on the claims of gay men who might be described as gender-conforming and then move to discuss the challenge of what Valerie Purdie-Vaughns and Richard Elback have called "intersectional invisibility"[5] for lesbian asylum seekers. It is entirely possible that male-identifying trans applicants or gender nonbinary asylum applicants have sought and won asylum through affirmative asylum processes in the United States,[6] but there are no defensive asylum cases to draw on in order to analyze the nuances of the reading practices of the judges in these cases, so any comment on these claimants' legibility and would be mere speculation. As we will see in this chapter, while gender-normative gay men experience challenges to their claims because of the way their styling strays from the conventions, they are ultimately incorporable as credible applicants on the basis of sexuality. Gay women[7] often fail at being legible against all three narrative conventions—making their navigation of the refugee system infinitely more difficult. In both instances, I read the challenges against the one-sex, one-gender system and the racialization of gender violence to further understand the institutional life of the category of gender in U.S. law and politics.

Normative Sexuality

While style is figured as a key element in the success of trans and gender nonnormative sexuality cases, gender-normative cisgender gay men may experience challenges from the court for their genre (gender) failures. In these cases, gay men do not follow the logics of "inversion" through their style, and thus their eligibility for refugee protection is questioned. Judges in these cases do not doubt that the applicants are gay; rather, they push back on whether these gay male applicants are likely to be persecuted in the future because of their sexuality. The judge hearing Jorge Soto Vega's claim recognized that Soto Vega was gay but denied the claim. He said, "[I] didn't see anything in his appearance, his dress, his manner, his demeanor, his gestures, his voice, or anything of that nature that remotely approached some of the stereotypical things that society assesses to gays, whether those are legitimate or not. I certainly would not be able to tell, just from his testimony and his appearance here in Court today that he was a homosexual."[8] This ruling came after Soto Vega testified to a childhood of abuse from his father and brother because he needed to "become 'a man, not a joto,'"[9] taunts and physical abuse at school for his "cullioni," "girly behavior,"[10] and the near-death beating he and a friend suffered at the hands of the police, who claimed that they were "ridding the streets of two more fags."[11] Soto Vega ultimately won asylum on appeal, but the first immigration judge found his gender performance more persuasive than his past experiences of persecution in rendering a negative decision. His ability to pass as "heterosexual" through the way that he did gender enabled, in the judge's mind, possibility of Soto Vega's safe return to Mexico as a gay subject.

The judge evaluating Serbian Mladen Zeljko Todorovic's case told him that he was not credible as a gay asylum seeker when Todorovic presented testimony in the court. The judge explained:

> The Court would first note that the respondent says that he is singled out for persecution because he is gay in his home country. The Court studied the demeanor of this individual very carefully throughout his testimony in Court today, and this gentleman does not appear to be overtly gay. The Court does not know whether he is or not, his testimony is that he is overtly gay and has been since he was 17 years old. Be that as it may, it is not readily apparent to a person who would see this gentleman for the first time that, that is the case, since he bears no effeminate traits or any other trait that would mark him as a homosexual.[12]

As in Soto Vega's case, the judge used the legibility of gender through an inversion logic, and in this instance a lack of audible, visible, or affective markers of femininity, to decide whether the claimant would be persecuted as a gay man. Similarly, Tarik Razkane of Morocco was questioned about his appearance as gay. The U.S. state lawyer cross examining him at his first asylum case asked Razkane whether people could identify him as gay "by the way he talked, dressed, and moved."[13] The lawyer asked a similar question to a Moroccan country-conditions expert testifying on behalf of Razkane. The expert retorted, "Ma'am, I'm sorry, I can't help you with that. I just don't know what it means to look like a gay."[14] The judge, however, seemed to have a very clear sense of what it meant to look gay. In his negative ruling the judge explained that the claimant's "appearance does not have anything about it that would designate [him] as being gay. [He] does not dress in an effeminate manner or affect any effeminate mannerisms."[15] Drawing on the inversion logic once again, the judge decidedly articulated that difference, as sexuality was not legible in Razkane's appearance. While not as drastic as the cases demonstrating this method of reading above, Mexican nationals Jose Patricio Boer Sedano and Leonardo Magdaleno Comparan were similarly figured as ineligible because the courts saw them as "low-profile, non-transvestite gay [men]" who could feasibly walk through the streets of Mexico and not be identified as gay.[16] Notably, each of these asylum claimants would later gain asylum on appeal as the appellate justices admonished the lower courts for relying primarily on stereotypes about gayness in their negative rulings. Yet it is these first instances of reading gender in the claimants' public performances where we see the genre conventions of style play out as a persuasive resource (or deficit) in winning asylum. While each of these claimants offered other substantive content toward demonstrating their eligibility for asylum—past physical and sexual assault that is animated by their sexuality,[17] and targeting as gay because of the places they frequent, people they associate with, and the way they live[18]—the claimants were first read as ineligible because of their inability to be legible against the rhetoric of style that shape judges' imaginations of what proper sexual orientation persecution claims look and sound like. Related to this and in line with the genre convention about early awareness of homosexuality and the singular-direction of sexual orientation, when male-assigned sexuality claimants had a record of heterosexual sexual/marital union, doubt was cast on the veracity of their claim.[19]

Despite these challenges, the logic of male rape discussed in the previous chapter supersedes any resistance that these claimants receive from the judges in being credibly received as eligible for asylum. Soto Vega, for example, was told first that he did not appear gay before the court. Yet because his claim involved physical and sexual assault at the hands of police, his case was more easily legible as a matter of state violence and power, entitling him to political asylum in the United States. This dynamic is evident across the record of case law. Sexual assault between those assigned as male is so imaginable as an abhorrent overpowering of someone and as a violation of one's sense of self that it can be nothing but political. This demonstrates the ways that intersections between gender and sexuality play out to privilege particular subjects who are closer to the norm because of their intersecting identities. In the next section of this chapter we will see the manifestations of the same intersections toward very different ends.

The Ampersand Problem

Gay women have been seeking asylum in the United States since at least the early 1990s, when Alla Pitcherskaia of Russia filed an asylum petition exclaiming that it was likely she would be further tortured or killed because of her lesbianism if she returned to Russia.[20] Pitcherskaia experienced early challenges to her claim for eligibility, including first being denied asylum and having the immigration judge tell her that the forced institutionalization and electroshock therapy she endured was done in an attempt to "cure," not persecute her. In 1997 the Ninth Circuit reversed this decision and granted her asylum in accordance with Janet Reno's then-recent declaration in *Matter of Toboso Alfonso* that gays and lesbians constituted recognized social groups in U.S. asylum law.[21]

Despite this early individual success, lesbian asylum seekers face numerous hurdles in gaining access to refuge in the United States on account of their sexual orientation.[22] First, gay women, as a whole, file fewer asylum claims under the *Toboso-Alfonso* ruling than gay men do. As Cynthia Cooper reports, between 1994 and 2007, "62 lesbians [were] permitted to stay in the United States out of 435 inquiries, compared to 643 gay men among 4,134 inquiries. In other words, only one lesbian applies for every 10 gay men."[23] This disparity in who files for asylum is in the context of already deep gender disparities wherein women account for only 37 percent of all asylum claimants in the United States despite persistent identification as the largest category of displaced persons around the world by refugee aid agencies.[24] Even arrival in a country of asylum that recognizes sexual orientation as a basis for refuge, however, does not mean that lesbian asylum seekers will be hospitably welcomed.[25] Gay women also struggle to win asylum claims because, as Victoria Neilson explains, "sexual orientation-based jurisprudence has been built on a male model of public activities resulting in public persecution, a paradigm that the facts of lesbian asylum claims do not often follow."[26] This falls in line with what Cheshire Calhoun, nearly twenty years ago, articulated as the problematic reception of lesbians from around the world *as* lesbians.[27] Gay women are sometimes recognized as women, and sometimes as gay, but rarely both at the same time. The institution of U.S. law is particularly guilty in producing what Elizabeth Spelman refers to as the "ampersand problem," where gender and sexuality (or any other intersection for that matter) cannot be seen as mutually informing one's experiences and identity.[28] While some are successful in demonstrating their need for refuge as gay women, for many the logics enforcing the genre conventions position gender and sexuality as discrete categories while still invisibly reading these claimants' applications for their gendered significance. This means that gay women's requests for refuge *as* gay are either interpreted as not gay enough or "too woman" (read: gendered) to warrant incorporation as sexuality-based asylum seekers.

LESBIANS WITH STYLE

Where style is overtly present as an inventional resource for some sexuality applicants and as a method of reading for immigration judges, in the cases of lesbian asylum seekers, style is virtually absent in the archive. This absence is strange, given the record in asylum cases that evidences immigration judges' often near obsession with determining whether asylum claimants are publicly recognizable as the vulnerable subjects they say they are.[29] This absence is further marked when read against the corpus of scholarship about lesbian migration that finds similar strange vacancies. In her historical work on the monitoring and exclusion of gays and lesbians through U.S. immigration processes, Eithne Luibhéid could find only one case of a woman being excluded from entrance at U.S. borders as a "sexual deviate" because she "looked, spoke, and acted 'like a lesbian.'"[30] This singular instance stands alongside a historical record ripe with evidence that the Immigration and Naturalization Service targeted men for exclusion as "sexual deviates" because of their bodily comportment and style. While we might read this stark difference in the record of immigration policing as demonstrative of more lax regulation around lesbian identity and subjectivity, Luibhéid calls on readers to consider the different modalities of policing used to target men and women. She writes, "We should not treat this dearth of court cases as further evidence that lesbians were unaffected by immigration policing; instead, we need to remain attuned to the ways that women are historically excluded/unrepresented within official documents but were present historically and had an impact."[31] In building on this important insight, I read the paucity of discussion of lesbian style in asylum cases not as evidence that their appearance was not evaluated, monitored, and regulated, but rather that lesbians' outward style *as* lesbians frequently disappears under the sign of "normal" heterosexual femininity.

This disappearance is most evident in reading what is silent and absent in these cases as moments rich with rhetorical significance. At age fourteen, Yesenia Marisol Maldonado Lopez of El Salvador was forced by her parents into marriage with a man fifty-four years her senior to "'cure' her of her lesbianism and masculine appearance";[32] the marriage continued from 1996 until 2009, when the man died of old age. Over the course of these thirteen years, the man drugged, beat, and raped Maldonado Lopez, resulting in two pregnancies. She fled numerous times—at one point living with a woman with whom she had a romantic relationship—but her husband always found her. In 2006 she fled to the United States as an undocumented migrant; she was returned to El Salvador in 2010, and then, upon a violent attack in her hometown by four women who "punched and kicked her," "called her 'lesbian' and shouted vulgarities at her,"[33] she again fled to the United States. This time, when apprehended by U.S. border officials, Maldonado Lopez explained that she "feared being attacked and murdered if she were to return to El Salvador."[34] Her asylum bid thus commenced.

After being evaluated as possibly eligible for refuge during her reasonable-fear interview, Maldonado Lopez's case went before an immigration judge for review. She explained to the judge that "in addition to the psychological harm and social isolation she was subjected to as a lesbian in El Salvador—including being drugged and raped as a child by the 68-year-old man who her family forced her to marry—she continues to fear physical harm from individuals in her home country who do not accept lesbians."[35] The judge found Maldonado Lopez credible, but he ultimately denied the claim, explaining that one assault (by the women on the streets) did not constitute persecution, that the claimant could not verify her attackers' motivations, and that there was not evidence that El Salvador was unable or unwilling to secure her safety. The Board of Immigration Appeals affirmed this ruling, explaining that her record neither showed past persecution nor supported the belief that she would be persecuted as a lesbian in El Salvador. Toward the former point, the BIA "characterized her assault in March 2011 as 'minor' and said that her 'arranged' marriage to Pineda was not persecution because it lasted 'for about 13 years, until his death in 2009'";[36] they also refused to acknowledge the rape as rape. Arguing that the immigration judge and BIA missed the clear intersections between gender-based violence (forced marriage and sexual assault) and sexual orientation violence (harassment and physical assault by strangers for being a lesbian), the Ninth Circuit Court agreed that her case should be re-opened and re-evaluated.[37]

Maldonado Lopez was identified as having a "masculine mannerism" from an early age that prompted her parents' abuse and community's castigation, yet the adjudicators failed to consider whether this "style" as a lesbian heightened her fear of persecution, as they had often considered in male assigned sexuality cases.[38] To the contrary, the early courts decided that Maldonado Lopez did not have an adequate fear of future persecution. Similarly, Belinda Burog-Perez told the judge that she faced economic discrimination in the Philippines because of her "appearance as a lesbian," which meant that clients avoided coming to her for their dental-work needs.[39] It is left to the reader to surmise what it means to "look like a lesbian" in this instance. The judge never took the question up as a process of applying the genre conventions to read her style. In similar fashion, Roxanne Angela Isaacs of Guyana was denied immigration relief despite testifying that "people would assume she was a lesbian because of her appearance," likely leading to arrest, detainment, and physical abuse by Guyanese authorities.[40] In affirming the previous two negative rulings in Isaacs's bid, in their final appeal the Second Circuit justices admonished Isaacs, explaining that she may not gain relief "merely by stringing together a series of suppositions to show that it is more likely than not that torture will result where the evidence does not establish that each step in the hypothetical chain of events is more likely than not to happen."[41] Burog-Perez and Isaacs tried to use style to demonstrate their need for immigration relief. Immigration judges refused to apply the rhetoric to read lesbian asylum seekers in the courtroom. Rather, the women's "appearance as lesbian[s]" was a moot point in the judges' rulings.

This silence could signal the irrelevance of lesbians' styling in the courtroom. I argue, as a counterpoint, that the inverted convention of reading style in sexual orientation is immaterial when applied to female-assigned bodies and subjects. Style is already associated in the popular U.S. imagination with femininity, such that when the female-assigned subjects appear before the courts, the judges see first, and foremost, a woman enacting femininity. Additionally, there is arguably a wider range of gendered performances that are permissible as heterosexual femininity for cisgender female-assigned subjects than are available for male-assigned subjects enacting masculinity. This means that visible, audible, and affective differences that appear so stark in the cases of gender nonconforming subjects are negligible when lesbians "appear" as lesbians in their asylum cases. Based on the invisible intersections of gendered norms and the way gender becomes a privileged sign over sexuality in the court's reading practice of cisgender women, those "appearances" as lesbians may still be readable as a form of femininity. Lesbian, in other words, disappears under the sign of woman. And, as we will see in the next section, any potential to be legible as a lesbian is cast in further doubt when the content of gay women's claims is interpreted against the genre conventions that frame what immigration judges expect to hear as the details of one's life as a sexuality-related asylum seeker. These genre conventions, when read in relation, re-fashion gay women as both not gay enough and "too woman," or too similar to cisgender (presumed heterosexual) women's gendered claims to be intelligible as sexuality-related asylum claims.

SEXUAL AWARENESS

In the same way that male-assigned sexuality claimants must navigate expectations about awareness of sexuality, lesbian asylum seekers are also expected to have a history, a story that neatly fits Western biological constructs of sexual awareness. It is important to note that gay women's narratives of awareness often differ dramatically from the genre conventions present in cisgender and trans male sexuality persecution narratives. This difference in awareness instigates the doubt that immigration officials express regarding whether lesbian asylum seekers are actually gay and also whether their gayness is so fundamental that it cannot be changeable or hidden. The immigration judge evaluating her case told Zeng Qing Chang of China that "she had not 'established to the satisfaction of the Court that she is, in reality, a lesbian.'"[42] Toward this point he said that he "found it 'extremely important' that Zheng did not provide a letter from her ex-husband in China corroborating her claim that she is a lesbian."[43] Chang's former union with a man cast doubt in the judge's mind, and he went a step further to insist on evidence from that man about her sexual orientation. While in a post–REAL ID Act era the judge has the right to ask for such forms of evidence, the notion that the ex-husband, whom she feared, would somehow produce evidence of her lesbianism on behalf of her asylum claim seems to be a rather rigorous burden of proof to expect from the claimant.[44]

There were so many complex twists and turns in the case of Ingrida Mockeviciene from Lithuania that the judge went so far as to question whether she was, in fact, a lesbian.[45] In reviewing her case the immigration judge noted that he doubted her lesbian identity. First, he cited her heterosexual marriage and children in Lithuania as evidence to support his assertion. He also created the following list of reasons supporting his doubt:

> (1) Mockeviciene "defined" being a lesbian as "a woman who wants to be around other women and . . . it does not necessarily involve sexual relationships"; (2) although she had been in the United States for four years, she had not had a lesbian partner, so that she was "[a]t best . . . a non-practicing lesbian"; (3) she had "no documents to establish that she is a lesbian," and the letters or notes she did submit were not originals and did not "mention with any degree of specificity the lesbian relationships of [Mockeviciene], only addressing the conclusion that [Mockeviciene] is indeed a lesbian"; (4) she had "not joined any groups while being here in the United States for four years that involve[d] lesbian activities"; (5) she did not produce any witnesses to "attest to the fact that she is indeed a lesbian."[46]

Similarly, Olha Lyashchynska's narrative of awareness was complicated by the fact of her sexual and relational history. Lyashchynska claimed that she was persecuted because of her sexual orientation but had, while living in Ukraine, dated a man who, along with his friends, raped her to reportedly teach her "'how to be a real woman.'"[47] Also, after arriving in the United States, Lyashchynska "married a man, despite her sexual orientation, because the guy 'was like really nice' to her."[48] The judge denied her asylum claim, deciding that her credibility as a lesbian was no longer intact after the two marriages. Similarly, Latvian Margarita Michulena came to the United States as a student with her Latvian girlfriend after they both experienced physical assault, harassment, and vandalism of their personal property in Latvia. Michulena explained to the court "she was bi-sexual" but that she thought of herself "more as a lesbian."[49] This explanation confused the court because Michulena had not only been married to a man in Latvia (who raped her), but shortly after she broke up with her girl-friend, she married a man who was a U.S. citizen, a marriage that immigration authorities found to be fraudulent. When asked why she "as a lesbian decided to be married" in the United States, Michulena responded that she wanted to "live a normal life" and to have children.[50] The immigration judge and BIA took both heterosexual unions as the basis for finding her claim to be a lesbian not cred-ible. Indeed, the immigration judge believed that her two heterosexual unions "were so fundamentally inconsistent with her claimed social group that it shat-ters her credibility before the court."[51] In each of these cases the courts ignored the possibility that heterosexual relationality might be a question of force or convenience rather than desire. The courts also refused to consider that sexual desire may be oriented in multiple directions or may change over the course of one's life. When read through non-intersectional, heterosexual logics, it is hard to dispute that these women's relationships with men cast doubt on their sexual-orientation claims. Yet, when read against the scholarly record docu-menting lesbian sexuality, these claimant's experiences strongly resonate as *gay women's* experiences of *sexuality*. Not only does this scholarship demonstrate that gay women often come to an awareness of their homosexual desire much later in life than gay men, but they often do so after being in relationships with men or having children.[52] The courts' reading practices also gender the claim-ants as "too woman" by reading the claimants into discourses about rape cul-ture that frame women's claims of sexual assault in the context of heterosexual unions or relationships as impossible, false, or fake.[53] Instead of understanding the complexity of gay women's awareness and experience of sexuality and the complexities of the cultures of violence that play out in women's lives, judges are doubtful of the immutability of their claims. Gender and sexuality intersect invisibly in the reading practices of the judges who evaluate gay women's rela-tional and sexual histories. Read against the genre conventions that establish immutability as awareness early in one's life that does not change in orientation, these claimants are legible as, at most, "fake" or "non-practicing" lesbians.

Racializing discourses of suspicion also creep into the evaluations of Bal-tic, Central, and Eastern European gay women in these cases. One need not look too hard to find U.S. representations of Baltic, Central, and Eastern Eu-ropean women as subjects who use their femininity and sexuality for material exchanges. Popular U.S. media is rife with what Elza Ibroscheva calls "porno-chic" representations of these women with beautiful, eroticized, sexualized, and commodified bodies in the current post-Socialist moment—a sharp contrast to the Socialist representations of these same women.[54] Indeed, Baltic, Central, and Eastern European women have taken center stage in U.S. media as "fashion models, flooding the Western catwalks, and [as] top athletes, gracing the covers of magazines,"[55] and as prostitutes and "femme fatales" in television and film. These representations pair in the U.S. imagination with messages about Central and Eastern European women's use of sexuality and beauty (willingly or not) as a means to immigration through methods such as "mail-order brides," "prostitution rings," and "sex trafficking."[56] The pairing implies that Baltic, Central European, and Eastern European women might do anything—including the exchange of their bodies and sex—to accumulate material resources such as money, immigration status, and goods that might improve their social standing. These racialized gendered discourses linger in the background of the performative scene of the courtroom when Baltic, Central European, and Eastern European women make claims to asylum on the basis of their sexuality, casting doubt and suspicion on the veracity of their accounts about sexuality that already stray from the narrative convention of a sexuality-related persecution narrative.

One interpretation of this failure to conform to the convention is that gay women, when read against this convention, are gendered as "too woman" to be recognized as gay. Indeed, evidence of heterosexual unions, boyfriends, and children potentially position these claimants back into narratives of heterosexual femininity, making it hard for immigration judges to recognize the *gayness* in their experiences. This, I believe, partially explains the failure. Against this intersectional axis of gender and sexuality, though, lesbian asylum seekers are also read as not gay enough to meet the standard of immutability assumed by the court. Here, a male model is presumed for homosexuality and gay women necessarily fall short. As Adrienne Rich articulated, this exclusion happens because lesbians are often offered "'inclusion'" in political life "as female versions of male homosexuality." She writes: "To equate lesbian existence with male homosexuality because each is stigmatized is to erase female reality once again."[57] Here it is not that gay women are completely unimaginable but that the rhetoric of gayness used by the courts does not provide ample discursive maneuverability for a range of experiences of sexual desire and practice. What this creates is an intersectional invisibility for lesbian asylum seekers whereby lesbians can't be intelligible in the language of the law as both gay and women but are rather always audienced invisibly through the essentializing discourses about gender and sexuality that circulate in the judges' reading practices of gay women.[58] In this instance, gay women fail to meet the standard of the model of gayness and, at the same time, are read as "too woman" to be seen as persecuted because of their sexuality. As we see in the next section, the genre conventions for sexuality-based persecution position gay women as "too woman" yet again, rendering the complexities of their experiences as gay women triply invisible.

PERSECUTION

Unlike the previous genre conventions wherein there were also examples of gender-conforming gay men who experienced difficulties of fitting the convention, all male-assigned sexuality claimants I found in my archive described past physical or sexual violence as the basis for their claims. Read against the severity of violence that these claimants discuss, gay women's experiences are often interpreted as not severe enough to meet the standard of persecution necessary for winning asylum. For example, Zeng Qing Chang "testified that she and her girlfriend were once picked up by local village officials and dragged by their hair to a 'local office,' detained for the night" because they were lesbians.[59] The courts evaluating this case agreed that an "isolated incident of harassment does not rise to the level of persecution, which is defined as including 'threats to life, confinement, torture, [or] economic restrictions so severe that they constitute a real threat to life or freedom.'"[60] Burog-Perez, introduced earlier, did not experience threats to her life, but she did argue that her experiences in the Philippines were enough to warrant asylum on the basis of economic persecution. Not only did her patients leave her dentistry practice because she was a lesbian, but "she would not be able to find a job given her appearance as a lesbian" were she to return to the Philippines.[61] As the court explained in denying her case, "When persecution based on purely economic harm is alleged, we have required a showing of 'a probability of *deliberate* imposition of *substantial* economic disadvantage'" (emphases in original).[62] The evidence in Burog-Perez's case, the court continued, demonstrated that "some private individuals chose to bring their business to another dentist," but did not showcase deliberate and widespread harm.[63] They denied her claim. Unclear in the record is what exactly "private individuals" means in the court's logic as one might think of all patients of a dentist as "private individuals." Regardless of this, Burog-Perez's experience of economic disenfranchisement seems small or inconsequential when read against the record of sexual orientation persecution articulated in gay men's cases. Against this genre convention, Burog-Perez's experiences most logically read as "discrimination," not persecution.

Doris de la Inmaculad Tavera Lara also claimed to experience economic persecution in Colombia when she was fired after coming out as a lesbian to her co-workers. Tavera Lara had children earlier in her life and first started seeing a woman romantically when she was an adult working at the university.

One evening at a holiday party, her supervisor asked why she was never seen with men. He insinuated that she might be gay, and Tavera Lara responded affirmatively that she was a lesbian. After that night Tavera Lara reported that her co-workers were no longer friendly to her at work, and after a few months her supervisor let her know that her contract would not be renewed. When she asked why, he explained that "she was being fired because of her sexual preferences."[64] Not only was she fired from her job, but in looking for a new job she went around to the different architectural firms and no one would hire her (despite previous job offers at these firms). One potential employer explained to her over the phone that she "would not find a job in her specialization because she was a lesbian."[65] The judge ruled negatively against these points regarding persecution, citing that there was insufficient evidence to verify that she was fired because she was gay.[66]

Tavera Lara's reasons for leaving Colombia, though, did not only concern economic persecution. Not long after being fired, she began to receive threatening phone calls at home, and when she changed her phone number, she began to receive threatening notes at her home: "The notes included newspaper clippings about social cleansing and homosexuals along with handwritten 'vulgarities and threats.' She testified that the notes said '[she] was a dirty lesbian,' 'was expendable,' 'had no right to have children,' that it was shameful to be a lesbian with children, and that they 'could talk to the welfare institute' and have her children taken away, especially her daughter."[67] She went to the police with the notes but the officers laughed at her and ridiculed her. Then, in 2001 "she was attacked on the street by two men as she was returning home . . . one of them took her arms and the other started touching her 'privates' . . . they called her by name and said, in a vulgar manner, that a woman did not exist in order to be with another woman."[68] She reported the incident to the police, but again they refused to do anything because the assailants did not physically harm her or steal anything. Shortly after this Tavera Lara heard that one of her lesbian friends was found murdered. Having had enough, she left Colombia because she, too, feared for her life. In evaluating these elements of persecution, the judge also ruled negatively, explaining that Tavera Lara's experiences neither rose to the level of persecution nor proved that she had a reasonable fear of future persecution.

The BIA and federal court agreed with the immigration judge, explaining that "harassing or threatening calls and notes 'do not rise to the level of past persecution that would compel reversal of the IJ's decision.'"[69] Male-assigned cis and trans gay cases illustrate that sexual violence is the primary mode of violence imagined as sexual-orientation persecution, for sexual assault and torture are used as admonishments, repudiations against a person's nonheterosexual desires. Interpreted against the prevalence of sexual assault in male-assigned

gay cases, lesbians' experiences of harassment and economic disenfranchisement seem hardly capable of rising to the level of persecution expected in sexual
orientation cases. Instead, lesbians' experiences are seen as harassing or discriminatory, but not persecution.

Even when lesbians include experiences of sexual assault in evidencing their
need for asylum, they still struggle to be received in U.S. courts as eligible. Tsog-
zolmaa Densmaa fled Mongolia because "she and her partner, Chimgee, were
arrested and imprisoned because they are lesbians." As explained, "the police
falsely charged them with prostitution as a pretense for the arrest. During their
detention, the women were raped and beaten. Chimgee died as a result of the
beatings."[70] Furthermore, "during her interrogation, the inspector accused her of
being a 'lesbian pervert,' and told her that she would be released to a psychiatric
hospital if she admitted it."[71] The judge in Densmaa's case did not believe the
story because prostitution was legal in Mongolia and her arrest papers indicated that she was arrested for "risk of recidivism and fugitive evasion."[72] The
judge denied her claim. Notably, the police assault in Chimgee's case was not
mentioned in the judge's decision, but the fact of the denial demonstrates that
the assault was either not political or violent enough to warrant considering an
asylum grant.

Mockeviciene, discussed earlier, also reported being physically assaulted
by police officers who broke into her home after they learned that she was gay.
Later, her then-husband raped her with the help of his friends. As the court
record notes, she told her husband and children she was gay, and her husband
"beat and raped her while his friends held her down." In evaluating these experiences, the judge ruled that "the incidents that Mockeviciene testified about
did not constitute a threat to her life or freedom, and the incidents perpetrated
by one police officer were insufficient to establish that, even if she suffered
persecution, that the persecution was caused by the government."[73] The judge's
decision completely ignored Mockeviciene's report of being gang raped by her
husband and his friends; it centered instead on the police harassment as her
primary evidence.[74] Though the judge never explicitly stated it, the omission
demonstrates, perhaps, that the judge didn't see the rape *as* rape, allowing the
marital contract to exclude the possibility that sexual assault happened, and
that the violation was politically motivated.[75] When marital rape is excluded
from the record, Mockeviciene's experiences with the police assaulting her and
breaking in to her mother's house to look for "homosexual literature" may be
harassing, yet they do not seem to rise to the severity of persecution evidenced
in male-assigned gay cases that constitute what judges expect to hear and read
in a sexuality-related asylum claim.

Similarly, the sexual assault that Olivia Nabulwala of Uganda experienced was evaluated as personal in nature by the judge hearing her claim. Nabulwala came to consciousness of her lesbian identity when she was in high school. She told her family, and they decided to send her to a co-ed school, "hoping she would stop being a lesbian."[76] Instead of turning straight, she joined a lesbian-rights activist group and protested for the rights of sexual minorities in her country. Homophobic protesters besieged one of the group's meetings, and Nabulwala was physically assaulted and hospitalized. After this incident, Nabulwala returned to her family, and they consequently realized that she was still a lesbian. Her father then proceeded to assault her and "two relatives forced her to have sex with a stranger. She was then expelled from her clan. Disowned by her family, she moved into the YMCA."[77]

In reviewing the case the judge noted that it was a difficult case to decide but ultimately gave the case a negative ruling. Regarding the incident with the lesbian organization, he cited that the event was "isolated and did not arise to that level of persecution." And of the physical and sexual assault: it was "private family mistreatment," he said, asserting that the Ugandan government was in no way involved.[78] The BIA affirmed this decision, but the Eighth Circuit judges took issue with the prior ruling concerning the Ugandan government's involvement and remanded the case to the BIA in 2007.

Proving persecution in the lesbian cases is so challenging because these cases are read against the precedent set through male-assigned sexuality cases, where sexual assault is not only prevalent but is often perpetrated by state officials such as the police and military who fit easily into the frame of political persecution that is necessary in winning asylum claims. Against this genre convention, gay women are "too woman," such that their experiences of violence are reordered into heterosexual scripts that frame the violence as personal in nature because it involves either male desire for a woman or male power over a woman. The assault positions the claimants back into heterosexuality and therefore along the intersectional axis as "too woman" to be persecuted on account of their sexuality. Indeed, gay women's experiences of violence sound too similar to those of their heterosexual counterparts who more frequently cite sexual assault by family members and intimate partners in evidencing their cases.[79] Such discursive alignments position gay women's experiences of violence as more personally motivated (for example, individual heterosexual sexual desire, or family members' punishment for breaking familial/social mores) than politically instigated (to dominate or overpower, or because of a hatred of gay people). Thus, while the claimants may experience violence because of their gendered identities, the courts struggle to recognize how their fears emanate from their sexuality. Gender erases the difference that sexuality makes, thus making gay women's intersectional experiences invisible once again; specifically, sexuality ceases to be legible as a primary modality of identity for gay women. Instead, against the genre conventions of sexuality-based persecution, these claimants are seen first and foremost as women.

CONTEXT

A final constraining factor for lesbian asylum seekers is a lack of information about geographical and cultural contexts to serve as supporting evidence in warranting gay women's claims. Quite simply, lesbian applicants are often denied asylum because there is not enough contextual evidence to affirm the veracity of their bids, and immigration judges frequently mandate such proof for gay women. Producing evidence of a context of persecution to fit the genre conventions for the situation is often nearly impossible for lesbian asylum seekers due to the almost complete radio silence about lesbian-targeted laws, abuse, and violence.

A number of LGBT-specific human rights groups have emerged in the last few decades. These organizations investigate and document the experiences of LGBT persons around the world, creating reports and archives of homophobic and transphobic peril, what I talk about in chapter 1 as transnational publicity, that serve as vital sources of evidence for asylum claimants in demonstrating a credible and justified need for refuge. Most of this work continues to focus on the experiences of male-assigned gay men and to some extent trans experiences, leaving lesbian and bisexual claimants largely in the lurch without documented evidence of abuse when they go to make their claims.[80] A search for the words "lesbian and gay" on Refworld, the leading database for information relating to refugees, pulled almost six thousand documents; doing the same search while excluding the word "gay" extracted fewer than three hundred sources. While this search's methods were by no means systematic or complete, it gives a rough sense of how infrequently lesbians are the sole focus of news media and investigative human rights reports.

Even when this contextual information is available, it is often interpreted as irrelevant to women's sexuality-related claims. As we saw in chapter 4, the universal recognition of male-male rape as a violation of one's self and as political renders need for corporeal or geographical specificity about persecution largely irrelevant in making a sexuality-related asylum case. No matter the continent, country, region, or political theater, male-male rape is imagined as a heinous act of power and control. For gay women, gender invisibly intercedes again to make the specificities of places and types of persecution they flee relevant. Burog-Perez, introduced earlier, included news reports about the persecution of gays throughout regions of the Philippines. The court evaluating her claim saw this evidence as pertaining mostly to men and consequently not persuasive in demonstrating her credible fear. Though Burog-Perez filed a sexuality-related claim, her gender invisibly intersected in the evaluation of her claim, making available contextual information unusable to her as evidence. Densmaa, also introduced above, struggled in proving a context of persecution in Mongolia. As the court wrote, "Densmaa failed to provide any evidence of a pattern or practice of persecution against homosexuals in Mongolia. Although, as noted above, she did submit a newspaper article that reflects some amount of societal discrimination against lesbians, this article does not establish a pattern or practice of persecution."[81] The judge evaluating the case of Egyptian national Salama Rababa Badawy told Badawy that she may experience discrimination, but evidence in the country reports did not indicate that she would be persecuted. The court explained,

> The State Department Country Reports indicate that there is discrimination and violence against women in Egypt, and that in the past the police have targeted homosexuals using "Internet-based 'sting' operations." The record also contains documents indicating that tattooing is prohibited by Islam, an article about the dangers faced by a homosexual man in an Egyptian prison, and a report describing increased punishments for drug violations. While this evidence suggests that an individual with Badawy's characteristics may face discrimination or harassment, it does not compel the conclusion that it is likely that she will be tortured if removed to Egypt.[82]

In each of these instances, the judges rely on the genre conventions as their primary method of reading, which functions to render the lesbian claimants as too-woman or not-gay-enough to be making eligible sexuality-related asylum claims. This means that when women do make sexuality-related claims, their narratives of fear are often diminished in importance. With their experiences of persecution relegated to discrimination and harassment, gay women are legible through gendered narratives that infantilize them or render them as hysterical and over-reactive in their fears.

Even the presence of homophobic laws in a gay woman's country of citizenship, such as anti-sodomy laws and buggery laws, do not guarantee that these claimants will be seriously received. Ellen Andreasian of Armenia was denied asylum relief because she could not provide evidence that the Armenian state supported or condoned the persecution of lesbians: "Although she presents evidence of the lack of acceptance of lesbians and enforcement of anti-sodomy laws in Armenia, she offers no evidence that lesbians are being persecuted, or that the situation is worse now than it was several years ago."[83] Here the court interpreted the anti-sodomy laws in Armenia as pertaining only to sex between men, discounting without justification how the presence of these laws within a country might also influence how gay women express their sexual desire and identity. While there certainly are state laws that affect women, such as wide-reaching anti-homosexuality laws, the buggery and sodomy laws that are frequently discussed are colonial-state architectures that figure male (read: public) subjects as those intended for surveillance and exclusion.

Together these cases demonstrate the difficulty of proving the context of persecution in asylum cases. Quite simply, there are no journalistic or human rights accounts to draw on in building cases about the persecution of gay women in these countries. Even when there is evidence of homophobic laws or social mores, the laws and practices are recognized as targeting men, thus excluding women from using such country-specific evidence to their advantage. In these instances, it is not so much that lesbians are not gay enough or "too woman" to be credibly received as lesbian asylum seekers, but it is the context that is gendered to reflect and privilege gay male experiences. What we know about context is always, already gendered to reflect a male model of sexuality. This male model for context is then assumed to reflect the experiences of women who may also experience persecution in that context. Here, gay women are both not gay enough and "too woman" to find representation in the record that articulates the context of persecution, thus rendering their experiences *as gay women* invisible. In this instance, there is an intersection, but the intersection leaves gay women frightfully without representation on the international stage of human rights advocacy for gays and lesbians.

Conclusion

This chapter illuminated the ways gender and sexuality invisibly interact for lesbian and gender-conforming gay male asylum seekers, shaping the possibilities for refuge that these claimants have in accordance with what I theorized in chapter 4 as the one-sex, one-gender system. While gender-conforming gay men experience challenges to their claims through this rhetoric and logic, gay women often fail at being legible through all three narrative conventions; their cases fall into the divide between gender and sexuality. Here, too frequently, gay women are either figured as not gay enough or as "too woman," against the genre conventions of sexual orientation persecution claims, to be recognized as worthy of asylum relief because of their sexuality.

Conclusion

The development of a gender discourse in U.S. asylum law since the 1980 Refugee Act has meant some exceptional "wins" for asylum applicants who experience or fear persecution relating to their gender. Yet, for most gender-related asylum applicants, gaining access to refugee reliefs has been an uphill battle. This book has tracked the emergence and development of gender as a political concept in U.S. law and politics, questioning what asylum acceptances and denials in the name of gender violence reveal about the institutional life of the term. I have shown gender to be a contingent and segregated category in refugee and asylum law that responds to cultural or relational violence against cisgender women. This is a legal category that racializes the forms of gender violence discussed in these cases and in public discourse, essentializing violence as a natural fact experienced by particular bodies in particular places of the world. While intending to open up asylum reliefs to a broader range of applicants, the development of the gendered reliefs in this institution further sediments the universality of the male-assigned subject as the neutral-sexed subject for which asylum reliefs are intended.

One challenge in analyzing the conceptual development of a term like *gender* in an institution like U.S. asylum is the perpetuity of the concept's life in jurisprudential citation; individuals will continue to arrive in the United States and claim that they have fears of returning to their home countries because of possible persecution relating to their gender. People will also continue to stand in immigration courts and call on U.S. officials to recognize that their experiences and fears make them eligible for refuge. A related challenge in tracking the development of this discourse is that this modality of law (as with all legal areas) is continuously developing and shifting. Just as there is no end in sight to peoples' need for asylum, there is no final word about who will be protected through these processes. As many of the chapters in this book reveal, asylum seekers who were at one point denied asylum may have had winning cases if their claims had been heard years or decades later. Changing reception demonstrates an evolving understanding of gender as a legal concept, but it also illustrates the state's shifting relationship to, use of, and involvement in the production of gendered concepts and subjects.

It is quite possible that new openings will emerge for asylum seekers to make winning gender-related arguments in the coming years, yet if the institutional life of gender in U.S. asylum should teach us anything, it is that gendered subjects and experiences are received problematically within the walls of U.S. law and politics. We must view liberal openings for wider inclusion of gender-related arguments not automatically as "wins." Instead, we must continue to question what the shifts in gender's intelligibility and applicability say about the legal and political context of that time. This means reflecting on the concept's rhetorical contours and hidden logic while also asking what the instantiation of the concept does as a revealing and concealing force.

A primary argument of this book has been that liberal openings for gender-related reliefs naturalize a one-sex and one-gender logic in U.S. asylum. Greater access to cisgender women, gays and lesbians, and transgender or gender nonconforming asylum seekers seems, on the surface, to open the system, challenging institutional norms so that greater ranges of persons who invoke their human rights to claim asylum may be welcomed. The actual development of the concept segregates gender into a category all its own and relegates it to cisgender, presumably heterosexual women who fear relational and cultural persecution, often in the form of sexual violence. As a consequence of this segregation, male-assigned subjects are naturalized as the sexed subjects for whom all of the other categories of refugee relief—race, religion, nationality, political opinion, and membership in a social group—are available. Asylum seekers must choose one of these categories to ground their claim of persecution in constructing their requests for refuge. It is often not simple to choose one category in which to base a claim—even for male-assigned asylum seekers. Yet because of the universality of male sex, male-assigned subjects are given wider rhetorical license in being recognizable as fleeing experiences of persecution that are both political and related to the category in which they ground their claim. Namely, the experiences and identities associated with male-assigned persons are in advance more legible in the one-sex, one-gender logic as valid, true, and political. Because of male-sex universality, male-assigned subjects are endowed with greater latitude to speak as credible subjects with political claims and to be received as persons who may be persecuted for their identities and opinions. As such, male-assigned subjects often need not articulate in elaborated fashion how their experiences and identities are political or how they fit these categories. As an enthymeme, the universality of male-sex is already legible in the rhetorical encounter. Indeed, as the claims of Chinese married men in chapter 3 illustrated, even a claim as gendered as fearing forced sterilization or abortion could be naturalized as rhetorical means for male-assigned subjects to gain access; the universality of their sex, along with the naturalization of heteropatriarchal notions of kin structures covered them, allowing male assigned husbands to "stand in the shoes" of their female spouses in making intimately gender-related claims.

For claimants who cannot be recognized in the realm of male-sex universality, the institution has added special means for incorporation. Through precedent, executive orders, and legislation, the experiences of subjects fleeing gender violence have been included as conditional addendums to the refugee definition. These exceptions enable particular persons entrance, but in solidifying and segregating legal categories they foreclose as much as they produce. In this, a paradox is created. Unlike claimants whose male-assigned sex acts silently as an enthymeme that buttresses the persuasiveness, political nature, and ethos of the claim, women making gender-related claims often only have gender in which to ground their claim. And they often have no enthymemes to rely on as supplemental arguments to persuade judges that their claims are political, that they themselves are credible, or that their experiences and fears warrant their incorporation. Women with gender-related claims have the double duty of negotiating the invisible intersecting experiences and identities that cannot be named in the argument construction (for example, race, class, sexuality, age) but that necessarily intervene in the audiencing of their cases, such that their claims are often evaluated in excess of the categories to which they have requested relief. Their experiences exceed the named category, they don't go far enough in fitting the category, or they fit cumbersomely. As revealed in chapter 2, Parastoo Fatin was received in excess of her gendered claim through the classed, religious, and national intersections of her identity and experience that shaped her fear of persecution. The judges agreed, deciding that she did not reasonably show that it was her gender alone that prompted her fear. Belinda Burog-Perez sought relief on the basis of her sexuality as a lesbian from the Philippines (chapter 5). The intersections of class, sexuality, and gender muddled her ability to be seen as legitimately fearing persecution on the basis of her sexuality alone. Unlike male-assigned claimants who rely on the universal recognition of their sex in the institution, Fatin and Burog-Perez did not have argumentative enthymemes to rely on as supplemental silent arguments in making their case for immigration relief as refugees. Where intersectionality does surface in asylum law, as chapter 4 and 5 illustrated is in the essentializing reading and audiencing practices of adjudicators.

One of the key ways essentializing happens in the reception of gender-related claimants is in the racialized association of certain forms of gender violence with particular bodies and geographies. Militarized sexual violence and femicide link to Central America (chapter 1), genital surgeries with Africa (chapter 2), social castigation for nonconformity to gendered norms with the Middle East (chapter 2), and invasive population control practices to China (chapter 3). While sexuality-based persecution seems to flatten in the U.S. imaginary onto the world as the geographical landscape (chapter 4), when female-assigned women make sexuality-related claims, the racialization of gender and gender violence returns again as a specter (Eastern European women in chapter 5). The claimants fleeing these forms of gender violence are fixed in the U.S. political imaginary through the racialization of the violence as essential to entire populations and geographies. Sometimes the racialized fixing enables asylum seekers' inclusion, as I showed for women from various African countries fleeing genital surgeries, Central American women fleeing fears of sexual assault and femicide, and married Chinese men who oppose state family-planning programs. In other instances, the racialization of gender violence fixed the subjectivities as either too threatening to be incorporated (Iranian women in chapter 2 and Chinese women in chapter 3) or not politically important enough to warrant concern or incorporation (lesbian asylum seekers in chapter 5). In addition to the discursive fixing of claimants who speak about gender violence, the locales the claimants flee are also racialized as volatile to women. Mapped in the U.S. imaginary, particular forms of gender violence are localized as essential to particular places. As I indicated in chapter 3, these aspects of racializing gender violence become important to pay attention to as the United States' geopolitical strategies shift from economic and political hegemony to consolidate around maintaining global moral authority through pastoral power in matters of human rights. If this book forecasts one thing, it is that there is mounting U.S. state interest in gender violence. Looking to the future, we must keep an eye on how the United States uses rhetoric around global instantiations of gender violence in order to maintain what it figures as its pastoral position at the helm of the world's global moral authority over women's rights.

Signed as an executive order on August 10, 2012, President Barack Obama charged numerous offices to act on a strategy titled "Preventing and Responding to Violence against Women and Girls Globally."[1] These offices focus their energies on implementing programs and metrics for putting "gender equality and the advancement of women and girls at the forefront of the three pillars of U.S. foreign policy—diplomacy, development, and defense."[2] Vice President Joe Biden outlined what the state envisions as the stakes of gender-based violence:

> Around the globe, violence against women is an epidemic. Violence robs women and girls of their full potential and causes untold human suffering. Violence against women impedes economic development, threatens peace and prosperity, and inhibits full participation in civic life. For every woman who has been beaten in her own home, for the millions of women who have been raped as a weapon of war, for every girl who has been attacked on her way to school, for all of the children—girls and boys—who have witnessed this brutality, we must do better.[3]

Metaphoric language of disease and war combine in this statement to illustrate a breathtakingly broad picture of the problem. Violence against women is the aggressor: "the globe" is under attack, and the threat is reaching "epidemic" proportions. Biden's statement is followed directly by Secretary of State Hillary Clinton giving the reader a sense of action: "It is time for all of us to assume our responsibility to go beyond condemning this behavior, to taking concrete steps to end it, to make it sociably unacceptable, to recognize it is not cultural; it is criminal."[4]

The implementation of this new strategy also has surprising breadth and reach, though the actual material support is arguably more performative than substantive.[5] The United States began by appointing the first Ambassador-at-Large for Global Women's Issues as a permanent position. Other steps involve partnering with NGO and supranational organizations like the UNHCR through programs such as *Call to Action on Protecting Women and Girls in Emergencies* and *Safe from the Start* to "prevent and respond to gender-based violence in the context of conflicts and natural disasters and to ensure such efforts are routinely prioritized as a life-saving intervention along with other vital humanitarian assistance."[6] Moreover, there are efforts to put gender-based violence in dialogue with rising concerns about the precariousness of life for LGBT people around the world.[7]

We may read these new programs as attempts to make the world more livable for girls, women, and LGBT persons, yet UN Ambassador Susan Rice explicitly figures these efforts as contributing to the U.S. goal of "Advancing American Interests and Values" around the world. Rice's comments are instructive. "We stand proudly for the rights of women, the LGBT community and minorities," she asserts. It is not we "strive to stand" or "will stand," but that we *do* stand. The use of present tense makes the defense of women, the LGBT community, and minorities a fact. It is happening in the United States and will continue to happen. That U.S. asylum cases and human rights discourse localize gender violence as happening elsewhere only solidifies the idea that the work to be done in addressing gender violence is beyond the borders of the United States. "Make no mistake, advancing democracy and respect for human rights is central to our foreign policy. It's what our history and our values demand, but it's also profoundly in our interests," Rice continues, which further orients the reader to the necessity of work and to the specifics of where the work still needs to be done.[8]

Frightfully missing in this global strategy for addressing gender violence is an analysis of the prevalence of gender-based violence within the United States (or of racist, homophobic, or transphobic violence, for that matter). Instead, readers are led to believe that the end of gender violence in the United States is *fait accompli*. Also strangely absent is a plan for admitting those fleeing gender-based persecution as refugees in the United States, or even mention of how immigration and refugee reliefs may figure in the implementation of this plan. The implication is that there is no interaction between national programs, such as immigration and naturalization law, and the more internationalist programs of the departments of defense, development, and diplomacy. While this absence might be read as mere oversight, my broader project demonstrates that national rhetoric concerning gender and gender-based violence is rarely innocent, nor is it ever only nationally attuned. International politics, aspirations, and anxieties are on the horizon, or just below the surface, of every national decision about human rights and migration. Just as the limited and conditional openings for gender-based asylum seekers to be granted asylum must be interpreted through the racial and geopolitical, this new initiative organizing around gender violence and human rights concerns must also be read as an effort to manage transnational racial anxieties and to maintain geopolitical moral authority.

First, we must attend to what this strategy does to the United States' need to grant refuge to those fleeing gender-based violence. If we are to take anything from the first three decades of U.S. asylum, it is that gendered subjects are received problematically as political subjects in the country. In the early years, gendered claims were managed by being cordoned off as individual and personal. By the mid-1990s, largely through transnational forms of publicity, the concept had generated enough momentum to receive contingent yet segregated incorporation in the institution. Meanwhile, cisgender, poor, and women of color of reproductive age were consistently racialized as threatening to the U.S. nation and consistently denied incorporation as refugees in the country.

This has happened while women's claims of gender violence have been politically mounted as rhetorical admonishments of other states' political, economic, and human rights practices. These admonishments are only possible through the racialization of gender violence as essential to the experiences of particular people and endemic to particular parts of the world. Femicide, genital surgeries, social repression, and forced sterilization become "knowable" in the U.S. imaginary and asylum law as part and parcel of Central America, Africa, the Middle East, and China. We come to know through these cases and broader mediated and political discourses that gender violence involves physical and sexual assault often in the context of relational or cultural dynamics. We also come to know where it happens. In the context of this record, the United States' global strategy might be read as a new method of managing and ordering gendered subjects by shifting the publicity garnered about their fears of gender violence to the geographies that have been racialized as violent to women. In an era of transnational publicity around women's issues where women's human rights concerns can no longer be relegated to the private, individual sphere, such a move functions to manage the state's anxieties around the incorporation of reproductive women of color to the United States through immigration and refugee processes.

This political move, though, serves a secondary function. Namely, it shifts Western states' responsibility for managing refugees from a national conversation to a global, externally oriented one. There is no clear estimation of just how many displaced, stateless, internally displaced, and refugee and asylum-seeking persons there are in the world, but by all accounts one thing is clear: the numbers are only mounting.[9] This uptick in global displacement attends with a leveling off (and arguable diminishment) in the number of people granted asylum and resettlement in the United States and elsewhere each year.[10] It also attends with amplifications of border militarization and fortressing strategies in Western states (including the use of detention, deportation, and dispossession) in order to detract, dissuade, and prevent those with legitimate refugee claims from making it to states of asylum. This new focus on preventing global gender violence is a further extension of this neoliberal technique of migration control. Now that there is a global strategy to deal with violence against women and girls, and there is certainty about who is most vulnerable and where forms of gender violence are most pervasive, questions about the state's treatment of gendered subjects in processes like national refugee and immigration systems can fall into the background.

Focusing on those places that have been racialized in U.S. discourse as violent to women, the state can enact its pastoral care as global moral authority without the risk of being overwhelmed with migrants. In this move the United States demonstrates that it is doing its due diligence in actively addressing women's issues around the world while continuing to reduce the risk of refugee subjects flooding its borders.

Notes

Introduction

1. The claimant's full name is not used in court proceedings.

2. The asylum system as we know it today was not an available protection prior to 1980, so those in need of political refuge requested withholding of removal. Similar to asylum, withholding of removal is a form of protection that allows noncitizens to stay in the United States if they fear persecution in their respective home countries. Notably, withholding is still a relief available to non-U.S. citizens, along with political asylum, humanitarian asylum, and convention against torture reliefs. Generally speaking, withholding of removal allows noncitizens to remain in the country and work legally, but they cannot apply for permanent residency. Also, those who win withholding cannot travel outside the United States. Interestingly enough, the standards for withholding are higher than they are for asylum cases. To win withholding, applicants must prove that they will "more likely than not" be persecuted if returned to their home country. But applicants do not have to file within one year of entering the country, and if they have been convicted of certain crimes in the United States, they can still qualify for the relief. For a thorough explanation of the difference between withholding and asylum, and of the historical shift from protections granted to individuals through withholding of removal proceedings prior to 1980 to the present-day system of asylum, see Kate Aschenbrenner, "Discretionary (In)Justice: The Exercise of Discretion in Claims for Asylum," *University of Michigan Journal of Law Reform* 45 (2012): 119–20.

3. Board of Immigration Appeals, *Matter of Pierre*, September 16, 1975, 462.

4. BIA, *Matter of Pierre*, 463.

5. I tried to track Pierre in the public and legal archive, but the record of Pierre begins and ends with this 1975 case. It is hard to say whether she remained in the United States or was deported to Haiti after the BIA denied her claim. For the rest of this book, when I have information from the public and legal record to share, I will make mention of what happened to the claimants after their final case decisions in the footnotes of the chapter. For most of the claimants I discuss in this book, there is, as with Pierre, no further record of their presence.

6. *Fatin v. INS*, 12 F.3d 1233, 1237 (3rd cir. 1993).

7. *Fatin v. INS*, 1237.

8. *Fatin v. INS*, 1237.

9. *Fatin v. INS*, 1240.

10. *Fatin v. INS*, 1240.

11. The INS's *Considerations for Asylum Officers Adjudicating Asylum Claims from Women*, which offers suggestions to immigration officials for evaluating the claims of women, differs with *Matter of Acosta* in both form and content. *Matter of Acosta* is the precedent that courts turn to in determining what counts as a social group. In this decision, sex is used as a mere example to demonstrate a broader point about immutability standards. *Considerations*, in contrast, comprises suggestions the INS published to guide asylum officers in evaluating whether women's claims to asylum on the basis of social group membership may fit the refugee standards. *Considerations* has no precedential weight and yet served as a powerful barometer of how gender was first articulated as a legal category for claiming asylum.

12. *Miranda v. INS*, 51 F.3d 767 (8th cir. 1995).

13. *Miranda v. INS*, 767.

14. Karen Musalo, "A Short History of Gender Asylum in the United States: Resistance and Ambivalence May Very Slowly Be Inching toward Recognition of Women's Claims," *Refugee Survey Quarterly* 29 (2010): 46.

15. Erin K. Baines, *Vulnerable Bodies: Gender, the UN and the Global Refugee Crisis* (New York: Ashgate, 2004).

16. Marian Kennady, "Gender-Related Persecution and the Adjudication of Asylum Claims: Is a Sixth Category Needed?" *Florida Journal of International Law* 12 (1998): 317–40; Mattie L. Stevens, "Recognizing Gender-Specific Persecution: A Proposal to Add Gender as a Sixth Refugee Category," *Cornell Journal of Law and Public Policy* 3 (1993): 179–219.

17. Canada was the first of these countries in 1993, offering guidelines to asylum officers for evaluating gender-based asylum cases. The Netherlands, Sweden, and Australia, among other countries, soon followed with their own articulations of gender as a politically protected category. The United States was actually the second country to offer a gender analysis through the 1995 Immigration and Naturalization Services guidelines "Considerations for Asylum Officers Adjudicating Asylum Claims from Women." However, as this document was a mere suggestion for asylum officers and

judges to follow, without any binding power, it was highly ineffectual in changing the conditions through which gender-based claimants could gain protection.

18. I use the term imaginary here and throughout this text to refer to a public's or a nation's shared repository of ideas, values, beliefs, and familiar symbols. This usage is derived from Cornelius Castoriadis, *The Imaginary Institution of Society* (Cambridge, Mass.: MIT Press, 1998).

19. Lewis R. Gordon, "Critical 'Mixed Race'?" *Social Identities* 1 (1995): f2.

20. Katherine M. Donato et al., "A Glass Half Full? Gender in Migration Studies," *International Migration Review* 40 (2006): 3–26; Brad Epps, Keja Valens, and Bill Johnson González, eds., *Passing Lines: Sexuality and Immigration* (Cambridge, Mass.: Harvard University Press, 2005); Pierrette Hondagneu-Sotelo, "Feminism and Migration," *Annals of the American Academy of Political and Social Science* 571 (2000): 107–20; Eithne Luibhéid, *Entry Denied: Controlling Sexuality at the Border* (Minneapolis: University of Minnesota Press, 2002); Eithne Luibhéid and Lionel Cantú, eds., *Queer Migrations: Sexuality, U.S. Citizenship, and Border Crossings* (Minneapolis: University of Minnesota Press, 2005); Sarah J. Mahler and Patricia R. Pessar, "Gender Matters: Ethnographers Bring Gender from the Periphery toward the Core of Migration Studies," *International Migration Review* 40 (2006): 27–63; Martin Manalansan IV, "Queer Intersections: Sexuality and Gender in Migration Studies," *International Migration Review* 40 (2006): 224–49; Denise A. Segura and Patricia Zavella, eds., *Women and Migration: In the U.S.-Mexico Borderlands* (Durham, N.C.: Duke University Press, 2007).

21. Hondagneu-Sotelo, "Feminism and Migration," 117.

22. Luibhéid, *Entry Denied*, xviii–xix.

23. Monisha Das Gupta, *Unruly Immigrants: Rights, Activism, and Transnational South Asian Politics in the United States* (Durham, N.C.: Duke University Press, 2006); Inderpal Grewal and Caren Kaplan, "Warrior Marks: Global Womanism's Neo-Colonial Discourse in a Multicultural Context," *Camera Obscura* 13 (1996): 4–33; Lisa Lowe, *Immigrant Acts: On Asian American Cultural Politics* (Durham, N.C.: Duke University Press, 1996); Aihwa Ong, *Buddha Is Hiding: Refugees, Citizenship, the New America* (Berkeley: University of California Press, 2003).

24. Sonia Akibo-Betts, "The Canada-U.S. Safe Third Country Agreement: Why the U.S. Is Not a Safe Haven for Refugee Women Asserting Gender-Based Asylum Claims," *Windsor Review of Legal and Social Issues* 19 (2005): 105–29; Megan Annitto, "Asylum for Victims of Domestic Violence: Is Protection Possible after in Re R-A-?" *Catholic University Law Review* 49 (2000): 785–823; Susan A. Berger, "Production and Reproduction of Gender and Sexuality in Legal Discourses of Asylum in the United States," *Signs: Journal of Women in Culture and Society* 34 (2009): 659–85; Jacqueline Bhabha, "Embodied Rights: Gender Persecution, State Sovereignty, and Refugees," *Public Culture* 9 (1996): 3–32; Tanya Domenica Bosi, "*Yadegar-Sargis v. INS*: Unveiling the Discriminatory World of U.S. Asylum Laws; The Necessity to Recognize a Gender Category," *New York Law School Law Review* 48 (2003): 778–814; Heaven Crawley, "Engendering the State in Refugee Women's Claims for Asylum," in *States of Conflict: Gender,*

Violence and Resistance, ed. Susie M. Jacobs, Ruth Jacobson, and Jennifer Marchbank (New York: Palgrave Macmillan, 2000), 87–104; Aubra Fletcher, "The Real ID Act: Furthering Gender Bias in U.S. Asylum Law," *Berkeley Journal of Gender, Law and Justice* 21 (2006): 111–32; Danette Gomez, "Last in Line: The United States Trails Behind in Recognizing Gender-Based Asylum Claims," *Whittier Law Review* 25 (2004): 959–88; Michael G. Heyman, "Domestic Violence and Asylum: Toward a Working Model of Affirmative State Obligations," *International Journal of Refugee Law* 17 (2005): 729–48; Katherine E. Melloy, "Telling Truths: How the Real ID Act's Credibility Provisions Affect Women Asylum Seekers," *Iowa Law Review* 92 (2007): 637–76; Musalo, "Short History," 46–63; Jennifer Podkul, "Domestic Violence in the United States and Its Effects on U.S. Asylum Law," *Human Rights Brief* 12 (2005): 16–20.

25. Baines, *Vulnerable Bodies*; Jane Freedman, *Gendering the International Asylum and Refugee Debate* (New York: Palgrave Macmillan, 2007); Jane Freedman, "Mainstreaming Gender in Refugee Protection," *Cambridge Review of International Affairs* 23 (2010): 589–607; Jane Freedman, "Protecting Women Asylum Seekers and Refugees: From International Norms to National Protection?" *International Migration* 48 (2010): 175–98; Wenona Mary Giles and Jennifer Hyndman, eds. *Sites of Violence: Gender and Conflict Zones* (Berkeley: University of California Press, 2004); Jennifer Hyndman, *Managing Displacement: Refugees and the Politics of Humanitarianism* (Minneapolis: University of Minneapolis, 2000); Thomas Spijkerboer, *Gender and Refugee Status* (Burlington, Vt.: Ashgate, 2000).

26. Lila Abu-Lughod, "Do Muslim Women Really Need Saving? Anthropological Reflections on Cultural Relativism and Its Others," *American Anthropologist* 104 (2002): 783–90; Cynthia Enloe, *Maneuvers: The International Politics of Militarizing Women's Lives* (Berkeley: University of California Press, 2000); Margo Okazawa-Rey, "Warring on Women: Understanding Complex Inequalities of Gender, Race, Class, and Nation," *Affilia* 17 (2002): 371–83; Sherene H. Razack, *Casting Out: The Eviction of Muslims from Western Law and Politics* (Toronto: University of Toronto Press, 2008).

27. Inderpal Grewal, *Transnational America: Feminisms, Diasporas, Neoliberalisms* (Durham, N.C.: Duke University Press, 2005); Wendy S. Hesford and Wendy Kozol, eds., *Just Advocacy? Women's Human Rights, Transnational Feminisms, and the Politics of Representation* (New Brunswick, N.J.: Rutgers University Press, 2005).

28. Rebecca Dingo, *Networking Arguments: Rhetoric, Transnational Feminism, and Public Policy Writing* (Pittsburgh, Pa.: University of Pittsburgh Press, 2012); Nicole Nguyen, "Education as Warfare? Mapping Securitised Education Interventions as War on Terror Strategy," *Geopolitics* 19 (2014): 1–31.

29. Elizabeth Bernstein, "Carceral Politics as Gender Justice? The 'Traffic in Women' and Neoliberal Circuits of Crime, Sex, and Rights," *Theory and Society* 41 (2012): 233–59; Kristin Bumiller, *In an Abusive State: How Neoliberalism Appropriated the Feminist Movement against Sexual Violence* (Durham, N.C.: Duke University Press, 2008).

30. Matthew J. Gibney, *The Ethics and Politics of Asylum: Liberal Democracy and the Response to Refugees* (Cambridge: Cambridge University Press, 2004); Emma Haddad, *The Refugee*

in International Society: Between Sovereigns (Cambridge: Cambridge University Press, 2008); David W. Haines, *Safe Haven? A History of Refugees in America* (Sterling, Va.: Kumarian Press, 2010); Philip A. Holman, "Refugee Resettlement in the United States," in *Refugees in America in the 1990s,* edited by David W. Haines (Westport, Conn.: Greenwood, 1996), 3–27; Gil Loescher, *Beyond Charity: International Cooperation and the Global Refugee Crisis* (Oxford: Oxford University Press, 1996); Nevzat Soguk, *States and Strangers: Refugees and Displacements of Statecraft* (Minneapolis: University of Minnesota Press, 1999).

31. Emma Haddad, "The Refugee: The Individual between Sovereigns," *Global Society: Journal of Interdisciplinary International Relations* 17 (2003): 297–323; Soguk, *States and Strangers.*

32. Gibney, *Ethics and Politics.*

33. UN, "The Refugee Convention," (1951), 36.

34. Spijkerboer, *Gender and Refugee Status.*

35. Atle Grahl-Madsen, "Commentary on the Refugee Convention 1951," (Geneva, Switzerland: Division of International Protection of the United Nations High Commissioner for Refugees, 1997), 9; Spijkerboer, *Gender and Refugee Status,* 1.

36. Spijkerboer, *Gender and Refugee Status,* 1.

37. Spijkerboer, *Gender and Refugee Status,* 1.

38. Baines, *Vulnerable Bodies,* 24.

39. UNHCR, "Policy on Refugee Women," (UNHCR, 1990).

40. *The Convention on the Elimination of All Forms of Discrimination against Women,* 20378.

41. UNHCR, "Policy on Refugee Women," 5.

42. Luibhéid, *Entry Denied,* 148.

43. B. S. Chimni, "The Geopolitics of Refugee Studies: A View from the South," *Journal of Refugee Studies* 11 (1998): 350–74; Bill Ong Hing, *Making and Remaking Asian America through Immigration Policy: 1850–1990* (Palo Alto, Calif.: Stanford University Press, 1993); Kamala Visweswaran, "Gendered States: Rethinking Culture as a Site of South Asian Human Rights Work," *Human Rights Quarterly* 26 (2004): 483–511.

44. Gibney, *Ethics and Politics.*

45. INS, "Considerations."

46. INS, "Considerations," 4–5.

47. Emily Love, "Recent Developments: Equality in Political Asylum Law: For a Legislative Recognition of Gender-Based Persecution," *Harvard Women's Law Journal* 17 (1993): 133.

48. Priscilla F. Warren, "Women Are Human: Gender-Based Persecution Is a Human Rights Violation against Women," *Hastings Women's Law Journal* 5 (1994): 315.

49. Stevens, "Recognizing Gender-Specific Persecution," 179.

50. Peter C. Godfrey, "Defining the Social Group in Asylum Proceedings: The Expansion of the Social Group to Include a Broader Class of Refugees," *Journal of Law and Policy* 3 (1994): 285.

51. Pierrette Hondagneu-Sotelo, *Gender and U.S. Immigration: Contemporary Trends* (Los Angeles: University of California Press, 2003). 6.

52. Akibo-Betts, "Canada-U.S."; Layli M. Bashir, "Female Genital Mutilation in the United States: An Examination of Criminal and Asylum Law," *American University Journal of Gender and the Law* 4 (1996): 415–54; Angélica Cházaro, "Witnessing Memory and Surviving Domestic Violence: The Case of Rodi Alvarado Peña," in Epps, Valens, and González, *Passing Lines*, 365–88; Heaven Crawley, *Refugees and Gender: Law and Process* (Bristol: Jordan, 2001); Lindsay A. Franke, "Not Meeting the Standard: U.S. Asylum Law and Gender-Related Claims," *Arizona Journal of International and Comparative Law* 17 (2000): 605–27; Gomez, "Last in Line"; Heyman, "Domestic Violence"; Kennady, "Gender-Related Persecution"; Linda A. Malone, "Beyond Bosnia and In re Kasinga: A Feminist Perspective on Recent Developments in Protecting Women from Sexual Violence," *Boston University International Law Journal* 14 (1996): 319–41; Karen Musalo, "The Center for Children, Families, and the Law Interdisciplinary Conference: 'Welcome to America: Immigration, Families and the Law'; Protecting Victims of Gendered Persecution: Fear of Floodgates or Call to (Principled) Action?" *Virginia Journal of Social Policy and the Law* 14 (2007): 119–44; Shannon Nichols, "American Mutilation: The Effects of Gender-Biased Asylum Laws on the World's Women," *Kansas Journal of Law and Public Policy* 6 (1997): 42–53; Leslye E. Orloff and Janice Kaguyutan, "Offering a Helping Hand: Legal Protections for Battered Immigrant Women; A History of Legislative Responses," *American University Journal of Gender, Social Policy and the Law* 10 (2001): 95–184; Podkul, "Domestic Violence"; Melanie Randall, "Refugee Law and State Accountability for Violence against Women: A Comparative Analysis of Legal Approaches to Recognizing Asylum Claims Based on Gender Persecution," *Harvard Women's Law Journal* 25 (2002): 281–319; Patricia A. Seith, "Escaping Domestic Violence: Asylum as a Means of Protection for Battered Women," *Columbia Law Review* 97 (1997): 1804–43; Hannah R. Shapiro, "Notes & Comments: The Future of Spousal Abuse as a Gender-Based Asylum Claim: The Implications of the Recent Case of *Matter of R-A-*," *Temple International and Comparative Law Journal* 14 (2000): 463–91; Amy Stern, "Female Genital Mutilation: United States Asylum Laws Are in Need of Reform," *American University Journal of Gender and the Law* 6 (1997): 89–111; Caryn L. Weisblat, "Gender-Based Persecution: Does United States Law Provide Women Refugees with a Fair Chance?" *Tulane Journal of International and Comparative Law* 7 (1999): 407–30.

53. Freedman, *Gendering*, 16.

54. Crawley, "Engendering the State," 88.

55. Donato et al., "Glass Half Full?" 6.

56. Judith Butler, *Gender Trouble: Feminism and the Subversion of Identity* (New York: Routledge, 1999).

57. Spijkerboer, *Gender and Refugee Status*, 6.

58. Gayle Rubin, "The Traffic in Women: Notes on the Political Economy of Sex," in *Toward an Anthropology of Women*, ed. Rayna Reiter (New York: Monthly Review Press, 1975), 157–209.

59. Rubin, "The Traffic in Women," 205.

60. Joan W. Scott, "The Evidence of Experience," *Critical Inquiry* 17 (1991): 792.

61. Kimberle Crenshaw, "Mapping the Margins: Intersectionality, Identity Politics and Violence against Women of Color," *Stanford Law Review* 43 (1991): 1251.

62. Crenshaw, "Mapping the Margins."

63. Sherene H. Razack, *Looking White People in the Eye: Gender, Race and Culture in Courtrooms and Classrooms* (Toronto: University of Toronto, 1998). 13.

64. Sara L. McKinnon, "Essentialism, Intersectionality and Recognition: A Feminist Rhetorical Approach to the Audience," in *Standing in the Intersection: Feminist Voices, Feminist Practices in Communication*, ed. Karma R. Chávez and Cindy L. Griffin (Albany: SUNY Press, 2012), 189–210.

65. Lowe, *Immigrant Acts*, 22.

66. Ong, *Buddha Is Hiding*, 14.

67. Deborah Anker, "Refugee Law, Gender, and the Human Rights Paradigm," in Epps, Valens, and González, *Passing Lines*, 105–36; Bhabha, "Embodied Rights"; Crawley, *Refugees and Gender*.

68. Anker, "Refugee Law."

69. Dingo, *Networking Arguments*.

70. Dingo, *Networking Arguments*, 7.

71. Raka Shome, "Transnational Feminism and Communication Studies," *Communication Review* 9 (2006): 256.

72. M. Jacqui Alexander and Chandra Talpade Mohanty, eds., *Feminist Genealogies, Colonial Legacies, Democratic Futures* (New York: Routledge, 1997), xxviii.

73. M. Jacqui Alexander, "Not Just (Any) Body Can Be a Citizen: The Politics of Law, Sexuality, and Postcoloniality in Trinidad and Tobago and the Bahamas," *Feminist Review* 48 (1994): 5–23; Eithne Luibhéid, "Heteronormativity, Responsibility, and Neo-Liberal Governance in U.S. Immigration Control," in Epps, Valens, and González, *Passing Lines*, 69–101.

74. Jessica Livingston, "Murder in Juarez: Gender, Sexual Violence, and the Global Assembly Line," *Frontiers* 25 (2004): 59–76.

75. Enloe, *Maneuvers*; Okazawa-Rey, "Warring on Women"; Inger Skjelsbæk, "Sexual Violence and War: Mapping out a Complex Relationship," *European Journal of International Relations* 7 (2001): 211–37.

76. The Board of Immigration Appeals is the body that creates precedent in asylum cases and is tasked with evaluating the decisions of lower-level immigration judges. The federal Court of Appeals judges, then, may evaluate the procedural decisions of the Board of Immigration Appeals and lower courts. Each of the thirteen federal circuit courts has somewhat unique case law histories, language preferences, and ways of interpreting past precedent. I make note throughout this text to the points where I see these differences mattering in the broader development of gender-related asylum case law, though in general I treat the courts as a part of a whole system that is evaluating, assessing, and ultimately deciding what gender means in the United States. I do this with the understanding that as officials nominated and appointed by the president of the United States, all Court of Appeals judges as well

as all Board of Immigration Appeals members who are appointed by the U.S. attorney general serve as state officials and reflect, in part, U.S. state interests in their decisions. For a thorough evaluation of the differences in the various immigration courts' decision-making patterns, see Jaya Ramji-Nogales, Andrew Schoenholtz, and Philip G. Schrag, *Refugee Roulette: Disparities in Asylum Adjudication and Proposals for Reform* (New York: New York University Press, 2011).

77. Carrie Crenshaw, "The 'Protection' of 'Woman': A History of Legal Attitudes towards Women's Workplace Freedoms," *Quarterly Journal of Speech* 81 (1995): 63–82; Katie L. Gibson, "Judicial Rhetoric and Women's 'Place': The United States Supreme Court's Darwinian Defense of Separate Spheres," *Western Journal of Communication* 71 (2007): 159–75; Katie L. Gibson, "The Rhetoric of *Roe v. Wade*: When the (Male) Doctor Knows Best," *Southern Communication Journal* 73 (2008): 312–31; Marouf Hasian Jr., "Critical Legal Rhetorics: The Theory and Practice of Law in a Postmodern World," *Southern Communication Journal* 60 (1994): 44–56.

78. Eithne Luibhéid, *Pregnant on Arrival: Making the Illegal Immigrant* (Minneapolis, MN: University of Minnesota Press, 2013); E. Valentine Daniel and John C. Knudsen, eds., *Mistrusting Refugees* (Berkeley: University of California Press, 1995).

79. Marouf Hasian Jr., *Colonial Legacies in Postcolonial Contexts: A Critical Rhetorical Examination of Legal Histories* (New York: Peter Lang, 2002). 9.

80. John Louis Lucaites, "Between Rhetoric and 'the Law': Power, Legitimacy, and Social Change," *Quarterly Journal of Speech* 76 (1990): 445.

81. Lucaites, "Between Rhetoric," 447.

82. Wendy Hesford, *Spectacular Rhetorics: Human Rights Visions, Recognitions, Feminisms* (Durham, N.C.: Duke University Press, 2011). 10.

Chapter 1. Transnational Publicity, Gender-Based Violence, and Central American Women's Asylum Cases

1. There are numerous variations in the spelling of Rody Alvarado's first and last names. I refer to her throughout the record with her single appellation of Alvarado, as that is what is used by the Center for Gender and Refugee Law, where she is a member of the board of directors.

2. Karen Musalo et al., "Brief of Amici Curiae" (Refugee Law Center and International Human Rights/Migration Project, 1997), 16.

3. Musalo, "Brief of Amici Curiae."

4. Karen Musalo, "Brief on Behalf of Rodi Alvarado Pena to the Attorney General of the United States" (Hastings College of Law, 2001), 7.

5. *Re R-A-*, 22 I. & N. Dec. 906 (Board of Immigration Appeals 2001).

6. CGRS, "Documents and Information on Rodi Alvarado's Claim for Asylum in the U.S.," http://cgrs.uchastings.edu/campaigns/alvarado.php.

7. Alvarado is on the board of directors for the Center for Gender and Refugee Studies at the Hastings School of Law at the University of California. Alvarado's case is now frequently discussed when advocates address the pervasiveness of in-

timate violence and the need of gender-sensitive asylum processes in the United States.

8. Sara L. McKinnon, "(In)Hospitable Publics: Theorizing Modalities of Access to U.S. Publics," in *Public Modalities: Rhetoric, Culture, Media, and the Shape of Public Life*, edited by Daniel C. Brouwer and Robert Asen (Tuscaloosa: University of Alabama Press, 2010), 131–53; Sara L. McKinnon, "Positioned in/by the State: Incorporation, Exclusion, and Appropriation of Women's Gender-Based Claims to Political Asylum in the United States," *Quarterly Journal of Speech* 97 (2011): 178–200.

9. Daniel C. Brouwer and Robert Asen, eds., *Public Modalities: Rhetoric, Culture, Media, and the Shape of Public Life* (Tuscaloosa: University of Alabama Press, 2010), 9.

10. Mimi Sheller and John Urry, "Mobile Transformations of 'Public' and 'Private' Life," *Theory, Culture and Society* 20 (2003): 114.

11. Wendy Hesford, *Spectacular Rhetorics: Human Rights Visions, Recognitions, Feminisms* (Durham, N.C.: Duke University Press, 2011). 65.

12. Rebecca Dingo, *Networking Arguments: Rhetoric, Transnational Feminism, and Public Policy Writing* (Pittsburgh, Pa.: University of Pittsburgh, 2012).

13. Inderpal Grewal, *Transnational America: Feminisms, Diasporas, Neoliberalisms* (Durham, N.C.: Duke University Press, 2005). 23.

14. *Gomez v. INS*, 947 F.2d 660 (2nd cir. 1991).

15. *Campos-Guardado v. INS*, 809 F.2d 285 (5th cir. 1987).

16. *Campos-Guardado v. INS*, 287.

17. *Campos-Guardado v. INS*, 287.

18. *Campos-Guardado v. INS*, 287.

19. *Campos-Guardado v. INS*, 287.

20. *Lazo-Majano v. INS*, 813 F.2d 1432 (9th cir. 1987).

21. *Lazo-Majano v. INS*, 1433.

22. *Lazo-Majano v. INS*, 1433.

23. *Lazo-Majano v. INS*, 1433.

24. *Lazo-Majano v. INS* 1433.

25. *Juarez-Lopez v. Gonzales*, 235 Fed. Appx. 361 (7th cir. 2007).

26. CGRS, "Cgrs Case No. 68," http://cgrs.uchastings.edu/law/detail.php.

27. CGRS, "Cgrs Case No. 264," http://cgrs.uchastings.edu/law/detail.php.

28. *Gomez v. INS*, 663.

29. *Gomez v. INS*, 664.

30. *Campos-Guardado v. INS*, 288.

31. *Lazo-Majano v. INS*, 1435.

32. *Lazo-Majano v. INS*, 1435.

33. Sara L. McKinnon, "Excavating Gender in Women's Early Claims to Political Asylum in the United States," *Women's Studies in Communication* 33 (2010): 91.

34. "The Guatemalan Military: What the U.S. Files Reveal. National Security Archive Electronic Briefing Book No. 32: Document 20," National Security Archive at the George Washington University, http://www.gwu.edu/~nsarchiv/NSAEBB/NSAEBB32/vol2.html.

35. "The Guatemalan Military: What the U.S. Files Reveal. National Security Archive Electronic Briefing Book No. 32: Document 23," National Security Archive at the George Washington University, http://www.gwu.edu/~nsarchiv/NSAEBB/NSAEBB32/vol2.html (cited hereafter as "Guatemalan Military, NSA 32:23.")

36. "Guatemalan Military, NSA 32:23."

37. "Guatemalan Military, NSA 32:23."

38. John Joseph Moakley, "Correspondence: Joe Moakley to President Reagan" (Washington D.C.: Suffolk University Moakley Archive and Institute, 1982).

39. Susan Gzesh, "Central Americans and Asylum Policy in the Reagan Era," *Migration Information Source*, April 2006.

40. Katherine Bishop, "U.S. Adopts New Policy for Hearings on Political Asylum for Some Aliens," *New York Times*, December 20, 1990; Ruth Ellen Wasem, "Central American Asylum Seekers: Impact of the 1996 Immigration Law," in *CRS Report for Congress* (Congressional Research Service of the Library of Congress, 1997), 1–26.

41. Gzesh, "Central Americans."

42. Beatriz Manz, *Refugees of a Hidden War: The Aftermath of Counterinsurgency in Guatemala* (Albany: SUNY Press, 1988); Patricia R. Pessar, "Women's Political Consciousness and Empowerment in Local, National, and Transnational Contexts: Guatemalan Refugees and Returnees," *Identities* 7 (2001): 461–501.

43. Kathleen Newland, "The Impact of U.S. Refugee Policies on U.S. Foreign Policy: A Case of the Tail Wagging the Dog?" in *Threatened Peoples, Threatened Borders: World Migration and U.S. Foreign Policy*, edited by Michael S. Teitelbaum and Myron Veiner (New York: American Assembly, 1995).

44. *Re R-A-*, 927.

45. U.S. Senate Judiciary Committee, "Correspondence to Janet Reno" (Washington, D.C., 2000). Available at http://cgrs.uchastings.edu/our-work/matter-r.

46. Bernie Sanders, "Correspondence to Janet Reno" (Washington, D.C., 2000). Available at http://cgrs.uchastings.edu/our-work/matter-r.

47. Amnesty International USA, "Refugee Action. USA: Guatemalan Women, Domestic Abuse, Asylum" (Washington, D.C.: Amnesty International, 2003).

48. Amnesty International, "Guatemala. No Protection, No Justice: Killings of Women in Guatemala," in *Stop Violence against Women* (London: Amnesty International, 2005).

49. Anthony Fontes, "Refuge from Femicide: Facing Gendered Violence in Guatemala," in *Berkeley Review of Latin American Studies* (Berkeley: Center for Latin American Studies, University of California, Berkeley, 2010), 2.

50. Katherine Ruhl, "Guatemala's Femicides and the Ongoing Struggle for Women's Human Rights" (San Francisco: Center for Gender and Refugee Studies, 2006), 9.

51. Julie Suarez and Mary Jordan, "Three Thousand and Counting: A Report on Violence against Women in Guatemala" (Washington, D.C.: Guatemala Human Rights Commission USA, 2007).

52. "Feminicidios No Ceden En El Salvador," *ContraPunto*, April 1, 2012.

53. Violence against Women is on the Rise, 2011," http://voiceselsalvador.wordpress.com/2011/03/04/violence-against-women-is-on-the-rise.

54. Ruhl, "Guatemala's Femicides," 2.

55. Erin Yates, "San Lucas Mission: Gender Issues," http://www.sanlucasmission.org/iss_gender.php.

56. "Human Rights Brief: Domestic Violence in Guatemala" (Immigration and Refugee Board of Canada, 1994).

57. Fontes, "Refuge from Femicide."

58. Amnesty International, "Guatemala."

59. Amnesty International, "Guatemala," 6.

60. Blanca Blanco and Lorna Hayes, "The Hidden Challenge to Development: Gender-Based Violence in Guatemala," *Trócaire Development Review* (2007): 50.

61. CGRS, "Guatemala: Documentation in Support of Asylum Applicants Based on Domestic Violence and Femicides" (Berkeley, Calif.: Center for Gender and Refugee Studies, 2006).

62. Ruhl, "Guatemala's Femicides," 2–3.

63. Michel Foucault, "The Subject and Power," *Critical Inquiry* 8 (1982): 784.

64. Foucault, "Subject," 782.

65. Kristin Bumiller, *In an Abusive State: How Neoliberalism Appropriated the Feminist Movement against Sexual Violence* (Durham, N.C.: Duke University Press, 2008); Catherine Cook and Margaret Brunton, "Pastoral Power and Gynaecological Examinations: A Foucauldian Critique of Clinician Accounts of Patient-Centered Consent," *Sociology of Health and Illness* 37 (2015): 545–60; Dingo, *Networking Arguments*.

66. Thomas Biebricher, "Faith-Based Initiatives and Pastoral Power," *Economy and Society* 40 (2011): 399–420; Ronald Walter Greene, "Lessons from the YMCA: The Materialist Rhetoric of Criticism, Rhetorical Interpretation, and Pastoral Power," edited by Jeremy Packer and Stephen B. Crofts Wiley, *Communication Matters: Materialist Approaches to Media, Mobility, and Networks* (New York: Routledge, 2012), 219–30; Nikolas Rose, "The Politics of Life Itself," *Theory, Culture and Society* 18 (2001): 1–30.

67. Aihwa Ong, *Buddha Is Hiding: Refugees, Citizenship, the New America* (Berkeley: University of California Press, 2003).

68. Iris Marion Young, "The Logic of Masculinist Protection: Reflections on the Current Security State," *Signs* 29 (2003): 2, 4.

69. Young, "Logic," 7.

70. *Castillo-Hernandez v. U.S. Attorney General*, 297 Fed. Appx. 894, 897 (11th cir. 2008).

71. *Castillo-Hernandez v. U.S. Attorney General*, 897.

72. *Perdomo v. Holder*, 611 F.3d 662; 2010 U.S. App. LEXIS 14171, 664 (9th cir. 2010).

73. *Perdomo v. Holder*, 665.

74. *Perdomo v. Holder*, 667.

75. *Perdomo v. Holder*, 663.

76. *Perdomo v. Holder*, 664.

77. Elise Foley, "Honduran Mom Fleeing 'Horrific Acts of Harm' Wins U.S. Asylum with Daughters," *Huffington Post*, November 25, 2014; U.S. Committee for Refugees and Immigrants, "Domestic Violence Based Asylum," http://www.refugees.org/resources/for-lawyers/asylum-research/domestic-violence-based-asylum/immigration-judge .html#Honduras; Karen Musalo, "Brief on Behalf of L-R-" (Hastings College of Law, 2010).

Chapter 2. Fixing Bodies, Fashioning Subjects

1. Charlotte Bunch, "Women's Rights as Human Rights: Toward a Re-Vision of Human Rights," *Human Rights Quarterly* 12 (1990): 6.

2. "Women Bring Concern about Rights to U.N." *New York Times*, March 14, 1992. Also see Charlotte Bunch and Niamh Reilly, *Demanding Accountability: The Global Campaign and Vienna Tribunal for Women's Human Rights* (New Brunswick, N.J.: Center for Women's Global Leadership 1994), 5.

3. Elisabeth Friedman, "Women's Human Rights: The Emergence of a Movement," in *Women's Rights, Human Rights: International Feminist Perspectives*, edited by Julie Peters and Andrea Wolper (New York: Routledge, 1995), 18.

4. Subcommittee on International Security, International Organizations, and Human Rights, *Human Rights Abuses against Women*, 103, September 28 1993. ISBN 0160446775, G.P.O. 1994.

5. *Human Rights Abuses against Women*, 1.

6. *Human Rights Abuses against Women*, 4.

7. *Human Rights Abuses against Women*, 4.

8. *Human Rights Abuses against Women*, 37.

9. *Human Rights Abuses against Women*, 4.

10. *Human Rights Abuses against Women*, 67.

11. *Human Rights Abuses against Women*, 67.

12. INS, "Considerations for Asylum Officers," (1995).

13. INS, "Considerations for Asylum Officers," 1.

14. INS, "Considerations for Asylum Officers," 4.

15. INS, "Considerations for Asylum Officers," 4.

16. INS, "Considerations for Asylum Officers," 4.

17. Fauziya Kasinga, "Affidavit of Fauziya Kasinga" (International Human Rights Law Clinic, 1995).

18. *Re Kasinga*, 21 I. & N. Dec. 357, 10 (BIA 1996).

19. Numerous feminist scholars who have addressed the way genital surgeries are imagined in U.S. discourse inform my reading of the public discourse leading up to Kassindja's asylum win. As exemplars of this work, see: Rogaia Mustafa Abusharaf, "Virtuous Cuts: Female Genital Circumcision in an African Ontology," *differences: A Journal of Feminist Cultural Studies* 12 (2001): 112–40; Inderpal Grewal and Caren Ka-

plan, "Warrior Marks: Global Womanism's Neo-Colonial Discourse in a Multicultural Context," *Camera Obscura* 13 (1996): 4–33; Isabelle R. Gunning, "Arrogant Perception, World-Travelling and Multicultural Feminism: The Case of Female Genital Surgeries," *Columbia Human Rights Law Review* 23 (1991): 189–248; Stanlie M. James and Claire C. Robertson, eds., *Genital Cutting and Transnational Sisterhood: Disputing U.S. Polemics* (Urbana: University of Illinois Press, 2002); Wairimu Ngaruiya Njambi, "Dualisms and Female Bodies in Representations of African Female Circumcision: A Feminist Critique," *Feminist Theory* 5 (2004): 281–303; Obiama Nnaemeka, ed., *Female Circumcision and the Politics of Knowledge: African Women in Imperialist Discourses* (Westport, Conn.: Praeger, 2005); Obioma Nnaemeka, "The Challenges of Border-Crossing: African Women and Transnational Feminisms," in Nnaemeka, *Female Circumcision*, 3–20; Courtney Smith, "Who Defines 'Mutilation'? Challenging Imperialism in the Discourse of Female Genital Cutting," *Feminist Formations* 23 (2011): 25–46; Lisa Wade, "Defining Gender Oppression in U.S. Newspapers: The Strategic Value of 'Female Genital Mutilation,'" *Gender and Society* 23 (2009): 293–314; Lisa Wade, "Learning from 'Female Genital Mutilation': Lessons from 30 Years of Academic Discourse," *Ethnicities* 12 (2011): 26–49.

20. Barbara Crossette, "Female Genital Mutilation by Immigrants Is Becoming Cause for Concern in the U.S.," *New York Times*, December 10, 1995.

21. Judy Mann, "When Judges Fail," *Washington Post*, January 19, 1996.

22. Celia Dugger, "Woman's Plea for Asylum Puts Tribal Ritual on Trial," *New York Times*, April 15, 1996.

23. Indeed, by 1996, when Kassindja was finally awarded asylum, almost all major national and regional newspapers, magazines, and televised news shows had covered the topic with at least one article or segment. Here are a number of the radio and television programs that covered the topic, for reference: *All Things Considered*, "Activists Denounce Female Genital Mutilation" (National Public Radio, 1993); *All Things Considered*, "Genital Mutilation May Await Two American-Born Girls" (National Public Radio, 1994); *CBS This Morning*, "African Fauziya Kasinga Talks about the Reason She Left Her Native Togo Seeking Asylum in the U.S. and Her Experience in a U.S Jail (CBS Inc., 1996); *ABC News*, "Day One: A Reporter's Notebook" (ABC News Television, 1993); *ABC News*, "Day One: Scarred for Life" (ABC News Television, 1993); *ABC World News Tonight*, "African Woman Seeks Asylum from Genital Mutilation" (American Broadcasting Companies, 1996); *CNN News*, "Beyond the Numbers—Part 2—Female Circumcision" (CNN, 1994); *CNN News*, "Nigerian Says Daughters Face Mutilation If Deported" (CNN, 1994).

24. Crossette, "Female Genital Mutilation."

25. Ellen Goodman, "Refugee Seeks Freedom from Mutilation," *Tampa Tribune*, April 9, 1996.

26. "Fight Genital Mutilation," *Providence Journal*, April 28, 1996.

27. A. M. Rosenthal, "On My Mind: Fighting Female Mutilation," *New York Times*, April 12, 1996.

28. Marie McCllough, "Asylum Is Granted in Circumcision," *Philadelphia Inquirer*, June 15, 1996.

29. Joan Beck, "The Ugliness Abroad: Abuse against Women Cannot Be Ignored," *Charleston Gazette*, February 13, 1994.

30. Crossette, "Female Genital Mutilation," 18.

31. *Re Kasinga*, 11.

32. Patricia Hill Collins, *Black Sexual Politics: African Americans, Gender, and the New Racism* (New York: Routledge, 2004); Evelynn M. Hammonds, "Toward a Genealogy of Black Female Sexuality: The Problematic of Silence," in *Feminist Genealogies, Colonial Legacies, Democratic Futures*, edited by M. Jacqui Alexander and Chandra Talpade Mohanty (New York: Routledge, 1997), 170–82; Shanara Rose Reid-Brinkley, "Mammies and Matriarchs: Feminine Style and Signifyin(g) in Carol Moseley Braun's 2003–2004 Campaign for the Presidency," in *Standing in the Intersection: Feminist Voices, Feminist Practices in Communication Studies*, edited by Karma R. Chávez and Cindy L. Griffin (Albany, N.Y.: SUNY Press, 2012), 35–58.

33. *Hassan v. Gonzales*, 484 F.3d 513, 518 (8th cir. 2007).

34. *Abebe v. Gonzales*, 432 F.3d 1037 (9th cir. 2005).

35. *Abay v. Ashcroft*, 368 F.3d 634, 642 (6th cir. 2004).

36. Aihwa Ong, *Buddha Is Hiding: Refugees, Citizenship, the New America* (Berkeley: University of California Press, 2003).

37. *Fatin v. INS*, 12 F.3d 1233, 1236 (3rd cir. 1993).

38. *Safaie v. INS*, 25 F.3d 636 (8th cir. 1994); *Fisher v. INS*, 79 F.3d. 955 (9th cir. 1995); *Sharif v. INS*, 87 F.3d 932 (7th cir. 1996).

39. *Fatin v. INS*, 1235.

40. *Fatin v. INS*, 1236.

41. *Safaie v. INS*, 638.

42. *Safaie v. INS*, 640.

43. Referred to as "Fisher" in court documents, the last name of the man the court denies she was ever really married to.

44. *Fisher v INS*.

45. *Fisher v. INS*, 960.

46. *Fisher v. INS*, 960.

47. *Fisher v. INS*, 959.

48. *Fisher v. INS*, 959.

49. John Kifner, "Cracks in the Wall of Khomeini's Power," *New York Times*, April 25, 1982.

50. "Four in Iran Executed by Stoning," *New York Times*, July 4, 1980.

51. Gayatri Chakravorty Spivak, "Can the Subaltern Speak?" in *Marxism and the Interpretation of Culture*, edited by Lawrence Grossberg and C. Nelson (Urbana: University of Illinois Press, 1988), 271–313.

52. Radha Hegde, "Eyeing New Publics: Veiling and the Performance of Civic Visibility," in *Public Modalities: Rhetoric, Culture, Media and the Shape of Public Life*, edited by

Daniel C. Brouwer and Robert Asen (Tuscaloosa: University of Alabama Press, 2010), 154–72; Sherene H. Razack, *Casting Out: The Eviction of Muslims from Western Law and Politics* (Toronto: University of Toronto Press, 2008); Joan W. Scott, *The Politics of the Veil* (Princeton, N.J.: Princeton University Press, 2009); Bradford Vivian, "The Veil and the Visible," *Western Journal of Communication* 63 (1999): 115–39.

53. Lila Abu-Lughod, "Do Muslim Women Really Need Saving? Anthropological Reflections on Cultural Relativism and Its Others," *American Anthropologist* 104 (2002): 783–90; Dana L. Cloud, "'To Veil the Threat of Terror': Afghan Women and the Clash of Civilizations in the Imagery of the U.S. War on Terrorism," *Quarterly Journal of Speech* 90 (2004): 285–306; Wendy Hesford, *Spectacular Rhetorics: Human Rights Visions, Recognitions, Feminisms* (Durham, N.C.: Duke University Press, 2011); Saba Mahmood, *Politics of Piety: The Islamic Revival and the Feminist Subject* (Princeton, N.J.: Princeton University Press, 2005); Robin L. Riley, Chandra Talpade Mohanty, and Minnie Bruce Pratt, eds., *Feminism and War: Confronting U.S. Imperialism* (London: Zed, 2008); Carol A. Stabile and Deepa Kumar, "Unveiling Imperialism: Media, Gender and the War on Afghanistan," *Media, Culture and Society* 27 (2005): 765–82.

54. Chandra Talpade Mohanty, "Under Western Eyes: Feminist Scholarship and Colonial Discourses," *Feminist Review* 30 (1988): 75.

55. Abu-Lughod, "Do Muslim Women Need Saving?"; Leila Ahmed, *A Quiet Revolution: The Veil's Resurgence, from Middle East to America* (New Haven, Conn.: Yale University Press, 2011); Cloud, "To Veil," 285–306; Nilifur Göle, "Islam in Public: New Visibilities and New Imaginaries," *Public Culture* 14 (2002): 173–90; Hegde, "Eyeing New Publics"; Mahmood, *Politics of Piety*; Minoo Moallem, *Between Warrior Brother and Veiled Sister: Islamic Fundamentalism and the Politics of Patriarchy in Iran* (Berkeley: University of California Press, 2005); Afsaneh Najmabadi, *Women with Mustaches and Men without Beards: Gender and Sexual Anxieties of Iranian Modernity* (Berkeley: University of California Press, 2005); Arzoo Osanloo, *The Politics of Women's Rights in Iran* (Princeton, N.J.: Princeton University Press, 2009); Scott, *Politics of the Veil*.

56. *Fatin v. INS*, 1237.

57. *Fatin v. INS*, 1241.

58. Julietta Hua, "Feminism, Asylum and the Limits of the Law," *Law, Culture and the Humanities* 6 (2010): 375–93.

59. Mia Bloom, *Bombshell: Women and Terrorism* (Philadelphia: University of Pennsylvania Press, 2011); Kelly Oliver, *Women as Weapons of War: Iraq, Sex, and the Media* (New York: Columbia University Press, 2007).

60. *Fisher v. INS*, 962.

61. *Safaie v. INS*, 640.

62. *Safaie v. INS*, 638.

63. *Safaie v. INS*, 638.

64. "Iranian Women Protest Dress Code," *New York Times*, July 6, 1980.

65. Jonathan C. Randal, "Iranian Women Foresee More Battles with Moslem Clergy," *Washington Post*, May 22, 1980.

66. Barbara Slavin, "Iranian Women's 'Reconstructed Lives' Unveiled at Length," *USA Today*, July 21, 1997.

67. Barbara Slavin, "Islamic Women's Power, out from under Wraps," *USA Today*, December 20, 1996.

68. Jay Ross, "Iranian Women Protest Dress Code; Demonstrators Defy Jeering Men," *Washington Post*, July 6, 1980.

69. Elaine Sciolino, "The Will to Adorn," *New York Times*, May 24, 1992.

70. Randal, "Iranian Women Foresee."

71. Elaine Sciolino, "The Chanel under the Chador," *New York Times*, May 4, 1997.

72. Patrick E. Tyler, "In Iran, Women's Fashion Ferment; Breaking of Traditional Dress Code Angers Radicals," *Washington Post*, February 8, 1989.

73. Nora Boustany, "In Iran, the Chador Has Begun to Chafe: With Little Organized Help, Women Seek to Wrest Their Rights," *Washington Post*, October 26, 1992.

74. Slavin, "Islamic Women's Power."

75. Boustany, "In Iran."

76. Boustany, "In Iran."

77. Caryle Murphy, "Iran: Reconciling Ideology and a Modern State," *Washington Post*, April 28, 1992.

78. Sciolino, "Will to Adorn."

79. Sciolino, "Chanel."

80. *Re Kasinga*.

81. *Mohammed v. Gonzales*, 400 F.3d 785, 789n2 (9th cir. 2005).

82. Kassindja now lives in the United States and is an advocate for women's rights through the Tahirih Justice Center. For more information on Tahirih, go to http://www.tahirih.org. For information about her experiences of exile see the narrative-based book she co-wrote: Fauziya Kassindja and Layli M. Bashir, *Do They Hear You When You Cry* (New York: Delta, 1998).

83. House of Representatives, *Introduction of Legislation to Prevent Female Genital Mutilation and the Dangers of the National Security Revitalization Act*, 1995, J1695.

84. *Introduction of Legislation to Prevent Female Genital Mutilation and the Dangers of the National Security Revitalization Act*, J1695.

85. Sara L. McKinnon, "Unsettling Resettlement: Problematizing 'Lost Boys of Sudan' Resettlement and Identity," *Western Journal of Communication* 72 (2008): 397–414.

86. Deborah Scroggins, "Women of the Veil," *Atlanta Journal and Constitution*, June 28, 1992.

87. Marlise Simons, "Cry of Muslim Women for Equal Rights Is Rising," *New York Times*, March 9, 1998.

88. Barbara Crossette, "Women's Rights Gaining Attention within Islam," *New York Times*, May 12, 1996.

89. Reena Shah Stamets, "Status of Women in Spotlight," *St. Petersburg Times*, August 28, 1995.

90. Barbara Slavin, "A Lifting of Veils as Iranians Try to Soften Image," *USA Today*, November 7, 1996.

91. Barbara Demick, "For Afghan Women, Iran Is a Better World," *Philadelphia Inquirer*, February 28, 1999.

92. Jack Kelly, "Taking on Tradition: Women Make a Stand," *USA Today*, January 4, 1994.

Chapter 3. Standing in Her Shoes

1. Wesley L. Hsu, "The Tragedy of the *Golden Venture*: Politics Trumps the Administrative Procedures Act and the Rule of Law," *Georgetown Immigration Law Journal* 10 (1996): 317–70.

2. Ian Fisher, "Smuggled to New York: The Scene; Waves of Panic Yield to Elation of Refugees," *New York Times*, June 7, 1993, 4.

3. Raymond Hernandez, "Finding of 3rd Body Rasies More Questions about Ship," *New York Times*, June 17, 1993, 8.

4. Ying Chan, "Town Lives Golden Rule: Supporters Cheer Order Freeing Last Venture Detainees," *New York Daily News*, February 23, 1997.

5. *Matter of Chang*, 20 I. & N. Dec. 38, 38 (BIA 1989).

6. It must be said that nowhere in the legislative deliberations about China's use of forced sterilization and abortion is there any mention of the way the United States has used the same bio-techniques to manage its citizenry. Jessica Enoch, "Survival Stories: Feminist Historiographic Approaches to Chicana Rhetorics of Sterilization Abuse," *Rhetoric Society Quarterly* 35 (2005): 5–30; Paul A. Lombardo, *Three Generations, No Imbeciles: Eugenics, the Supreme Court, and* Buck v. Bell (Baltimore, Md.: Johns Hopkins University Press, 2010); Nancy Ordover, *American Eugenics: Race, Queer Anatomy and the Science of Nationalism* (Minneapolis: University of Minnesota Press, 2003).

7. Kathleen Blanchard and Jan C. Ting, "Asylum Process Slights Chinese Refugees," *New York Times*, July 15, 1994.

8. Population Committee on Women, and the Environment, "International Anti-Abortion Research Project," *Political Environments* 3 (1996), available at http://www.cwpe.org/node/118.

9. Taking this point one step further, scholars of China studies rightly note that there is no actual uniform "one child policy." Instead, this term that has circulated most prominently in U.S. discourse about China. In reality, there have been vast differences, depending on local authorities and region, in the actual implementation of state reproductive policies. In 2014, China announced that it would completely abandon these programs. Susan Greenhalgh, *Just One Child: Science and Policy in Deng's China* (Berkeley: University of California Press, 2008).

10. I thank Annie Hill, assistant professor in the Department of Gender, Women and Sexuality Studies at the University of Minnesota, for guiding me to this point of analysis.

11. Subcommittee on International Operations and Human Rights of the Committee on International Relations, *Coercive Population Control in China*, 104th, First Session, May 17, June 22, June 28, July 19, 1995.

12. *Coercive Population Control in China*, 101.

13. *Coercive Population Control in China*, 2.

14. Mimi Thi Nguyen, *The Gift of Freedom: War, Debt, and Other Refugee Passages* (Durham, N.C.: Duke University Press, 2012).

15. Jacqueline Bhabha, "Embodied Rights: Gender Persecution, State Sovereignty, and Refugees," *Public Culture* 9 (1996): 3–32; Sherene H. Razack, *Looking White People in the Eye: Gender, Race and Culture in Courtrooms and Classrooms* (Toronto: University of Toronto, 1998); Mireille Rosello, *Postcolonial Hospitality: The Immigrant as Guest* (Stanford, Calif.: Stanford University Press, 2001).

16. *Illegal Immigration Reform and Immigrant Responsibility Act*, H.R. 3610.

17. *Re X-P-T*, 21 I. & N. Dec. 634 (BIA 1996).

18. *Xea v. Ashcroft*, 20 Fed. Appx. 640 (9th cir. 2001).

19. *Re C-Y-Z*, 21 I. & N. Dec. 915, 916 (BIA 1997).

20. Kitty Calavita, "The Paradoxes of Race, Class, Identity, and 'Passing': Enforcing the Chinese Exclusion Acts, 1882–1910," *Law and Social Inquiry* 25 (2000): 1–40.

21. Estelle T. Lau, *Paper Families: Identity, Immigration Administration, and Chinese Exclusion* (Durham, N.C.: Duke University, 2007). 115.

22. Lau, *Paper Families*, 131.

23. *Re C-Y-Z*, 918.

24. *Re C-Y-Z*, 918–19.

25. *Zhao v. Reno*, 265 F.3d 83 (2nd cir. 2001).

26. *Zhao v. Reno*, 86.

27. *Huang v. Ashcroft*, 113 Fed. Appx. 695 (6th cir. 2004).

28. *He v. Ashcroft*, 328 F.3d 593 (9th cir. 2003).

29. *Re C-Y-Z*.

30. Heidi Murphy, "Sending the Men Over First: Amending Section 601(a) of the Illegal Immigration Reform and Immigrant Responsibility Act to Allow for Asylum for Spouses and Partners," *Vermont Law Review* 33 (2008): 143–68.

31. There is an impressive body of scholarship addressing the historical lineage and contemporary manifestations of coverture in the United States. See Elizabeth Freeman, *The Wedding Complex: Forms of Belonging in Modern American Culture* (Durham, N.C.: Duke University Press, 2002); Linda K. Kerber, *No Constitutional Right to Be Ladies: Women and the Obligations of Citizenship* (New York: Hill and Wang, 1999); Kathleen S. Sullivan, *Constitutional Context: Women and Rights Discourse in Nineteenth-Century America* (Baltimore, Md.: Johns Hopkins University Press, 2007). For a review of legal scholarship on the subject see Claudia Zahar, "When a Woman's Marital Status Determined Her Legal Status: A Research Guide on the Common Law Doctrine of Coverture," *Law Library Journal* 94 (2002): 459–86.

32. Ann Marie Nicolosi, "'We Do Not Want Our Girls to Marry Foreigners': Gender, Race, and American Citizenship," *NWSA Journal* 13 (2001): 1–21.

33. Margot Canaday, "Heterosexuality as a Legal Regime," in *The Cambridge History of Law in America*, edited by Michael Grossberg and Christopher Tomlins (Cambridge: Cambridge University Press, 2008), 445.

34. Janet M. Calvo, "Spouse-Based Immigration Laws: The Legacies of Coverture," *San Diego Law Review* 28 (1991): 593–644; Elizabeth Cohen, F., "Neither Seen nor Heard: Children's Citizenship in Contemporary Democracies," *Citizenship Studies* 9 (2005): 221–40; Nancy Fraser and Linda Gordan, "A Genealogy of *Dependency*: Tracing a Keyword of the U.S. Welfare State," *Signs* 19 (1994): 309–36; Mary L. Heen, "From Coverture to Contract: Engendering Insurance on Lives," *Yale Journal of Law and Feminism* 23 (2011): 335–84; Linda K. Kerber, "The Stateless as the Citizen's Other: A View from the United States," *American Historical Review* 112 (2007): 1–34; Sandra R. Zagier Zayac and Robert A. Zayac, "Georgia's Married Women's Property Act: An Effective Challenge to Coverture," *Texas Journal of Women and the Law* 15 (2005): 81–105.

35. Kerber, *No Constitutional Right*, xxiii.

36. *Ma v. Ashcroft*, 361 F.3d 553 (9th cir. 2004).

37. *Ma v. Ashcroft*, 554.

38. *Lin v. US Department of Justice*, 416 F.3d 184 (2nd cir. 2005).

39. *Lin v. US Department of Justice*, 184.

40. Eithne Luibhéid, "Heteronormativity, Responsibility and Neo-Liberal Governance in U.S. Immigration Control," in *Passing Lines: Sexuality and Immigration*, ed. Brad Epps, Keja Valens, and Bill Johnson González (Cambridge, Mass.: Harvard University, 2005), 76.

41. Luibhéid, "Heteronormativity," 76.

42. Kerry Abrams, "Polygamy, Prostitution, and the Federalization of Immigration Law," *Columbia Law Review* 105 (2005): 641–716; Huping Ling, *Surviving on the Gold Mountain: A History of Chinese American Women and Their Lives* (Albany: SUNY Press, 1998); Eithne Luibhéid, *Entry Denied: Controlling Sexuality at the Border* (Minneapolis: University of Minnesota Press, 2002); Adam McKeown, "Transnational Chinese Families and Chinese Exclusion, 1875–1943," *Journal of American Ethnic History* 18 (1999): 73–110; Judy Yung, "'A Bowlful of Tears' Revisited," *Frontiers: A Journal of Women Studies* 25 (2004): 1–22.

43. Lau, *Paper Families*, 17.

44. Todd Stevens, "Tender Ties: Husbands' Rights and Racial Exclusion in Chinese Marriage Cases, 1882–1924," *Law and Social Inquiry* 27 (2002): 272.

45. Clare Sears, "All That Glitters: Trans-Ing California's Gold Rush Migrations," *GLQ: A Journal of Gay and Lesbian Studies* 14 (2008): 383–402.

46. Sears, "All That Glitters," 395.

47. I thank Jigna Desai, professor in the Department of Gender, Women and Sexuality Studies at the University of Minnesota for helping me tease out this point and guiding me to consider Eng's work. David L. Eng, *Racial Castration: Managing Masculinity in Asian America* (Durham, N.C.: Duke University Press, 2005).

48. Thomas K. Nakayama, "Show/Down Time: 'Race,' Gender, Sexuality, and Popular Culture," *Critical Studies in Mass Communication* 11 (1994): 162–79.

49. John Ruggie, "International Regimes, Transactions, and Change: Embedded Liberalism in the Postwar Economic Order," *International Organization* 36 (1982): 379–415.

50. Beverly J. Silver and Giovanni Arrighi, "Polanyi's 'Double Movement': The Belle Époques of British and U.S. Hegemony Compared," *Politics and Society* 31 (2003): 341.

51. Robert Brenner, *The Economics of Global Turbulence* (London: Verso, 2006).

52. Silver and Arrighi, "Polanyi's 'Double Movement,'" 345.

53. Adam Tickell and Jamie Peck, "Making Global Rules: Globalization or Neoliberalism," *Globalization and World Cities Study Group and Network Research Bulletin* 102 (2003): 1–17.

54. Many fantastic books have been written about China's entrance in the global economy. For more on the subject see Giovanni Arrighi, *Adam Smith in Beijing: Lineages of the Twenty-First Century* (London: Verso, 2009); Doug Guthrie, *China and Globalization: The Social, Economic and Political Transformation of Chinese Society* (New York: Routledge, 2012); Peter Nolan, *Transforming China: Globalization, Transition and Development* (London: Anthem, 2004); Aihwa Ong, *Flexible Citizenship: The Cultural Logics of Transnationality* (Durham, N.C.: Duke University, 1999); Kenneth Pomeranz, *The Great Divergence: China, Europe, and the Making of the Modern World Economy* (Princeton, N.J.: Princeton University Press, 2009); Hui Wang, *China's New Order: Society, Politics, and Economy in Transition* (Cambridge, Mass.: Harvard University Press, 2003); Yongnian Zheng, *Globalization and State Transformation in China* (Cambridge: Cambridge University Press, 2004).

55. "Stock Offerings Bring Chinese out En Masse," *USA Today*, March 28, 1994.

56. Elaine Sciolino, "Clinton and China: How Promise Self-Destructed," *New York Times*, May 29, 1994.

57. Associated Press, "Clinton's Call: Avoid Isolating China," *New York Times*, May 27, 1994.

58. John Williamson, "What Washington Means by Reform," in *Latin American Adjustment: How Much Has Happened?* edited by John Williamson (Institute for International Economics, 1990).

59. Paul Blustein, "Clinton's Trade Challenge: Playing the China Card Correctly," *Washington Post*, November 7, 1996.

60. David E. Sanger, "China Faces Test of Resolve to Join Global Economy," *New York Times*, March 1, 1997.

61. Sanger, "China Faces Test."

62. John Pomfret, "Chinese Are Split over WTO Entry: Monopolies Fear Western Influence," *Washington Post*, March 13, 2000.

63. Paul Blustein and Clay Chandler, "WTO Approves China's Entry: Move Expected to Speed Beijing's Transition to Capitalism," *Washington Post*, November 11, 2001.

64. Blustein and Chandler, "WTO Approves China's Entry."

65. Blustein and Chandler, "WTO Approves China's Entry."

66. Tickell and Peck, "Making Global Rules."

67. Though beyond the scope of the historical record I am discussing in this chapter, it is perhaps even more emblematic of the geopolitical struggle between these two

countries that China announced in 2014 it is ending state family-planning programs throughout the nation.

68. Wendy Brown, *Walled States, Waning Sovereignty* (Brooklyn, N.Y.: Zone, 2010).

Chapter 4. The Rhetoric and Logic of One Sex, One Gender

1. *Arabillas Morales v. Gonzales*, 478 F.3d 972 (9th cir. 2006).

2. *Arabillas Morales v. Gonzales*, 693–94.

3. Scott Barclay, Mary Bernstein, and Anna-Maria Marshall, eds., *Queer Mobilizations: L.G.B.T. Activists Confront the Law* (New York: New York University, 2009); Kimberle Crenshaw, "Mapping the Margins: Intersectionality, Identity Politics and Violence against Women of Color," *Stanford Law Review* 43 (1991): 1241–99; Martha Fineman, Jack E. Jackson, and Adam P. Romero, eds., *Feminist and Queer Legal Theory: Intimate Encounters, Uncomfortable Conversations* (Surrey, UK: Ashgate, 2009); Trina Grillo, "Anti-Essentialism and Intersectionality: Tools to Dismantle the Master's House," *Berkeley Women's Law Journal* 10 (1995): 16–30; Angela P. Harris, "Race and Essentialism in Feminist Legal Theory," *Stanford Law Review* 42 (1990): 581–616; Francisco Valdes, "Unpacking Hetero-Patriarchy: Tracing the Conflation of Sex, Gender and Sexual Orientation to Its Origins," *Yale Journal of Law and the Humanities* 8 (1996): 161–211; Leti Volpp, "Talking 'Culture': Gender, Race, Nation, and the Politics of Multiculturalism," *Columbia Law Review* 96 (1996): 1573–617.

4. Myriad sources exist documenting the experiences of gay men, transgender asylum applicants, or LGBT asylum seekers more broadly, but in my archival work I could only find one law review article that focused exclusively on the experiences of lesbian asylum seekers in the United States. Victoria Neilson, "Homosexual or Female? Applying Gender-Based Asylum Jurisprudence to Lesbian Asylum Claims," *Stanford Law and Policy Review* 16 (2005). A few more essays add to this scant research from outside the field of legal studies and outside the U.S. legal context. Susan A. Berger, "Production and Reproduction of Gender and Sexuality in Legal Discourses of Asylum in the United States," *Signs: Journal of Women in Culture and Society* 34 (2009); Rachel Lewis, "The Cultural Politics of Lesbian Asylum: Angelina Maccarone's *Unveiled* (2005) and the Case of the Lesbian Asylum Seeker," *International Feminist Journal of Politics* 12 (2010); Rachel Lewis, "Deportable Subjects: Lesbians and Political Asylum," *Feminist Formations* 25 (2013): 174–94; Jenni Millbank, "Gender, Sex and Visibility in Refugee Claims on the Basis of Sexual Orientation," *Georgetown Immigration Law Journal* 18 (2003): 71–110.

5. Edwin Black, *Rhetorical Criticism a Study in Method* (New York: MacMillan, 1965).

6. Lloyd F. Bitzer, "The Rhetorical Situation," *Philosophy and Rhetoric* 1 (1968): 13.

7. Karlyn Korhs Campbell and Kathleen Hall Jamieson, *Form and Genre: Shaping Rhetorical Action* (Annandale, Va.: Speech Communication Association, 1978), 17.

8. Karlyn Korhs Campbell and Kathleen Hall Jamieson, *Deeds Done in Words: Presidential Rhetoric and the Genres of Governance* (Chicago: University of Chicago Press, 1990);

John M. Murphy, "'Our Mission and Our Moment': George W. Bush and September 11th," *Rhetoric and Public Affairs* 6 (2003): 607–32; Mary E Stuckey, "Legitimating Leadership: The Rhetoric of Succession as a Genre of Presidential Discourse," *RSQ: Rhetoric Society Quarterly* 22 (1992): 25–38; Tammy R. Vigil, "George W. Bush's First Three Inaugural Addresses: Testing the Utility of the Inaugural Genre," *Southern Communication Journal* 78 (2013): 427–46.

9. B. L. Ware and Wil A. Linkugel, "They Spoke in Defense of Themselves: On the Generic Criticism of Apologia," *Quarterly Journal of Speech* 59 (1973): 273–83.

10. Rita C. Hubbard, "Relationship Styles in Popular Romance Novels, 1950 to 1983," *Communication Quarterly* 33 (1985): 113–25; Janice A. Radway, "Women Read the Romance: The Interaction of Text and Context," *Feminist Studies* 9 (1983): 53–78.

11. Karlyn Kohrs Campbell, "Gender and Genre: Loci of Invention and Contradiction in the Earliest Speeches by U.S. Women," *Quarterly Journal of Speech* 81 (1995): 479.

12. Karlyn Kohrs Campbell, "Style and Content in the Rhetoric of Early Afro-American Feminists," *Quarterly Journal of Speech* 72 (1986): 434–45; Campbell, "Gender and Genre"; Bonnie J. Dow and M. B. Tonn, "'Feminine Style' and Political Judgment in the Rhetoric of Ann Richards," *Quarterly Journal of Speech* 79 (1993): 286–302.

13. Shanara Rose Reid-Brinkley, "Mammies and Matriarchs: Feminine Style and Signifyin(g) in Carol Moseley Braun's 2003–2004 Campaign for the Presidency," in *Standing in the Intersection: Feminist Voices, Feminist Practices in Communication Studies*, edited by Karma R. Chávez and Cindy L. Griffin (Albany: SUNY Press, 2012), 38.

14. Amy Shuman and Carol Bohmer, "Representing Trauma: Political Asylum Narratives," *Journal of American Folklore* 117 (2004): 396–97.

15. Sara L. McKinnon, "Citizenship and the Performance of Credibility: Audiencing Gender-Based Asylum Seekers in U.S. Immigration Courts," *Text and Performance Quarterly* 29 (2009): 205–21.

16. Deborah Cohler, *Citizen, Invert, Queer: Lesbianism and War in Early Twentieth-Century Britian* (Minneapolis: University of Minnesota Press, 2010); Nancy Ordover, *American Eugenics: Race, Queer Anatomy, and the Science of Nationalism* (Minneapolis: University of Minnesota Press, 2003); Jennifer Terry, *An American Obsession: Science, Medicine, and Homosexuality in Modern Society* (Chicago: University of Chicago Press, 1999).

17. Lisa Walker, *Looking Like What You Are: Sexual Style, Race, and Lesbian Identity* (New York: New York University Press, 2001), 2.

18. Jennifer Terry, "Lesbians under the Medical Gaze: Scientists Search for Remarkable Differences," *Journal of Sex Research* 27 (1990): 318.

19. George Chauncey, "From Sexual Inversion to Homosexuality: Medicine and the Changing Conceptualization of Female Deviance," *Salmagundi* 58/59 (1983): 114–46; Terry, "Lesbians under the Medical Gaze."

20. David France, "The Science of Gaydar," *New York Magazine*, June 17, 2007; Dean H. Hamer and Peter Copeland, *The Science of Desire: The Search for the Gay Gene and the Biology of Behavior* (New York: Simon and Schuster, 1994); Regina Nuzzo, "What Does Gay Look Like? Science Is Working on It," *Los Angeles Times*, June 16, 2008;

Joshua A. Tabak and Vivian Zayas, "The Science of 'Gaydar,'" *New York Times*, June 3, 2012.

21. Margot Canaday, *The Straight State: Sexuality and Citizenship in Twentieth-Century America* (Princeton, N.J.: Princeton University Press, 2011).

22. Rudolf P. Gaudio, "Sounding Gay: Pitch Properties in the Speech of Gay and Straight Men," *American Speech* 69 (1994): 30–57; Simon LeVay, *Gay, Straight, and the Reason Why: The Science of Sexual Orientation* (Oxford: Oxford University Press, 2010); Richard A. Lippa, "Sex Differences in Sex Drive, Sociosexuality, and Height across 53 Nations: Testing Evolutionary and Social Structural Theories," *Archives of Sexual Behavior* 38 (2009): 631–51.

23. Fadi Hanna, "Punishing Masculinity in Gay Asylum Claims," *Yale Law Journal* 114 (2005): 913–21; Joseph Landau, "'Soft Immutability' and 'Imputed Gay Identity': Recent Developments in Transgender and Sexual-Orientation-Based Asylum Law," *Fordham Urban Law Journal* 32 (2005): 237–63; Alice M. Miller, "Gay Enough: Some Tensions in Seeking the Grant of Asylum and Protecting Sexual Diversity," in Epps, Valens, and González, *Passing Lines*, 137–88; Timothy J. Randazzo, "Social and Legal Barriers: Sexual Orientation and Asylum in the United States," in *Queer Migrations: Sexuality, U.S. Citizenship, and Border Crossings*, edited by Eithne Luibhéid and Lionel Jr. Cantú (Minneapolis: University of Minnesota Press, 2005), 30–60.

24. Hanna, "Punishing Masculinity," 913.

25. *Grijalva v. Gonzalez*, No. 05–3520, 544 (6th cir. 2007).

26. *Vitug v. Holder*, 723 F.3d 1056, 1060 (9th cir. 2013).

27. *Ozmen v. Attorney General*, 219 Fed. Appx. 125, 126 (3rd cir. 2007).

28. *Liong v. Attorney General*, 276 Fed. Appx. 232 (3rd cir. 2008); *Castro-Martinez v. Holder*, 641 F.3d 1103 (9th cir. 2011).

29. *Hernandez-Montiel v. INS*, 225 F. 3d 1084 (9th cir. 2000); *Reyes-Reyes v. Ashcroft*, 384 F.3d 782 (9th cir. 2004); *Ornelas-Chavez v. Gonzales*, 458 F.3d 1052 (9th cir. 2006).

30. For a fantastic discussion of the difficulties in demonstrating this nexus see Karen Musalo, "Symposium: Beyond Belonging; Challenging the Boundaries of Nationality: Revisiting Social Group and Nexus in Gender Asylum Claims; A Unifying Rationale for Evolving Jurisprudence," *DePaul Law Review* 52 (2003): 777–808.

31. *Halmenschlager v. Holder*, 331 Fed. Appx. 612, 617 (10th cir. 2009).

32. Gayle Salamon, *Assuming a Body: Transgender and Rhetorics of Materiality* (New York: Columbia University Press, 2010).

33. *Grijalva v. Gonzalez*, 544.

34. *J.P.S. v. U.S. Attorney General*, 384 Fed. Appx. 185 (3rd cir. 2010).

35. *Shahinaj v. Gonzales*, 481 F.3d 1027, 2 (8th cir. 2007).

36. It is important to note, as Carlos Decena demonstrates, that this question of the point of coming out may be irrelevant in certain cultural contexts, as sexual "outness" may be tacit knowledge or, in other words, known but agreed not to be talked about. As Decena explains, in the Spanish language (and for Dominican immigrant men in particular), "the 'sujeto tácito' suggests that coming out may sometimes be

redundant. In other words, coming out can be a verbal declaration of something that is already understood or assumed—tacit—in an exchange. What is tacit is neither secret nor silent." Carlos Ulises Decena, *Tacit Subjects: Belonging and Same-Sex Desire among Dominican Immigrant Men* (Durham, N.C.: Duke University Press, 2011). 19.

37. *Matter of Acosta*, 19 I&N Dec. 211 (BIA 1985).

38. Landau, "Soft Immutability."

39. *Ayala v. US Attorney General*, 605 F.3d 941, 944 (11th cir. 2010).

40. *Karouni v. Gonzales*, 399 F.3d 1163, 2846 (9th cir. 2005).

41. *Halmenschlager v. Holder*, 615.

42. *Hernandez-Montiel v. INS*; *Reyes-Reyes v. Ashcroft*; *Boer-Sedano v. Gonzales*, 418 F.3d 1082 (9th cir. 2005); *Comparan v. Gonzales*, 144 Fed. Appx. 673 (9th cir. 2005); *Maldonado v. Attorney General*, 188 Fed. Appx. 101 (3rd cir. 2006); *Ornelas-Chavez v. Gonzales*.

43. Salamon, *Assuming a Body*.

44. Writing about people's preferred gender identities using primarily secondary evidence that is not written or spoken by the people themselves is necessarily tricky. While the court record makes many appellations and attributions, I attempt to use pronouns in my own descriptions of the applicants' cases only when I know, in fact, that they are self-avowed. Conjointly, I maintain the pronouns used by court officials within quotations in order to highlight the complexities and complications of naming sex, gender, and sexuality present in the cases. These choices certainly make for slipperier and fuzzier articulations, which I hope will further highlight the messiness of articulating gender.

45. Randazzo, "Social and Legal Barriers: Sexual Orientation and Asylum in the United States," 30–60.

46. *Hernandez-Montiel v. INS*, 1088.

47. *Hernandez-Montiel v. INS*, 1089.

48. *Hernandez-Montiel v. INS*, 1089.

49. It is important to note that all of the transgender and gender nonconforming cases where the claimants are named as "gay men with female sexual identities" come out of the Ninth Circuit. This same circuit has also indicated that Nancy Arabillas Morales, a trans woman who has had partial gender-confirming surgery, may qualify for immigration relief under the Hernandez Montiel precedent (see *Arabillas Morales v. Gonzales*). Neither the BIA nor any of the other circuit courts have developed their own precedential language for evaluating trans and gender nonconforming cases. Indeed, the only additional mention of trans asylum seekers was the Tenth Circuit's denial of immigration relief to a woman identified as N- A- M- because of a prior criminal record in the United States. The court never took up the question of whether she would have qualified for asylum. *N-A-M- v. Holder*, 587 F.3d 1052 (10th cir. 2009).

50. Notably, this amicus brief is co-written by two leading scholars and advocates of LGBT asylum, Suzanne Goldberg and Shannon Minter: see Suzanne Goldberg et al., "Brief of Amici Curiae," (American Civil Liberties Union of Southern California, Lambda Legal Defense and Education Fund Inc., National Center for Lesbian Rights, International Gay and Lesbian Human Rights Commission, 1998).

51. *Hernandez-Montiel v. INS.*

52. Susan Stryker, "Transgender History, Homonormativity, and Disciplinarity," *Radical History Review* (2008): 145–57.

53. *Ulane v. Eastern Airlines*, 742 F.2d 1081 (7th Cir. 1984).

54. *Hernandez-Montiel v. INS*, 1095.

55. *Hernandez-Montiel v. INS*, 1095.

56. For an excellent explanation of the application of gender identity as a legal concept see Paisley Currah, "Gender Pluralism under the Transgender Umbrella," in *Transgender Rights*, edited by Paisley Currah, Richard M. Juang, and Shannon Price Minter (Minneapolis: University of Minnesota Press, 2006).

57. *In Re Grossman*, 127 1974 N.J. Super. LEXIS 701 19 (Superior Court of New Jersey 1974).

58. *Pinneke v. Preisser*, 623 F.2d 546 (8th Cir. 1980).

59. *South v. Gomez*, 129 F.3d 127; U.S. App. LEXIS 30063 (9th Cir. 1997).

60. *Hernandez-Montiel v. INS*, 1089.

61. *Hernandez-Montiel v. INS*, 1089.

62. Tomás Almaguer et al., "Revisting Activos and Pasivos: Towards New Cartographies of Latino and Latin American Male Same-Sex Desire," in *Latino/a Sexualities: A Reader*, edited by Marysol Ascencio (New Brusnwick, N.J.: Rutgers University Press, 2009); Lionel Cantú Jr., *The Sexuality of Migration: Border Crossings and Mexican Immigrant Men* (New York: New York University Press, 2009).

63. *Hernandez-Montiel v. INS*, 1094–95.

64. *Hernandez-Montiel v. INS*, 1095.

65. *Hernandez-Montiel v. INS*, 1095.

66. Vivienne C. Cass, "Homosexual Identity Formation: A Theoretical Model," *Journal of Homosexuality* 4 (1979): 219–35; For a sample of this work see Anthony R. D'Augelli, "Identity Development and Sexual Orientation: Toward a Model of Lesbian, Gay, and Bisexual Development," in *Human Diversity: Perspectives on People in Context*, edited by Edison J. Trickett, Roderick J. Watts, and Dina Birman (San Francisco: Jossey-Bass, 1994), 312–33; Lisa M. Diamond, "Sexual Identity, Attractions, and Behavior among Young Sexual-Minority Women over a 2-Year Period," *Developmental Psychology* 36 (2000): 241–50; Eric M. Dubé and Ritch C. Savin-Williams, "Sexual Identity Development among Ethnic Sexual-Minority Male Youths," *Developmental Psychology* 35 (1999): 1389–98.

67. Milton Diamond, "Sexual Identity and Sexual Orientation in Children with Traumatized or Ambiguous Genitalia," *Journal of Sex Research* 34 (1997): 207.

68. Diamond, "Sexual Identity and Sexual Orientation," 207.

69. *Ulane v. Eastern Airlines*, 7–8.

70. *Ulane v. Eastern Airlines*, 10.

71. *Littleton v. Prange*, 9 S.W. 3d 223 (Tex. App. 1999); *In Re Estate of Gardiner*, 273 Kan. 191; 42 P.3d 120 (Supreme Court of Kansas 2002); *Kantaras v. Kantaras*, 884 So. 2d 155 (Fla. Ct. App. 2004).

72. For an excellent review of this point see Marybeth Herald, "Explaining the Differences: Transgender Theories and Court Practices," in *Queer Mobilizations: LGBT*

Activists Confront the Law, edited by Scott Barclay, Mary Bernstein, and Anna-Maria Marshall (New York: New York University Press, 2009), 187–206.

73. *Reyes-Reyes v. Ashcroft*, 786.

74. *Ornelas-Chavez v. Gonzales*, 1054.

75. *Ornelas-Chavez v. Gonzales*, 1054.

76. *Ornelas-Chavez v. Gonzales*, 1054.

77. *Ornelas-Chavez v. Gonzales*, 1055.

78. *Hernandez-Montiel v. INS*, 1089.

79. Monique Wittig, "The Category of Sex," *Feminist Issues* 2 (1982): 66.

80. Valdes, "Unpacking Hetero-Patriarchy," 168.

81. Thomas Laqueur, *Making Sex: Body and Gender from the Greeks to Freud* (Cambridge, Mass.: Harvard University Press, 1990). 8.

82. Barbara Young Welke, *Law and the Borders of Belonging in the Long Nineteenth Century United States* (New York: Cambridge University Press, 2010).

83. Monique Wittig, *The Lesbian Body*, translated by David LeVay (New York: Beacon, 1986), 10.

84. Erin K. Baines, *Vulnerable Bodies: Gender, the UN and the Global Refugee Crisis* (New York: Ashgate, 2004); Jacqueline Bhabha, "Embodied Rights: Gender Persecution, State Sovereignty, and Refugees," *Public Culture* 9 (1996): 3–32; Heaven Crawley, *Refugees and Gender: Law and Process* (Bristol: Jordan, 2001); Eithne Luibhéid, *Entry Denied: Controlling Sexuality at the Border* (Minneapolis: University of Minnesota Press, 2002); Thomas Spijkerboer, *Gender and Refugee Status* (Burlington, VT: Ashgate, 2000).

85. Patricia Hill Collins, *Black Sexual Politics: African Americans, Gender, and the New Racism* (New York: Routledge, 2004); Thomas K. Nakayama, "Show/Down Time: 'Race,' Gender, Sexuality, and Popular Culture," *Critical Studies in Mass Communication* 11 (1994): 162–79.

86. Kristin Bumiller, "Rape as a Legal Symbol: An Essay on Sexual Violence and Racism," *University of Miami Law Review* 42 (1987): 75–91; Kristin Bumiller, *In an Abusive State: How Neoliberalism Appropriated the Feminist Movement against Sexual Violence* (Durham, N.C.: Duke University Press, 2008); Patricia Hill Collins, "Assume the Position: The Changing Contours of Sexual Violence," in *Black Sexual Politics* (New York: Routledge, 2004), 215–45; Cynthia Enloe, *Maneuvers: The International Politics of Militarizing Women's Lives* (Berkeley: University of California Press, 2000); Sylvanna M. Falcón, "Rape as a Weapon of War: Militarized Rape at the U.S.-Mexico Border," in *Women and Migration in the U.S.-Mexico Borderlands*, edited by Denise A. Segura and Patricia Zavella (Durham, N.C.: Duke University Press, 2007), 203–24; Jessica Livingston, "Murder in Juarez: Gender, Sexual Violence, and the Global Assembly Line," *Frontiers* 25 (2004): 59–76; Merril D. Smith, *Sex without Consent: Rape and Sexual Coercion in America* (New York: New York University, 2002).

87. Hilmi M. Zawati, "Impunity or Immunity: Wartime Male Rape and Sexual Torture as a Crime against Humanity," *Torture: Quarterly Journal on Rehabilitation of Torture Victims and Prevention of Torture* 17 (2007): 27–47.

88. Cantú, *Sexuality of Migration*, 62–63.

89. Sandesh Sivakumaran, "Male/Male Rape and the 'Taint' of Homosexuality," *Human Rights Quarterly* 27 (2005): 1281.

90. Sivakumaran, "Male/Male Rape," 1281.

91. *Juarez-Lopez v. Gonzales*, 235 Fed. Appx. 361 (7th cir. 2007).

Chapter 5. The Reading Practices of Immigration Judges

1. Dan Bilefsky, "Gays Seeking Asylum in U.S. Encounter a New Hurdle," *New York Times*, January 29, 2011.

2. Bilefsky, "Gays Seeking Asylum."

3. Bilefsky, "Gays Seeking Asylum."

4. Victoria Neilson and Lori Adams, "Gay Asylum Seekers," *New York Times*, February 6, 2011.

5. The authors define intersectional invisibility as "the general failure to fully recognize people with intersecting identities as members of their constituent groups. Intersectional invisibility also refers to the distortion of the intersectional persons' characteristics in order to fit them into frameworks defined by prototypes of constituent identity groups." Valerie Purdie-Vaughns and Richard P. Eiback, "Intersectional Invisibility: The Distinctive Advantages and Disadvantages of Multiple Subordinate-Group Identities," *Sex Roles* 59 (2008): 381. For an elaborated example of the workings of the concept see Devon W. Carbardo, "Colorblind Intersectionality," *Signs* 38 (2013): 811–45.

6. I found two anecdotal instances of transgender men gaining asylum through affirmative processes. For more information about the challenges of male signifying trans asylum seekers see Laurie Berg and Jenni Millbank, "Developing a Jurisprudence of Transgender Particular Social Group," in *Fleeing Homophobia: Sexual Orientation, Gender Identity, and Asylum*, edited by Thomas Spijkerboer (New York: Routledge, 2013).

7. I use the terms lesbian and gay women in this chapter to refer to women who identify sexually as desiring or loving other women with the understanding that these may not be the terms that the asylum claimants themselves use but are used nonetheless in the women's applications for asylum. For example, Rachel Lewis recounts from her analysis of the documentary *Unveiled*, about an Iranian lesbian asylum seeker in Germany, that Fariba, the asylum seeker, explained to the immigration officer, "I was with a woman," never using either the term gay or lesbian to identify herself to immigration officials. Rachel Lewis, "The Cultural Politics of Lesbian Asylum: Angelina Maccarone's *Unveiled* (2005) and the Case of the Lesbian Asylum Seeker," *International Feminist Journal of Politics* 12 (2010): 429. Moreover, Susan Berger notes in her analysis of Latin American gender and sexuality cases that "the term 'lesbian' does not enjoy the same currency in many Latin American contexts that it does in the United States. Sexual activity between women is still nascent as an identity marker in many parts of Latin America." Susan A. Berger, "Production and Reproduction of Gender and

Sexuality in Legal Discourses of Asylum in the United States," *Signs: Journal of Women in Culture and Society* 34 (2009): 674n15.

8. Jon W. Davidson, "Brief for the Respondent in Re: Jorge Soto Vega," (Los Angeles: Lamda Legal Defense and Education Fund, Inc., 2005), 41.

9. Davidson, "Brief for the Respondent," 6.

10. Davidson, "Brief for the Respondent," 6–7.

11. Davidson, "Brief for the Respondent," 8–9.

12. *Todorovic v. Attorney General*, 621 F.3d 1318, 1322–23 (11th cir. 2010).

13. *Razkane v. Holder*, 562 F.3d 1283, 1286 (10th cir. 2009).

14. *Razkane v. Holder*, 1286.

15. *Razkane v. Holder*, 1286.

16. *Boer-Sedano v. Gonzales*, 418 F.3d 1082, 1089 (9th cir. 2005); *Comparan v. Gonzales*, 144 Fed. Appx. 673, 674 (9th cir. 2005).

17. *Boer-Sedano v. Gonzales*; *Maldonado v. Attorney General*, 188 Fed. Appx. 101 (3rd cir. 2006); *Todorovic v. Attorney General*; Davidson, "Brief for the Respondent."

18. *Maldonado v. Attorney General*; *Razkane v. Holder*.

19. *Safadi v. Gonzales*, 148 Fed. Appx. 372 (6th cir. 2005); *Joaquin Porras v. Gonzales*, 435 F.3d 172 (2nd cir. 2006); *Eke v. Mukasey*, 512 F.3d 372 (7th cir. 2008); *Ndiaye v. Attorney General*, 304 Fed. Appx. 974 (3rd cir. 2008).

20. *Pitcherskaia v. INS*, 118 F.3d 641 (9th cir. 1997).

21. Janet Reno, "Attorney General Order Designating Board of Immigration Appeals Case as Precedent," Office of the Attorney General (Washington, D.C., 1994).

22. In this chapter, sexual orientation will most directly refer to gay men and lesbians, leaving other orientations such as bisexuality almost absent. Bisexual asylum claimants also face challenges, though the body of cases is arguably too small to demonstrate themes in the way bisexual claimants are received by U.S. immigration judges. In my very precursory analysis I found that cisgender male bisexual claimants often framed their sexual orientation as self-avowed bisexual but were ascribed by others with a homosexual identity. For example, Jamaican Arthur White identifies in his case as "bisexual" but argues to the court that he was "known in Jamaica as being a homosexual." *White v. Attorney General*, 447 Fed. Appx. 405, 406 (3rd cir. 2011). Other male-assigned bisexual claimants demonstrate similar reasoning: *Awuku v. Attorney General*, 331 Fed. Appx. 167 (3rd cir. 2009); *Sempagala v. Holder*, 318 Fed. Appx. 418 (6th cir. 2009); *Doe v. Holder*, 736 F.3d 871 (9th cir. 2013); *Powell v. Holder*, 507 Fed. Appx. 666 (9th cir. 2013). I could find no cisgender female bisexual cases to compare these cases against. All female sexual orientation cases that I found—whether the individuals identified as bisexual or not—argued that their sexual orientation social group membership was as a lesbian. These cases are discussed in this chapter.

23. Cynthia L. Cooper, "U.S. Court Considers Political Asylum for Lesbians," http://www.womensenews.org/article.cfm/dyn/aid/3218.

24. UNHCR, "Women," http://www.unhcr.org/pages/49c3646c1d9.html.

25. As Jenni Millbank demonstrates in her work on asylum in Australia and Canada, lesbian asylum seekers receive asylum at a significantly lower rate than their gay male

counterparts (36 percent success rate for gay men versus a 25 percent for lesbians). In Australia, lesbians are particularly disadvantaged because of the way their persecution is interpreted as "private" instead of "public." She explains, "While the Australian tribunal did view sexual violence as gendered in the sense that it was something that happened to 'women,' they were often unable to see the sexuality component in that violence in that it was directed specifically at lesbians *as lesbians*. The tribunal was often unable to see rape as a sexualized attack upon lesbians as a punishment for their sexual and social nonconformity. In several cases there was evidence to show that rape was a punishment for being a lesbian or was intended by the perpetrator to 'set her straight.'" Jenni Millbank, "Gender, Sex and Visibility in Refugee Claims on the Basis of Sexual Orientation," *Georgetown Immigration Law Journal* 18 (2003): 77.

26. Victoria Neilson, "Homosexual or Female? Applying Gender-Based Asylum Jurisprudence to Lesbian Asylum Claims," *Stanford Law and Policy Review* 16 (2005): 442.

27. Cheshire Calhoun, "The Gender Closet: Lesbian Disappearance under the Sign of 'Women,'" *Feminist Studies* 21 (1995): 7–33.

28. Elizabeth Spelman, *Inessential Woman: Problems of Exclusion in Feminist Thought* (Boston: Beacon, 1988).

29. Joseph Landau, "'Soft Immutability' and 'Imputed Gay Identity': Recent Developments in Transgender and Sexual-Orientation-Based Asylum Law," *Fordham Urban Law Journal* 32 (2005); Karen Musalo, "Symposium: Beyond Belonging; Challenging the Boundaries of Nationality: Revisiting Social Group and Nexus in Gender Asylum Claims; A Unifying Rationale for Evolving Jurisprudence," *DePaul Law Review* 52 (2003); Michele A. Voss, "Young and Marked for Death: Expanding the Definition of 'Particular Social Group' in Asylum Law to Include Youth Victims of Gang Persecution," *Rutgers Law Journal* 37 (2005): 235–75.

30. Eithne Luibhéid, *Entry Denied: Controlling Sexuality at the Border* (Minneapolis: University of Minnesota Press, 2002). 80. As Luibhéid points to, Shannon Minter details one other known case of lesbian exclusion as "sexual deviate." Shannon Minter, "Sodomy and Public Morality Offenses under U.S. Immigration Law: Penalizing Lesbian and Gay Identity," *Immigration and Nationality Law Review* 15 (1993): 428–74.

31. Luibhéid, *Entry Denied*, 206n13.

32. Karen Musalo, Lisa Frydman, and Blaine Bookey, "Brief as Amici Curiae on Behalf of Maldonado Lopez," (Center for Gender and Refugee Studies, 2013), 2.

33. Rocky C. Tsai et al., "Opening Brief in Support of Petition for Review for Maldonado Lopez," (2013), 9.

34. Tsai et al., "Opening Brief," 10.

35. Tsai et al., "Opening Brief," 10.

36. Tsai et al., "Opening Brief," 12.

37. National Immigrant Justice Center, "Groundbreaking Federal Court Settlement Gives Asylum Seeker Facing Reinstatement of Removal a Chance to Present Her Case in Court" (2014), http://immigrantjustice.org/press_releases/maldonado-lopez-settlement#.VR189GYigXh.

38. Tsai et al., "Opening Brief," 6.

39. *Burog-Perez v. Ins*, 95 Fed. Appx. 886, 889 (9th cir. 2004).

40. *Isaacs v. Holder*, 353 Fed. Appx. 515, 517 (2nd cir. 2009).

41. *Isaacs v. Holder*, 517.

42. *Chang v. Attorney General*, 397 Fed. Appx. 812, 814 (3rd cir. 2010).

43. *Chang v. Attorney General*, 814n1.

44. Aubra Fletcher, "The Real ID Act: Furthering Gender Bias in U.S. Asylum Law," *Berkeley Journal of Gender, Law and Justice* 21 (2006): 111–32; Sara L. McKinnon, "Citizenship and the Performance of Credibility: Audiencing Gender-Based Asylum Seekers in U.S. Immigration Courts," *Text and Performance Quarterly* 29 (2009); Katherine E. Melloy, "Telling Truths: How the Real ID Act's Credibility Provisions Affect Women Asylum Seekers," *Iowa Law Review* 92 (2007): 637–76.

45. *Mockeviciene v. Attorney General*, 237 Fed. Appx. 569 (11th cir. 2007).

46. *Mockeviciene v. Attorney General*, 572.

47. *Lyashchynska v. U.S. Attorney General*, 676 F.3d 962, 964 (11th cir. 2012).

48. *Lyashchynska v. U.S. Attorney General*, 965.

49. *Michulena v. Attorney General*, 382 Fed. Appx. 187, 189n3 (3rd Cir. 2010).

50. *Michulena v. Attorney General*, 189n3.

51. *Michulena v. Attorney General*, 189n3.

52. Carmen de Monteflores and Stephen J. Schultz, "Coming Out: Similarities and Differences for Lesbians and Gay Men," *Journal of Social Issues* 34 (1978): 59–72; Maria J. Kahn, "Factors Affecting the Coming out Process for Lesbians," *Journal of Homosexuality* 21 (1991): 47–70; Jessica F. Morris, "Lesbian Coming out as a Multidimensional Process," *Journal of Homosexuality* 33 (1997): 1–22; Paula C. Rust, "'Coming Out' in the Age of Social Constructionism: Sexual Identity Formation among Lesbian and Bisexual Women," *Gender and Society* 7 (1993): 50–77.

53. Lisa M. Cuklanz, *Rape on Trial: How the Mass Media Construct Legal Reform and Social Change* (Philadelphia: University of Pennsylvania Press, 1996).

54. Elza Ibroscheva, "Selling the Post-Communist Female Body: Portrayals of Women and Gender in Bulgarian Advertising," *Feminist Media Studies* 13 (2013): 456.

55. Ibroscheva, "Selling Post-Communist," 445.

56. Rutvica Andrijasevic, "Beautiful Dead Bodies: Gender, Migration, and Representation in Anti-Trafficking Campaigns," *Feminist Review* 86 (2007): 24–44.

57. Adrienne Rich, "Compulsory Heterosexuality and Lesbian Existence," *Signs* 5 (1980): 649.

58. Purdie-Vaughns and Eiback, "Intersectional Invisibility."

59. *Chang v. Attorney General*, 814.

60. *Chang v. Attorney General*, 814.

61. *Burog-Perez v. Ins*, 889.

62. *Burog-Perez v. Ins*, 888.

63. *Burog-Perez v. Ins*, 888.

64. *Tavera Lara v. Attorney General*, 188 Fed. Appx. 848, 850 (11th cir. 2006).

65. *Tavera Lara v. Attorney General*, 851.

66. *Tavera Lara v. Attorney General*.

67. *Tavera Lara v. Attorney General*, 851.

68. *Tavera Lara v. Attorney General*, 851–52.

69. *Tavera Lara v. Attorney General*, 858.

70. *Densmaa v. Attorney General*, 283 Fed. Appx. 889, 891 (3rd cir. 2008).

71. *Densmaa v. Attorney General*, 892.

72. *Densmaa v. Attorney General*, 892.

73. *Mockeviciene v. Attorney General*, 572.

74. As I mention above, Lyashchynska and Michulena were similarly assaulted by their boyfriends/husbands. The justices in each of these cases also ignored these experiences as evidence of persecution and proceeded to deny them immigration relief. *Michulena v. Attorney General*; *Lyashchynska v. U.S. Attorney General*.

75. As Jill Hasday explains, this refusal to see marital rape as rape is a perpetual theme in U.S. legal challenges. Jill Elaine Hasday, "Contest and Consent: A Legal History of Marital Rape," *California Law Review* 88 (2000): 1373–505.

76. *Nabulwala v. Gonzalez*, 479 F.3d 972, 1116 (8th cir. 2007).

77. *Nabulwala v. Gonzalez*, 1117.

78. *Nabulwala v. Gonzalez*, 1118.

79. *Gomez v. INS*, 947 F.2d 660 (2nd cir. 1991); *Re R- A-*, 22 I. & N. Dec. 906 (BIA 2001); *Perdomo v. Holder*, 611 F.3d 662 (9th cir. 2010).

80. As early as 1995 LGBT asylum advocates, activists, and lawyers recognized the gaps in information regarding lesbian human rights abuses. Toward closing this information gap, the International Gay and Lesbian Human Rights Commission, in partnership with numerous other Gay and Lesbian and Women's Rights organizations, published the first known report to center on the experiences of lesbians. Almost thirty years later, it is startling to see just how little information and analysis from this report surfaces in lesbian asylum seeker's cases. I thank Rachel Rosenbloom for alerting me to this report: Rachel Rosenbloom, ed. *Unspoken Rules: Sexual Orientation and Women's Human Rights* (San Francisco: International Gay and Lesbian Human Rights Commission, 1995).

81. *Densmaa v. Attorney General*, 882.

82. *Badawy v. Attorney General*, 390 Fed. Appx. 165, 167–68 (3rd cir. 2010).

83. *Andreasian v. Ashcroft*, 94 Fed. Appx. 624, 625 (9th cir. 2004).

Conclusion

1. Barack Obama, "Executive Order—Preventing and Responding to Violence against Women and Girls Globally" (Washington, D.C.: The White House, 2012).

2. U.S. Department of State and USAID, "United States Strategy to Prevent and Respond to Gender-Based Violence Globally" (2012), 6.

3. State and USAID, "United States Strategy," 3.

4. State and USAID, "United States Strategy," 3.

5. "Remarks at the Center for Strategic and International Studies Lecture and Roundtable on Advancing Policy and Programs on Global Women's Issues" (Washington, D.C.: Office of the Secretary of State, 2014); "U.S. Funding for Safe from the Start Announced at the Call to Action on Protection from Gender-Based Violence in Emergencies" (Washington, D.C.: U.S. Department of State, 2014).

6. "Obama Administration Leadership on International Human Rights" (2013), https://www.whitehouse.gov/the-press-office/2013/12/04/fact-sheet-obama-administration-leadership-international-human-rights.

7. "Obama Administration Leadership on International Human Rights."

8. Susan E. Rice, "Human Rights: Advancing American Interests and Values" (2013), https://www.whitehouse.gov/the-press-office/2013/12/04/remarks-national-security-advisor-susan-e-rice-human-rights-advancing-am.

9. As the United Nations High Commissioner for Refugees notes, globally there are an estimated 42.5 million refugees: this number, they explain, includes 28.8 million internally displaced persons and some 928,000 asylum seekers. They note that this figure is the highest since 1994, when there were an estimated 47 million people forcibly displaced worldwide. UNHCR, "2012 Statistical Yearbook" (Geneva: United Nations High Commissioner for Refugees, 2012), 6.

10. Daniel C. Martin and James E. Yankay, "Refugees and Asylees: 2012," (Washington, D.C.: Department of Homeland Security, 2012).

Index

SARA L. MCKINNON is an assistant professor of rhetoric, politics, and culture in the Department of Communication Arts and affiliate faculty in global studies and gender and women's studies at University of Wisconsin–Madison.

FEMINIST MEDIA STUDIES

Queer Migration Politics: Activist Rhetoric and Coalitional Possibilities
    Karma R. Chávez
Sexting Panic: Rethinking Criminalization, Privacy, and Consent
    Amy Adele Hasinoff
*Cupcakes, Pinterest, and Ladyporn: Feminized Popular Culture
    in the Early Twenty-First Century*   Edited by Elana Levine
Gendered Asylum: Race and Violence in U.S. Law and Politics
    Sara L. McKinnon

The University of Illinois Press
is a founding member of the
Association of American University Presses.

_____

University of Illinois Press
1325 South Oak Street
Champaign, IL 61820-6903
www.press.uillinois.edu

Printed by Printforce, United Kingdom